D1233954

MILTON STUDIES IN HONOR OF HARRIS FRANCIS FLETCHER

Harris Francis Fletcher

MILTON STUDIES

IN HONOR OF HARRIS FRANCIS FLETCHER

. . . neque enim nisi charus ab ortu
Diis superis poterit magno favisse poetae.

—MILTON, *Mansus*

UNIVERSITY OF ILLINOIS PRESS, URBANA, 1961

CONTENTS

PREFATORY NOTE

This collection of Milton studies in honor of Harris Francis Fletcher originally appeared as the October 1961 issue of *The Journal of English and Germanic Philology.* It has been repaged to form a separate volume.

HARRIS FRANCIS FLETCHER

Harris Fletcher would hesitate to call any fellow scholar "dedicated" and he would never apply the term to himself; yet I can think of no better word to describe his life-long devotion to Milton.

I had been in Urbana nearly six months before I found out what drove Fletcher from classroom to library and then back to the library after lunch. It was in the spring of 1927. The head of the Department of English had called four young assistant professors into his office and offered all four the job of directing freshman rhetoric. He gave us twenty-four hours in which to think it over. We wondered at the time what he would do if two of us accepted the offer. (We are still wondering, for no one did.)

Fletcher's reaction as we left the office was characteristic: "Let's go look at the bulls." It seemed an appropriate thing to do, so he and I walked to a field on the south campus, leaned on the fence, looked at the bulls, and talked. I had no intention of accepting the offer and I soon discovered that Fletcher had no intention of accepting it either, but for a different reason. I was a foot-loose bachelor, eager to see more of the world, and I was not going to settle down anywhere to any such job, not for a while, anyway. Fletcher had already made up his mind to spend the rest of his life finding out all he could about John Milton.

That summer I left the University of Illinois on my travels, which were to last ten years. I ran across Fletcher from time to time, sometimes at a meeting of the Modern Language Association, where he would be reading a paper on Milton. I was a little surprised to learn that he had all but quit teaching to become the associate dean of Liberal Arts and Sciences, but I heard that he still went to the library when he could and I suspected that Milton had been deferred to the night shift.

When I returned to Urbana in 1937, Fletcher was still hot on the trail. He had his professorship now and was resigning from the administration to devote full time to teaching and research. By this time he had inherited both the undergraduate and graduate courses in Milton and was in charge of graduate work in the seventeenth century. He now haunted the library, from seven in the morning until five in the evening.

In 1961, looking back over thirty-five years, it is easier, of course, to assess Fletcher's work than it was in 1927 or in 1937. Now we can see and measure his stature as teacher, as scholar, as collector of books, and as a member of the community (both town and gown).

Although Fletcher's work centered on Milton, he never shirked teaching; he never asked for relief from the classroom in order to devote more time to research, but accepted his teaching assignments as they came. Before coming to Illinois he had taught classes in elementary school and high school, and, at the University of Michigan, freshman English and a popular course in the contemporary novel. When he first came to Illinois he assisted Chauncey Baldwin, who taught the Bible and Milton. He took his turn with the large elementary course in Shakespeare and worked hard at it. Even after he attained full status in the graduate college he continued to teach an undergraduate course in the Bible and one in Milton, and he taught these until his retirement. He regarded the undergraduate as a more receptive, more stimulating student than were most of the candidates for the master's and doctor's degree, and he never lost the sense of excitement that comes with introducing a young mind to the sublime thought and sonorous music of *Isaiah* and *Paradise Lost*.

As a scholar, Fletcher's record of publications speaks for itself, and impressively—three early monographs on Milton's Semitic studies and use of the Bible; a 166-page bibliography; a revised college text of Milton's poetical works; a critical facsimile text, in four volumes, of Milton's poetical works; and two large volumes entitled *The Intellectual Development of John Milton*. In addition, there are some twenty-five articles on Milton in the learned journals and some thirty reviews of books on Milton or on seventeenth-century literature. Unpublished, there is a complete word index to Milton's prose, prepared years ago, which Fletcher has been using in his own work, and has made available to other scholars who come to his workroom in the University Library.

This record of publications, however, gives no hint of the many hours spent in conference with graduate students and with younger colleagues who came to him for help. I have seen him spend half the morning going from Rare Book Room to Reference Room to classical seminar to stacks, trying to run down a term or an allusion that had baffled a colleague. Moreover, he somehow managed to direct fourteen doctoral dissertations and to serve on examining committees of other candidates.

The record of scholarly publications gives no hint of the many hours spent in reading manuscripts submitted to the editors of the *Illinois Studies in Language and Literature*. With great care Fletcher would go over the manuscripts that he, as editor-in-chief, assigned to himself. He usually emerged with pages of questions, suggestions, and comments, which he would type before sending them to the author. Always his criticism emphasized clarity and common sense. "What does this mean?" "Then why not say so?" More often than not, his best criticism, certainly his most picturesque criticism, was delivered orally.

Fletcher's work as a collector of books arose from the needs of teacher and scholar. When he came to Illinois in the fall of 1926 he had already made up his mind that he would find out everything he could about Milton. He needed books. He needed editions of Milton's poetry and prose, the books that Milton himself had read, and the books that Milton's teachers had read. He needed sixteenth- and seventeenth-century poetry, fifteenth-, sixteenth-, and seventeenth-century books on poetry, rhetoric, grammar, logic, theology, history, music, astronomy, mathematics, and geography. He needed the textbooks that were used in the Elizabethan and Jacobean grammar schools and colleges. And, of course, he needed books about Milton.

Every man who starts an ambitious enterprise needs some luck, and Fletcher was fortunate in both time and place. The great economic depression had driven prices down in England and Germany as well as in the United States. Books were cheap. And books were plentiful, for World War II had not yet destroyed whole libraries and warehouses. The director of the University Library, Phineas L. Windsor, was an understanding man who quickly saw that Fletcher knew what he wanted and how to get it, so he gave him virtual *carte blanche*. Robert D. Carmichael, Dean of the Graduate College, was also an understanding man; he found the money for purchases beyond the means at the librarian's disposal. So Fletcher bought books. He bought hundreds of books, thousands of books, especially old books and rare books, including many incunabula. Of course many of these books were not Milton or even Miltoniana, for one thing led to another and then to still another as Fletcher's knowledge deepened and broadened. By 1937 his workroom was getting out of hand.

In 1937–38, a selection of seventeenth-century books from the general stacks was added to the books, pamphlets, and photostats collected by Fletcher for his own personal use and the "Seventeenth Century Room" was established on the top floor of the University Library. Some German books of the seventeenth century were added, then French, Italian, Greek, and Latin until there were 5,700 books and pamphlets on the overcrowded shelves. A few of Fletcher's colleagues and graduate students working on doctoral dissertations began to use the room.

In 1940–41, the sixteenth-century books gathered by T. W. Baldwin for his researches on Shakespeare were added and the whole collection moved to larger quarters down the hall. Then all books in the general library that were printed before 1700 were gradually added. Faculty and graduate students in English, Greek, Latin, German, French, history, music, mathematics, and science were now using the 15,000 books, pamphlets, and letters in the new room.

In 1943, when the numbers had risen to 26,000, the name was changed to Rare Book Room. Robert B. Downs was now Director of the University Library and he gave Fletcher the same encouragement that Windsor had given him throughout the 1930's.

By 1961 the Rare Book Room contained over 77,000 books, pamphlets, and letters, and thousands of microfilms. Fletcher did not collect all of these, to be sure, for colleagues were also ordering books and microfilms, but he alone was responsible for starting the collection and he remained the prime mover. No weekday passed that he did not stop at least once in the Acquisition Department to look at book catalogues. He knew from long experience that the book-collector can never let up. His office and workroom were just around the corner from the Rare Book Room.

How did a man engaged in full-time teaching or full-time administrative work, in laborious research, in writing, in directing doctoral dissertations, in editing manuscripts submitted to the *Studies*, in searching book catalogues and corresponding with booksellers, find time for any social life? Somehow Fletcher did find time. For years he was an active member of the University Club, of a duplicate-bridge club, of the Greek Club, of the Saturday-afternoon hikers, of the Urbana Country Club, where he played an energetic though erratic game of golf. As passing years began to demand more conservation of energy his social life naturally became more limited, so that his main contacts with town and gown came in the daily meetings of the Ten O'Clock Scholars. Fletcher was a charter member of this informal colloquium that started in a campus coffee-shop and then moved to a nearby drugstore. Its membership, except for Fletcher, changed from year to year; it contained not only University men, such as a few choice administrators, colleagues from English, Speech, classics, French, history, economics, political science, and physical education, physicians from the Health Service, athletic coaches, editors from the University Press, but also businessmen from Champaign and Urbana. Almost every conceivable subject was explored: campus politics, town politics, state politics, national politics, education, art, music, literature, medicine, theology, life insurance, retail merchandising, football, basketball, railroads, automobiles, and the American Civil War. No one knew, upon joining the group in the drugstore, what information or misinformation might be forthcoming. Sometimes the talk was very good. When it was at its best, Fletcher was sure to be at the center of it. As time went on he acquired an almost oracular standing and was consulted on nearly every subject that could arise among his various friends. "Ask Fletcher; find out what he thinks." "What does Fletcher have to say about it?"

Now the teaching and directing of doctoral dissertations will have to stop, but the research and collecting of books will not stop. Now it is time for Fletcher's colleagues and fellow Milton scholars to offer a tribute to the man who has so devotedly and so ably served teaching and scholarship for over forty years. A volume of scholarly essays is surely a proper addition to the monument that he has already built for himself in his writings, in the great Milton and Renaissance collections in the Rare Book Room, in the memories of the many students who still speak of him with gratitude and affection, and in the friendship of many men and women who trust that they will not only speak of him but with him for years to come.

Marvin T. Herrick

MILTON AND THE DESCENT TO LIGHT

D. C. Allen, The Johns Hopkins University

I

Though the English Protestants of the seventeenth century were, to their ultimate spiritual distress, so devoted to the literal interpretation of the Bible that they considered it the primary and superior reading, their affection for the letter and the historical sense did not prevent them from searching the text for types and allegories. This practice, of course, bore the taint of popery and hindered the full powers of the *fides divina;* yet it often yielded excellent results and enabled one to skirt the marsh of a troublesome passage. Though not addicted to the allegorical method, Milton was no stranger to it. He might scorn Amaryllis and Neaera, but he could spend an occasional moment of leisure with what Luther called "these whores of allegory." The latter books of *Paradise Lost* and the tragedy of *Samson* proved that he was quite a talented typologist, who could find foreshadowings of the great Advocate of Grace in the biographical records of the advocates of the Law. More than this, Milton, unlike many of his contemporaries who were inclined to be universal in their analogical researches, made fine discriminations between types because he believed in what we might now call "typological evolution."

An example of Milton's interpretative discretion is his refusal to accept—although in this he was contrary to theological opinion—the patriarch Aaron as a full type of Christ. He contended that this first priest simply adumbrated the priestly offices of Jesus.[1] When he came to this conclusion, Milton was flatly correcting the assertions of the Anglican prelates; but on another similar occasion he was mentally flexible enough to correct himself.[2] Since he also believed in a dynamic typology that changed as the sacred history was unrolled, he was quick to admit that symbols valid before the Law[3] were afterwards worthless.[4] He could also insist on the gradual revelation of types and symbols because he believed that the thunder and trumpets' "clang"

---

[1] *Church Government, Works* (New York, 1931–38), III, 202–205; hereafter I shall cite only volume and page.
[2] *Hirelings*, VI, 55, 58; *Christian Doctrine*, XIV, 311.
[3] *Christian Doctrine*, XVI, 191.
[4] *Ibid.*, XVI, 197.

on Mt. Sinai proclaimed, among other things, a new form of typology
and established Moses, who was, in a guarded sense, "the Divine
Mediator" and "the type of the Law,"[5] as a master typologist. This
evaluation had more than human worth because it was Jehovah who
instructed Moses so that he could teach this mode of interpretation to
men.

> Ordaine them Lawes; part such as appertaine
> To civil Justice, part religious Rites
> Of sacrifice, informing them by types
> And shadowes, of that destind Seed to bruise
> The Serpent, by what meanes he shall achieve
> Mankinds deliverance.   (*P.L.*, XII, 230–35)

These words are placed in the mouth of the Archangel Michael, who at
this moment is manipulating the magic lantern of holy shadows and
who is also an experienced exegete skilled in all four senses. Shortly
after speaking this gloss, he announces that the main purpose of the
Old Testament is to prepare the sons of Adam for a "better Cov'nant,
disciplin'd / From shadowie Types to Truth, from Flesh to Spirit"
(XII, 302–303). The mighty angel thus suggests that man can ascend
(as humbled Adam has ascended from the Vale of Despond to the
Mount of the Visions of God) from the darkness of sin and ignorance
into the light of truth, from the shadow of type and symbol into the
white blaze of the eternal literal.

It must be confessed that typology, even at its finest, is little more
than hindsight prophecy; it points surely to the Advent, but it is best
understood when the Word is made Flesh. Allegory—a game that
even Jehovah plays[6]—is, in Milton's somewhat reluctant opinion, a
possible form of revealed knowledge. This knowledge may be useful in
some instances and not in others. When, for example, Moses urges the
Israelites not to plow with an ox and an ass, Milton, who has been
searching Deuteronomy for divorce evidence, perceives that the
Hebrew lawgiver has the Miltons in mind,[7] an interpretation that
speaks better for a sense of mystery than for a sense of humor. In his
poetry Milton uses allegory with somewhat better artistry than a modern reader might imagine. An illustration of this skill appears when he
shows Satan, orbiting in space and viewing the margin of Heaven and
the angelic ladder of which "Each stair mysteriously was meant"

---

[5] *Ibid.*, XVI, III.
[6] *Ibid.*, XV, 145.
[7] *Doctrine and Discipline*, III, 419; *Colasterion*, IV, 265.

(III, 516). By reminding us that Jacob's ladder had allegorical force, Milton prepares us for Raphael's subsequent description of the *scala perfectionis*, "the common gloss of theologians." There is likewise poetic irony resident in the fact that Satan, who is totally without hope, is permitted to see what will be interpreted as Adam's way of assuming angelic nature.

In general Milton probably defined allegory as a downward descent of knowledge, a revealing of suprarational information that enabled the humble learner to ascend. Raphael's well-known comment on his account of the celestial battles (V, 570–76; VI, 893–96) and Milton's open admission that he can only accept the six days of Creation allegorically (VII, 176–79) make the Miltonic conception of allegory plain. For the poet, allegory is the only means of communication between a superior mind aware of grand principles, such as the enduring war between Good and Evil, and a lesser mind incapable of higher mathematics. It is essentially a form of revelation, or, as Vaughan would put it, "a candle tin'd at the Sun."

To burnish this observation, I should like to point to events within the confines of the epic that could be called an allegory about allegory. This sacred fiction begins to be written in Book II when Satan, leaving Hell for Eden, retains, except for his momentary ventures into several forms of symbolic wildlife, the literalness of satanship, never putting on the ruddy complexion, the horns, hoof, and tail by which he was recognized in the allegorical world. The celestial messengers, however, are real creatures and stay feathered and decorous so that Adam, unlike his sons, does not "entertain angels unawares." It is otherwise with Satan's strange relative, Death. At first he "seems" to be crowned and to shake his ghastly dart; actually, he is a vast black shadow, formless, not "Distinguishable in member, joynt, or limb, / Or substance" (II, 668–69). He is by no means the symbolic person who writes the dreary colophon to all human stories or who is stonily portrayed in ecclesiastical monuments. Once he has crossed his bridge into our world, he is better known. Although he is "not mounted yet / On his pale horse," we are familiar with his "vaste unhide-bound Corps" and we understand his hearty hunger for whatever "the Sithe" of his companion Time "mowes down" (X, 588–606). The bridge between the two worlds is a convention of infernal histories; but in *Paradise Lost*, it could also be called the Bridge of Allegory.

There is no doubt that at times Milton read the Scriptures for meanings other than the literal one, but he also was aware, thanks to a long tradition, that the pagans had a glimmer of Christian truth.

Their lamp was scantily fueled and the wick smoked, but with proper adjustments it could be made to give off a "pale religious light." It took almost four centuries to light this lamp in the Church; the pagan philosophers and their idolatrous legends had first to be suppressed. Then, taking over the methods of the same heathen brethren, the Christian scholars began searching the mythology for physical, moral, and spiritual notions that had been bequeathed to men by the sons of Noah. The moral commentaries of Bishops Fulgentius and Eustathius on pagan literature encouraged others to unshell these truths, and in Renaissance England Chapman, Bacon, Reynolds, Sandys, Ross, and Boys searched the pagans for what had been better revealed in the Bible or was narrated in the Books of Creation. All of them were infected to some degree with the current confidence in a universal philosophical system, a disease nourished by earlier mystagogues such as Ficino, Pico della Mirandola, and Agostino Steuchio, and best known to us in the fine clinical case of Theophilus Gale. Given the virulence of the epidemic, we are, consequently, not surprised when the daemon from "the threshold of Jove's Court" touches on it.

> Ile tell ye, 'tis not vain or fabulous
> (Though so esteem'd by shallow ignorance)
> What the sage Poets taught by th' heavenly Muse,
> Storied of old in high immortal verse
> Of dire *Chimaeras* and enchanted Isles,
> And rifted Rocks whose entrance leads to Hell,
> For such there be, but unbelief is blind. (*Comus*, ll. 512–18)

After reading this speech in *Comus*, we understand why the mythological remembrances in *Paradise Lost* are sometimes more than ornamental, why their submerged moral or spiritual meanings enable them to consort with and support the braver Christian myths. The multicolored phoenix, first underwritten by Clement of Rome as a Christ symbol, adorns Milton's own adventual allegory: the descent of Raphael through the air, "a *Phoenix*, gaz'd by all" (V, 272). Eden, expressed in vegetable grandeur, is quickly seared with evil foreboding when Milton likens it to the meadows of Enna, those sinister fields "where *Proserpin* gath'ring flow'rs / Herself a fairer Flow'r by gloomy *Dis* / Was gather'd" (IV, 269–71). When Milton compares Adam and Eve to Deucalion and Pyrrha (XI, 8–14), even we do not need a whole series of pious mythologizers to make the point; and foolish Pandora hardly needs the testimony of a Father as old as Tertullian[8] to inform us that she is the pagan half-memory of silly Eve (IV, 712–19).

[8] *Liber de Corona, Patrologia Latina,* II, 85.

Milton is quite conventional in permitting pagan legend to lend its soft biceps to Christian power. His method of searching for metaphoric support in heathen culture also enables him to stand aside from the other characters of the epic and act as a commentator on the pre-Christian world from the vantage point of a postclassical man. Among the various pagan figures with whom Milton plants his poetry, two rise above the rest; they are the poet-theologian Orpheus and the demigod Hercules. Both are attractive to him because of their Christian meaning.

From the flats of the first *Prolusion* through the latter ranges of *Paradise Lost*, Milton accents the legend of Orpheus in a way that suggests self-identification. The Greek hero was praised in antiquity and by men of later ages for softening the human heart and turning it through his higher magic to the useful and the good.[9] Christian as these achievements were, Orpheus, as Milton knew, enlarged them by singing of Chaos and Old Night and by teaching Musaeus the reality of the one God. St. Augustine, a Father beloved by Milton when he agreed with him, complained that Orpheus' theology was very poor stuff;[10] but other primitive theologians from Athenagoras onward hailed the Greek as unique among the unelect in explaining divine matters as a Christian would.[11] There is, as I have said, little doubt that Milton thought of the murdered poet as one of his own grave predecessors, and this view was probably enhanced by that of the Christian mythologists who described Orpheus as a pagan type of Christ.[12]

Clement of Alexandria is the first to bring both harrowers of Hell together, although his comments are actually an angry rejection of pagan complaints about Christian imitativeness. He brands the Christian doctrines of Orpheus as spurious and mocks the alleged majesty of his songs; then he turns with a "not so my singer" (ἀλλ' οὐ τοιόσδε ὁ ὁδὸς ὁ ἐμός) to praise the new Orpheus, who tamed

[9] J. Wirl, *Orpheus in der englischen Literatur* (Vienna and Leipzig, 1913). Milton's orphic imagery has been studied by Caroline Mayerson, "The Orpheus Image in *Lycidas*," *PMLA*, LXIV (1949), 189–207. The Columbia *Index* may be consulted for Milton's references to Orpheus.

[10] *Contra Faustum, PL*, XLII, 282; *De Civitate*, XVIII, 14.

[11] *Legatio pro Christianis, Patrologia Graeca*, VI, 928.

[12] Fulgentius, *Philosophi Mythologiarum libri tres* (Basel, 1536), pp. 77–79; Berchorius, *Metamorphosis Ovidiana Moraliter* (s.l., 1509), fol. lxxiii; Boccaccio, *Della Genealogia degli Dei*, tr. Betussi (Venice, 1585), p. 87; dell'Anguillara and Horologgi, *Le Metamorphosi* (Venice, 1584), pp. 357, 387; Comes, *Mythologiae* (Padua, 1616), pp. 401–402, 548; Ross, *Mystagogus Poeticus* (London, 1648), pp. 334–37.

the lions of wrath, the swine of gluttony, the wolves of rapine.[13] Religious Eusebius makes a similar comparison in a more kindly fashion:

> The Saviour of men through the instrument of the human body which he united to his divinity shows himself all saving and blessing, as Greek Orpheus who by the skillful playing of his lyre tamed and subdued wild animals. The Greeks, I say, sang of his miracles and believed that the inspired accents of the divine poet not only affected animals but also trees who left their places at his singing to follow him. So is the voice of our Redeemer, a voice filled with divine wisdom which cures all evil received in the hearts of men.[14]

The history of Orpheus as a pagan type of Christ can be traced for many centuries;[15] by Milton's time it was such a part of the symbolic fabric of Christianity that one had only to think of "lyre" to say "cross." It is, for example, Orpheus who comes into John Donne's mind when he writes in "Goodfriday," "Could I behold those hands which span the Poles, / And tune all spheares at once, peirc'd with those holes?" This is the occasional image of Christ on the lyre, but the open comparison is conventionally stated for us by Giles Fletcher:

> Who doth not see drown'd in Deucalion's name
> (When earth his men, and sea had lost his shore)
> Old Noah; and in Nisus lock, the fame
> Of Sampson yet alive; and long before
> In Phaethon's, mine owne fall I deplore:
> But he that conquer'd hell, to fetch againe
> His virgin widowe, by a serpent slaine,
> Another Orpheus was the dreaming poets feigne.[16]

Thus Christians hallowed Orpheus for his half-success as a saviour of men and for his frustrated attempt to lead a soul out of Hell's darkness.

Tatian, in his *Oration Against the Greeks*, had argued that Orpheus

---

[13] *Cohortatio ad Gentes, PG*, VIII, 56–57.

[14] *Panegyric to Constantine, PG*, XX, 1409.

[15] Lampridius informs us in his life of Alexander Severus (a work cited by Milton in *Of Reformation*) that this Emperor erected shrines to Abraham, Christ, and Orpheus: see *Historiae Augustæ Scriptores* (Frankfurt, 1588), II, 214. Antonio Bosio has a chapter on why Christians compared Orpheus and Christ in *Roma Sotterano* (Rome, 1630). For an account of the Orpheus-Christ metaphor in Spanish literature see Pablo Cabanas, *El Mito de Orfeo en la literatura Española* (Madrid, 1948), pp. 153–76.

[16] *The Poetical Works*, ed. F. Boas (Cambridge, Eng., 1908), I, 59–60. One of the earliest English comparisons is found in Gavin Douglas: see *Poetical Works*, ed. Small (Edinburgh, 1874), II, 18. Wither objects to these comparisons in *A Preparation to the Psalter*, 1619 (Spenser Society, 1884), pp. 77–78.

and Hercules were the same person;[17] Milton would hardly say this, though he found in the demigod foreshadowings of both Samson and Christ. His admission of the Christian Hercules to his pantheon begins with the "Nativity Ode," where we are shown the infant Jesus "in his swaddling bands" ready to control the snaky Typhon and the rest of "the damned crew." It is Hercules, too, who is praised in *The Tenure of Kings* for his suppression of tyrants,[18] a superb Miltonic exploit; and he is recalled in the twenty-third sonnet for his rescue of Alcestis from the dark floor of Hell. He was, of course, attractive to Christians for other reasons. Begotten by Jove of a mortal woman, he early chose the right path, eschewing "the broad way and the green"; and, according to the almost Christian Seneca, "Jove's great son" devoted his whole life, in the best Stoic manner, to the conquest of his passions and the suppression of vice.[19] His major exploits were against the forces of darkness. We first hear of him in the *Iliad* (V, 397) as he strikes Hades with his "swift arrow" to leave him in anguish among the dead. No wonder that he thrice descended into Hell with somewhat better fortunes than those of Orpheus.

When Milton read the Orphic poems, he read the one that praises Hercules as a human saviour, but the comparison between Christ and Hercules, like the comparison between Christ and Orpheus, had been made before Milton's birth. "Ipse Christus verus fuit Hercules, qui per vitam aerumnosam omnia monstra superavit et edomuit."[20] The analogy was firmly established across the Channel, where Hercules Gallus was a stern rival of Francus, by d'Aubigne's *L'Hercule Chrestien*,[21] a moral prose on the labors Christianly read. This book inspired the *Hercule Chrestien*[22] of Ronsard, who advises his reader to swim a little below his surface:

[17] *PG*, VI, 885.

[18] *Op. cit.*, V, 19; for other references to Hercules see the Columbia *Index*. The Samson-Hercules-Christ identification is explored by Krouse, *Milton's Samson and the Christian Tradition* (Princeton, 1949), pp. 44–45.

[19] *Dial.*, II, 2, 2; see also Apuleius, *Florida*, 14, and Servius on *Aeneid*, VI, 119–23. The moral mythologers who read Christ into Orpheus also found the same connections between Christ and Hercules: see Fulgentius, pp. 32, 39–42; Boccaccio, pp. 210–14; Gyraldus, *Hercules*, in *Opera* (Leyden, 1696), I, 571–98; Alciati, *Emblemata* (Leyden, 1593), pp. 50–54, 505–508; Valeriano, *Hieroglyphica* (Basel, 1556), fols. 23ᵛ, 109ᵛ, 247ᵛ, 386; Comes, pp. 372–74.

[20] G. Budé, *De Asse et partibus* (Paris, 1532), p. lxix.

[21] *Oeuvres*, ed. Reaume and de Caussade (Paris, 1877), II, 226–31. Annibal Caro writes the Duchess of Castro: "Sotto il misterio d'Ercole si dinota Cristo, il quale estrinse il vizio, come Ercole uccise Cacco" (*Lettere Familiari* [Padua 1763], I, 253).

[22] *Oeuvres*, ed. Vaganay (Paris, 1924), VI, 137–45.

> Mais ou est l'oeil, tant soit-il aveugle,
> Ou est l'esprit, tant soit-il desreigle,
> S'il veut un peu mes paroles comprendre,
> Que par raison je ne luy face entendre,
> Que la plus-part des choses qu'on escrit
> De Hercule, est deve a un seul Jesuschrist.

Chaplain Ross, a good Scot, can put it bluntly: "Our blessed Saviour is the true Hercules."[23]

There is little question that these two pagan Christ-types were congenial to Milton not only for their Christian grace notes but for their reflection of Miltonic ideals. Both heroes were received in the "sweet Societies / That sing, and singing in their glory move," because, as Boethius made clear,[24] they early chose the proper ascent to Heaven. Their accomplishments and their exploits were the sort that Milton himself might read in his own book of hope. But there is more to it than this. Hercules and Orpheus were types—not so good as Moses or Enoch, of course—of the strong Son of God and the Singer of the New Song. The event in their story that tied the hard knot of analogy was their descent into the darkness, their triumphs or half-triumphs in Hell, and their return into the light and, eventually, to the holy summits. In this process of descent and ascent, of entering the dark to find the light, the two halves of the coin of allegory were united.

II

The visual imagery of *Paradise Lost*, as I suggested some years ago, depends to some extent on verbs of rising and falling, of descent and ascent, and on contrasts between light and darkness. These modes of expression coil about the demands of the central theme as the serpent coils about the forbidden tree so that we may be urged to abandon the horizontal movement of human history for the vertical motion of the spiritual life, the dark nothingness of ignorance and evil for the light of ultimate truth and reality. The descent of Milton into the darkness of Hell before he rises to the great "Globe of circular light" is a sound Christian rescript. "Descend," says St. Augustine, "that you may ascend." "Descende ut ascendas, humiliare ut exalteris."[25] Christ's double descent—first into the flesh and then into the dark Saturday of

---

[23] *Op. cit.*, p. 169.

[24] *Consolations*, III, met. 12; IV, met. 7.

[25] *Sermo* CCXCVII, *PL*, xxxix, 2313–14; *Confessiones*, IV, 12; *De Civitate*, VII, 33; *Enarratio in Psalmos*, *PL*, xxxvii, 1596–1600, 1606.

Hell—furnished those who humbled themselves with a map of Christian progress. One goes down in humility into the dark so that one may ascend in triumph to the light. Satan and his squires know this course well enough to pervert it.

When the black tyrant, who has been "Hurl'd headlong" down, addresses his companions, he pretends, contrary to fact, that the descent was voluntary and a preparation for ascension. "From this descent / Celestial Virtues rising, will appear / More glorious and more dread than from no fall" (II, 14–16). Satan's prideful qualification is enough to make the word *rising* ironic; but his falsehood is not only believed but seconded by the deluded Moloch, who describes with desperate wit the millions that "longing wait / The Signal to ascend" and boastfully asserts "That in our proper motion we ascend / Up to our native seat: descent and fall / To us is adverse" (II, 55–77). Moloch's knowledge is no better than his grammar, for he, like his fellows, has gone about it the wrong way. He has already ascended in pride; been guilty of a "sursum cor contra Dominum,"[26] and so he has "frozen and fallen like a flake of snow."[27] The literature of the Church knows all these phrases for the fate of the prideful aspirant; it tells us that those who descend in humility arise to those heights, "Unde Satan elatus cecidit, fidelis homo sublevatus ascendat."[28] The humble ascend to the light; the proud enter the depths, the "caligo tenebrarum densissima."[29] For those in hope of seeing the light that Satan truly detests, the road is easily followed, because both roads, as Bernard of Clairvaux puts it, are the same:

The same steps lead up to the throne and down; the same road leads to the city and from it; one door is the entrance of the house and the exit; Jacob saw the angels ascending and descending on the same ladder. What does all this mean? Simply that if you desire to return to truth, you do not have to seek a new way which you do not know, but the known way by which you descended. Retracing your steps, you may ascend in humility by the same path which you descended in pride.[30]

Augustine's descent in humility is paralleled by Bernard's descent in pride, because both are dark ways that lead upward to the light. Had Milton's Adam been humble in obedience, he would have

---

[26] *Sermo XXV, PL,* xxxviii, 168.
[27] *In Job, PL,* xxxiv, 875.
[28] Cassiodorus, *Exposition in Psalter, PL,* lxx, 1036.
[29] Anselm, *Liber de Similitudinibus, PL,* clix, 664–65.
[30] *De Gradibus Humilitatis,* ed. Burch (Cambridge, Mass., 1940), p. 176.

ascended, as Raphael, who had read the Church Fathers,[31] made plain (V, 490–505). But Adam sacrificed his prospects of angelic perfection for the immediate rewards of romantic love; even then, however, his subsequent humility guarantees his ascension. The demons also talk of ascending, but "self-tempted," they are secure in their fall. The bitter pride and the prideful unrepentance that governs them is embossed by Satan in his soul-revealing soliloquy:

> O foul descent! that I who erst contended
> With Gods to sit the highest, am now constrain'd
> Into a Beast, and mixt with bestial slime,
> This essence to incarnate and imbrute,
> That to the hight of Deitie aspir'd:
> But what will not Ambition and Revenge
> Descend to? who aspires must down as low
> As high he soar'd . . . .   (IX, 163–70)

Satan, in other words, knows the rules. In time his legions will rise far enough to occupy the middle air, but they will not advance into the "precincts of light." Depth and dark are really their "native seat." Their master is very honest about this, admitting, as he returns from the grand seduction, that he finds descent "through darkness" an easy road (X, 393–98).

It is darkness, as well as descent, even though it is "darkness visible" that plagues the newcomers to Hades. They sit in the gloom, as Gregory the Great tells us, "inwardly dark amidst the everlasting darkness of damnation."[32] Behind them are "the happy Realms of Light" (I, 85), which they have exchanged for a dreary plain, "void of light" (I, 180). Once they were famed as God's "Bright-harness'd Angels"; now they spend their time plotting how to "affront" God's holy light "with thir darkness" (I, 389–91), confounding "Heav'n's purest Light" "with blackest Insurrection" (II, 136–37). In alternate moments they console themselves with foolish or violent plans for an escape to light (II, 220, 376–78), but Satan, who has read the sixth book of the *Aeneid*, reminds them that "Long is the way / And hard, that out of Hell leads up to Light" (II, 432–33). In Satan's church—

---

[31] For patristic comments on the perfectibility of an unfallen Adam, see Hugo of St. Victor, *De Vanitate Mundi*, *PL*, CLXXVI, 723; St. Thomas, *Summa*, I, Q.102, a.4; Pico della Mirandola, *De Hominis Dignitate*, ed. Garin (Florence, 1942), pp. 104, 106; J. Donne, *Sermons*, ed. Potter and Simpson (Berkeley, Calif., 1953–60), II, 123, VII, 108.

[32] *In Ezechielem*, *PL*, LXXVI, 1290.

and theology informs us that he has one—this might be called the diabolique of darkness; the counter-Church opposes to this opaqueness the sublime metaphysic of light.

We need not scratch through the Bible or the smaller gravel of the theologians to find the moral interpretation of the blackness of Hell, of the mind of evil, or what Milton's Jehovah calls the "dark designs." The Christian conscience is fully aware of the dark symbols. Ignorance, sin and sinner, damnation, Hell and its provost are festooned with black against a midnight ground, and the speculations of Beatus Jung are seldom required to expound the Christian tradition. Opposed to this night of negation is what might be called the *tenebrae in bono* which is consonant with the descent in humility and is explained by the divine darkness that even Mammon knows.

> This deep world
> Of darkness do we dread? How oft amidst
> Thick clouds and dark doth Heav'n's all-ruling Sire
> Choose to reside, his Glory unobscur'd,
> And with the Majesty of darkness round
> Covers his Throne; from whence deep thunders roar
> Must'ring thir rage, and Heav'n resembles Hell?
> As he our Darkness, cannot we his Light
> Imitate when we please?   (II, 262–70)

If these were not English devils, we would put this down to conscious humor; but the absence of jest is proclaimed when Pandaemonium is lighted with sputtering gas lamps that badly imitate Heaven's essential light. The dark with which God mantles himself is as different from Hell-dark as Hell-fire is from Heaven's blazing cressets. Moses, who ascended Mt. Sinai to enter the dark folds of God's light, could lecture the swart Mammon in hermeneutics.

Though Orpheus and Hercules enter the dark and arise to the light, the basic Christian idea of the dark god in the divine night is a totally different concept. For the ancients, light was the essence of existence and the sun shone in their temples, bathing the clear gods in bright gold. Death was the greatest of horrors, not because it deprived one of limb and motion but rather because it extinguished the mortal world of light. Dying Antigone weeps because never again will she see the holy light (ll. 879–80), and her lamentation is heard again and again in Greek tragedy.[33] Light was life, and it was also wisdom. For Plato

---

[33] See also Sophocles, *Aias*, 854–65, *Oedipus Col.*, 1549–51, and Euripides, *Iph. Aul.*, 1281–82, 1506–1509.

φῶς is the means by which men who live in the realm of shadow almost place their hands on the unknown and unknowable.[34] The Roman stoics soothed themselves with the same consolation of light; hence Seneca can remind the suffering Helvia that "The gleams of night" enable one to commune with celestial beings and keep one's mind "always directed toward the sight of kindred things above."[35] The Christians, too, saw Jehovah as a bright God, the Father of Lights, and in his human manifestation, the *Lux Mundi*;[36] but they also knew him as a god in darkness,[37] assuming his cloak of clouds.[38] The figure of a darkened god visible only in the soul's night demanded an explanatory inscription on the entablature.

The Christian doctrine of the light in darkness begins when Philo Judaeus, the stepfather of exegesis, interpreted Exodus 20:21. The broad cloud on Mt. Sinai, he writes, is the allegory of Moses' attempt to understand the invisible and incorporeal nature of Jehovah;[39] it is also, in a more general sense, the symbolic exposition of the process by which the contemplative mind tries to comprehend the immaterial.[40] More than a century later, Roman Plotinus compared man's perception of common experience to wandering through the statues of the gods that crowd the outskirts of a temple.[41] The luminous soul has, truly enough, descended into darkness[42] when it has entered the flesh, but it still provides an inner light.[43] Once it has reached its limit this light is also changed into an obscurity;[44] but this limit does not blind the inner sight by which one may ascend to the light in the shadows (ἐλλαμψις ἡ εἰς το σκοτος), the spiritual habitation which is the goal of the wise.[45] Philo, accounting for the experience of Moses, and Plotinus, elaborating on the light metaphysic of Plato, offered to western man an esoteric explanation of divine light:

[34] *Republic*, VI, 508–509, VII, 518; *Phaedo*, 99; see J. Stenzel, "Der Begriff der Erleuchtung bei Platon," *Die Antike*, II (1926), 235–37.

[35] *Ad Helviam*, VIII, 5–6; see also Plutarch, *De Genio Soc.*, 590 B.

[36] Psalms 36:9, 104:2; Wisdom, 7:21–25; I Timothy 6:16; I John 1:5.

[37] Exodus 20:21, II Chronicles 6:1, II Samuel 22:12, Psalms 18:11–12, 97:2, Job 22:14.

[38] Ezekiel 1:4, Revelation 1:7.

[39] *Vita Mosis*, I, 28.

[40] *De Poster. Caini*, 5.

[41] *Enneads*, VI, 9, 11, 8–22.

[42] *Ibid.*, IV, 3, 9, 23–29.

[43] *Ibid.*, V, 3, 17, 27–37.

[44] *Ibid.*, IV, 3, 9, 23–26.

[45] *Ibid.*, II, 9, 12, 31; I, 6, 9, 22–24; see M. de Corte, "Plotin et la nuit de l'esprit," *Études Carmélitaines*, II (1938), 102–15.

it hides itself in the dark and one must enter the cloud to find it.

Milton, who had only the rudimentary chronology of his age to guide him, would probably think of Plato as a contemporary of Moses. He would certainly accept the Pseudo-Dionysius, the great exponent of this philosophy, as the disciple of St. Paul and the coeval of Philo. He would, consequently, assign all these similar doctrines to the first Christian era. The facts, as we now know and as I intend to relate them, were otherwise, and it is Gregory of Nyssa, whom Milton was reading before he wrote *An Apology*, who was the precursor of the Areopagite and who brought this doctrine into the fold of the Church. Gregory invented the poignant oxymoron "bright darkness" (λαμπρός γνόφος),[46] a trope that haunts the rhetoric of mystics ever afterward. In his *Life of Moses* he is troubled by the god who first showed himself in light and then in a dark shroud. He sought and found a solution for this strangeness. The Logos is first seen as light, but as one ascends, it becomes dark because one realizes that it surpasses ordinary knowledge and is separated from mortal comprehension by the *tenebrae*.[47] This is why Moses first saw God as light. Becoming more perfect in understanding by putting aside false knowledge of the divine, he passed from the primary light of the Logos, which dissipates impiety, into the divine dark. In this night, his mind, rejecting "the simple aspects of things," was fixed in a stasis of contemplation so that here he saw the true light where God is.[48] In this way Gregory wrote out the Christian explanations of the dark experience which the person who called himself Dionysius would some centuries later make an intrinsic part of Christian knowledge.

The light metaphysic of the Pseudo-Dionysius also owes much to Origen's doctrine of the double vision obtained through the eyes of the sense and the eyes of the mind. In order that the external eyes of men may be blinded, Origen writes, and that the inner eyes may see, Christ endured the humility of incarnation. By this descent, he, who healed the blind by miracle, blinded our external eyes so that he could cure our inner sight.[49] The Pseudo-Dionysius begins his *Mystical Theology* with the request that he may be allowed to ascend to those

---

[46] *In Cantica Canticorum*, PG, XLIV, 1000–01. It should be noted that Tertullian prior to his polemic against Montanism describes an "obumbratio mentis" as a preface to divine knowledge; see *Ad Marcion*, PL, II, 413, and *De Anima*, ed. Waszink (Amsterdam, 1947), p. 62 and notes. Ambrose considers the *tenebrae* as a requirement of the prophetic state: *De Abraham*, PL, XIV, 484.

[47] *Op. cit.*, PG, XLIV, 376–77.

[48] *In Cantica, ibid.*, 1001.

[49] *Contra Celsum*, PG, XI, 1476.

oracles where the mysteries of theology are seen in a darkness brighter than light.[50] He yearns to enter the "divine darkness" (θειος γνόφος),[51] where the human handicap of seeing and being seen is removed and all forms of external perception are blinded in the sacred darkness that is inaccessible light.[52] For him the *tenebrae* is a ἀγνωσία; and when the searcher has arrived at its limits, which are complete negation, he will see at last without veils.[53] The Pseudo-Dionysius supports this doctrine with the example of Moses, who penetrated into "the cloud of unknowing" by closing his human eyes to all the vanities of mortal knowledge.[54] Moses, it is true, did not see God's face but only the divine place;[55] nonetheless, his intellectual eyes, like those of the supercelestial Intelligences and Seraphim,[56] were cleansed of the "mass of obscurity."[57]

After the tenth century the vogue of the Pseudo-Dionysius and his doctrine was enormous. Hilduin, John Scot, Hincmar, Radebert, John of Salisbury, Sarrazin, Hugo of St. Victor, Albert the Great, and St. Thomas found spiritual fascination in his writings.[58] The excitement of the Middle Ages was shared by the members of the Florentine Academy, by Ficino, who translated the Areopagite and wrote his own *De Lumine*, and by Pico della Mirandola, who discovered in the Pseudo-Dionysius a fellow exotic. But the light metaphysic of this fifth-century Greek was particularly illuminating to those who followed the upward mystic road, to John of the Cross, Ruusbroec, Tauler, and Suso, all of whom walked the way marked out by Richard of St. Victor[59] and St. Bonaventura. The manuals of the latter saint are rubricated with the paradoxical notion that to see one must become blind: "Excaecatio est summa illuminatio." One must search, says Bonaventura, for the night of light, but only those who have found it know what it is.

Jacob's ladder is placed on these three levels, the top reaching Heaven and so is Solomon's throne where sits the king wise and in peace, lovable as the most precious husband and most desirable. Upon him the angels desire

---

[50] *Op. cit., PG*, III, 997.
[51] *Ibid.*, 1000.
[52] *Epistolae, ibid.*, 1073.
[53] *T.M., ibid.*, 1000–1001.
[54] *Ibid.*, 1001.
[55] *Ibid.*, 1000.
[56] *De Coelesti Hierarchia, ibid.*, 205.
[57] *De Divinis Nominibus, ibid.*, 700–701; see H. C. Peuch, "La Ténèbre mystique chez le Pseudo-Denys," *Études Carmélitaines*, II (1938), 33–53.
[58] P. G. Théry, "Denys au moyen age," *Études Carmélitaines*, II (1938), 68–74.
[59] *Benjamin Minor, PL*, CXCVI, 52.

to look and the love of holy souls yearns for him just as the stag seeks fountains of water. Hither in the manner of fire, our spirit is made skillful by a most fervent desire for the ascent but is carried by a wise ignorance beyond itself into darkness and delight so that it not only says with the bride: "We will run after thee to the odor of thy ointments," but also sings with the prophet: "and night shall be my light in my pleasure." What this nocturnal and delightful illumination is no one knows unless he tries it, and unless grace is given divinely no one tries it; and no one is given it unless he trains himself for it.[60]

The same mode of expression is found in Dante, who like Virgil and Milton descended into Hell, who went into the dark in order to see the light. The poetic allegory comes at the beginning when Dante leaves the forest of this world and having endured the night with piety prepares to enter the dark downward path so that he may ascend to the triple circle of final illumination.

> Ma poi ch'io fui al piè d'un colle giunto,
> Là dove terminava quella valle
> Che m'avea di paura il cor compunto,
> Guardai in alto, e vidi le sue spalle
> Vestite già de' raggi del pianeta
> Che mena dritto altrui per ogni calle.
> Allor fu la paura un poco queta
> Che nel lago del cor m'era durata
> La notte ch' io passai con tanta pièta.   (I, 13–21)

Milton's poetic realization of the themes of descent and ascent, of the necessity of entering the dark in order to see the light, of the descent of light itself so that men may see, and of the inner eye that knows only when the exterior sight is gone, is constantly before us as we read him. These themes were carried to exorbitant excess by the mystics, but we must remember that in spite of the emphasis given them by this nervous faith they have a simple Christian provenience. It is in the plain sense, which seems nowadays to be extravagant, that Milton puts them to use. The descent of humility comes before us as early as the "Nativity Ode" when we are told how the Son of God forsook the "Courts of everlasting Day" to choose "with us a darksome House of mortal Clay." The same theme comes forward again when Christ is assured that he will not degrade his nature "by descending" to assume that of man. "Therefore thy Humiliation shall exalt / With thee thy Manhood also to this Throne" (*P.L.*, III, 303–14). On the human level the poet seeking perfection rises from the day

---

[60] *Breviloquium, Opera Omnia* (Florence, 1891), V, 260.

of "L'Allegro" and enters the night, "the high lonely Tow'r," of "Il Penseroso." Thus he, too, enters the dark, as Moses did, in order to reach the dawn and the "Prophetic strain." As Milton leaves the light of the first poem that reveals only the "aspects of things," Orpheus lifts his head, but in the night of the second he hears the singing of both Orpheus and his son Musaeus. It is in darkness, too, that fallen Adam descends so that the day of fleshly surrender can be followed by the night of remorse and humility; through this course, the father of men ascends to God, first, in prayer and, then, in vision.

The theme of the inner eyes, so comforting to the blind man, makes its appearance as early as the *Second Defence*,[61] where Milton compares his blindness with his opponent's spiritual dark: "mine keeps from my view only the colored surfaces of things, while it leaves me at liberty to contemplate the beauty and stability of virtue and truth." *Samson Agonistes*, if it is the last work, almost depends on this idea. At the bottom of despair Samson, "a moving grave," doubts that "light is in the Soul" (l. 92) and sees only "double darkness nigh at hand" (l. 593). But Samson's night becomes day when in the complete negation of himself he yields humbly to the "rousing motions in me" (l. 1382); then the Semichorus can sing:

> But he though blind of sight,
> Despis'd and thought extinguish'd quite,
> With inward eyes illuminated
> His fiery virtue rous'd
> From under ashes into sudden flame.   (ll. 1687–91)

We must turn, however, to *Paradise Lost*, and especially to two of its invocations, to find all of this in flower.

The epic opens with the great address recalling Moses' ascent from the low vale to the summit of Sinai to enter the clouded light that awaits him. The experience of "that Shepherd, who first taught the chosen Seed" reminds Milton of the brook of Siloa which flowed into Siloam's pool, "fast by the Oracle of God," where Christ healed the blind man, curing at once both the inward and the exterior eyes. The types of both Old and New Testament are then personally read as the poet prays for the ascent toward light. "What in me is dark / Illumine, what is low raise and support; / That to the highth of this great Argument. . . . " Prayer is itself the humble act, a preface to Milton's descent into the dark underground of Satan's province.

---

[61] *Op. cit.*, VIII, 71.

It is possible that Milton begins in Hell because he who met Casella "in the milder shades of Purgatory" began there. There is, however, a difference between the two poets and their purposes. Dante enters Hell (although the allegorical process of conversion and Christian education is a reader's requirement) because the literal demanded it. Milton's descent is an artistic voluntary. In a moral sense Dante descends that he may ascend; he enters the dark to find the light. In doing so he takes Milton by the hand, but the reason is doctrinal rather than poetic. Having explored the dark bottom of pride, Milton rises toward the light. The preface to Book III recounts this ascension:

> Thee I revisit now with bolder wing,
> Escap't the *Stygian* Pool, though long detained
> In that obscure sojourn, while in my flight
> Through utter and through middle darkness borne
> With other notes than to th'*Orphean* Lyre
> I sung of *Chaos* and *Eternal Night*,
> Taught by the heav'nly Muse to venture down
> The dark descent, and up to reascend,
> Though hard and rare.   (III, 13–21)

Milton, like Moses, sees the "Holy Light," but like the great type of the Redeemer he must descend to his "Native Element." Light, however, is given the inner eye, and, like Vaughan's Nicodemus, he can "at mid-night speak with the Sun!" It is more than sixteen hundred years after the typified event; yet the English poet joins himself to the procession, heathen and Christian, of those who acted in the great allegory of faith, who descended to ascend, who entered the darkness to see the light.

IRONIC AND AMBIGUOUS ALLUSION
IN *PARADISE LOST*

Douglas Bush, Harvard University

Criticism of *Samson Agonistes* has taken full account of the irony that invests the total structure, the outcome of the successive "acts," and the texture: ironic ambiguity begins with the title and the first line, "A little onward lend thy guiding hand." While Miltonic criticism has reached such bulk that one cannot readily take a precautionary review of it, ambiguity and irony in *Paradise Lost* seem to have been much less discussed, perhaps because these elements are less conspicuous in the more complex work or because they are accepted as obvious. Most of the examples I shall mention have been noted individually and incidentally but they have not, I think, been brought together. Those given here are only a sampling, especially on the biblical side, and they represent mainly one kind of ambiguity, that expressed through a particular but veiled allusion.

This technique seems to be regarded by some critics as the invention of Ezra Pound and T. S. Eliot, but it was used with subtle success by Spenser. The most exalted tribute Spenser paid to his bride is indirect:

> Open the temple gates unto my love,
> Open them wide that she may enter in.

The lines have their own emotional charge, but it is greatly heightened by our recollection of Psalm 24:7: "Lift up your heades ye gates, and be ye lift up ye everlasting dores, and the King of glorie shal come in." One example in *The Faerie Queene* (I, xii, 13, and 22–23) is the way in which the Red Cross Knight and Una merge with Christ and his "wife" through echoes of Christ's entry into Jerusalem and the marriage of the Lamb (Rev. 19:7–8).

The kind of allusion that we have in *Paradise Lost* had appeared in Milton as early as *In quintum Novembris* (1626). In the opening lines Satan, the roving exile from heavenly Olympus, counts over his faithful followers in crime, *sceleris socios*, a phrase Cicero used at least twice of Catiline's associates (*In Catilinam*, I, iv, 8, III, i, 4; cf. Lucretius, III, 61, *socios scelerum*). In line 11 these followers are described as *Participes regni post funera moesta futuros*, an ironical echo of Hebrews, 3:14, "For we are made partakers of Christ"; the echo is made still clearer by Tremellius' translation, *Participes enim facti sumus cum Christo* (cf. *De Doctrina Christiana, Works*, XVI, 4: *Christi participes facti sumus*).

There is a frequent difference between old and new methods, since in modern poets the whole significance may depend upon an allusion, sometimes a more or less esoteric allusion, which the reader may not catch and without which he is lost (until the critics have had time to hunt it down). In Spenser and Milton, however, the allusion is normally public, often biblical or classical, and supposedly within the ordinary reader's compass. Besides, even if it and its intensifying or complicating effect are missed, the loss, though real, is not fatal, since the main drift is clear without it.

Against this generality one partial exception might be lodged. Some lines in the epilogue to *Comus* are difficult in the modern way because—though the total context is a general guide—the meaning here is given through allusive symbols without anything in the way of "prose statement." The allusion to Venus and Adonis seems—as Professor Woodhouse showed in his well-known study (*University of Toronto Quarterly*, XI, 1941)—to be especially to Spenser's interpretation of the myth (*F.Q.*, III, vi, 46–49) in terms of the cycle of physical generation, the perpetual union of matter and form. Milton's allusion to Cupid and Psyche, which follows immediately (and is marked off by a distinct change of rhythm), is in a more fully orthodox tradition, since this late "myth" had long been understood as the marriage of Christ and the human soul, though it is uncertain here whether the poet is thinking of the life of grace on earth or of the full felicity of heaven.

While this short paper is concerned with particulars in *Paradise Lost*, we may remind ourselves of the larger ironies to which such details contribute. These larger and more familiar ironies are of the same dramatic kind that we have in *Samson:* that is, characters speak and act in ignorance of the outcome, which the reader already knows. But, because of the central theme of conflict in *Paradise Lost*, this dramatic irony has a further or clearer basis in the absolutes of Christian faith: Absolute Good, embodied in the Father and the Son, is completely and unshakably invincible, so that Satan—although he achieves a degree of success disastrous for man—can never be even imagined as winning. While in soliloquies he can recognize at least part of the truth, in his public harangues and actions he, like his followers, is in a state of spiritual blindness concerning the real issues. Thus all their futile activities are seen in an ironic light—"Hatching vain Empires," in Beelzebub's words.

This general conception, natural enough in a Christian writer, is carried out through a dramatic method, a character's self-revelation, which reminds us more of Shakespeare than of Sophocles. Like Shakespeare, Milton could rely on the moral and religious reactions of his audience, and he could also guide those reactions through his own comments. This sort of dramatic irony had been used in the speeches of Comus, as when he declares

> We that are of purer fire
> Imitate the Starry Quire . . . ;

and with him as with Satan we are not always certain of the line between unconscious and conscious self-deception. In *Paradise Lost* the first example of dramatic irony is Satan's first speech, delivered to Beelzebub—the place at which early romantic readers and their modern successors begin to show their inability to comprehend a Christian poem. Even if we had heard nothing of Satan's egocentric pride and hate, every phrase he utters reveals a completely perverted view of God and himself and the issues between them. In his second speech Satan is allowed to see the conflict between evil and good, even to state Milton's own conception of his epic theme (ll. 162–65; cf. 214–20), but only from the standpoint of Satan's own corruption. There is no need of remarking on the heterogeneous ironies and ambiguities that punctuate Satan's speeches, here and later, since we are, as I said, concerned with only one kind.

Paradise Lost has many certain and some uncertain examples of the veiled allusion. One of the most arresting is in the first two lines of Satan's first speech:

> If thou beest he; But O how fall'n! how chang'd
> From him, who in the happy Realms of Light . . . .

Milton's fusions of the Hebraic and the classical have usually a more than double potency, and here Isaiah's "How art thou fallen from heaven, O Lucifer, son of the morning" (14:12) is joined with Virgil's phrase about the bloodstained ghost of Hector, *quantum mutatus ab illo Hectore* who had been *lux Dardaniae* (*Aeneid*, II, 274, 281). Most of the general ironic ambiguities of Satan's speeches are quite clear, since they turn on two opposed sets of traditional values, religious and irreligious; but sometimes one is not sure how far the modern appetite

for this sort of thing is entitled to go. One major premise at least is that
Milton and his early readers knew the Bible and the common classics
far better than we do and were far more likely to use and to catch
overtones from both sources. For instance, when Satan grandly pro-
claims

> and thou profoundest Hell
> Receive thy new Possessor,

we know that he is really a prisoner, and in a mental as well as a local
hell. We know that "Better to reign in Hell, then serve in Heav'n" em-
bodies a false conception of power and freedom (and an echo in re-
verse of Achilles' shade in the *Odyssey*, XI, 489–91). But when in the
same speech Satan refers to "this unhappy Mansion" (I, 268; cf.
"this ill Mansion," II, 462), are we intended to remember "In my
Father's house are many mansions" (John, 14:2)? (So too in *Samson*,
where religious belief is kept within the Hebraic frame, are we to hear
an ambiguous overtone in the grieving Manoa's "Home to his Fathers
house"?) For another doubtful item, while the Red Sea's overwhelm-
ing of the Egyptians is the material of an elaborate simile (I, 304 ff.),
we cannot be sure, a little earlier, if we are intended to see an ironic
contrast with the Israelites' miraculous crossing when Satan

> rears from off the Pool
> His mighty Stature; on each hand the flames
> Drivn backward slope thir pointing spires, and rowld
> In billows, leave i' th' midst a horrid Vale.   (I, 221 ff.)

A longer passage (I, 549 ff.) prompts the question how far Milton,
when utilizing a source not likely to come to everyone's mind, gives it
an ironic effectiveness that is not dependent on recognition:

> Anon they move
> In perfect *Phalanx* to the *Dorian* mood
> Of Flutes and soft Recorders; such as rais'd
> To hight of noblest temper Hero's old
> Arming to Battel, and in stead of rage
> Deliberate valour breath'd, firm and unmov'd
> With dread of death to flight or foul retreat,
> Nor wanting power to mitigate and swage
> With solemn touches, troubl'd thoughts, and chase
> Anguish and doubt and fear and sorrow and pain
> From mortal or immortal minds. Thus they
> Breathing united force with fixed thought
> Mov'd on in silence to soft Pipes that charm'd
> Thir painful steps o're the burnt soyle; and now

> Advanc't in view, they stand, a horrid Front
> Of dreadful length and dazling Arms, in guise
> Of Warriers old with order'd Spear and Shield,
> Awaiting what command thir mighty Chief
> Had to impose.

Commentators have noted that Milton is adapting a passage in Plutarch's *Lycurgus*, and North will serve our purpose (Temple Classics, I, 203–204):

So that it was a marvellous pleasure, and likewise a dreadful sight, to see the whole battell march together in order, at the sound of the pipes, and never to break their pace, nor confound their ranks, nor to be dismayed nor amazed themselves, but to go on quietly and joyfully at the sound of these pipes, to hazard themselves even to death. For it is likely, that such courages are not troubled with much fear, nor yet overcome with much fury: but rather they have an assured constancy and valiantness in good hope, as those which are backed with the assisting favour of the gods.[1]

Dr. Tillyard, writing without reference to Plutarch, said long ago (*Milton*, p. 269) what he probably would not say now, that "In this passage if anywhere Milton is on the Devils' side." The poet does certainly acknowledge, with a heightening of Plutarch, the order, courage, and dignity of the marching angels. At the same time he makes most of the borrowed matter into a simile and implies a contrast between the "Deliberate valour" of ancient heroes arming for battle in assurance of divine help and the "rage" that has inspired the defeated and evil host of hell; and after the simile the last lines (containing a bit of Plutarch) bring us back to these marchers and what and where they are. All this is made subtly clear even if we do not know of the "source."

A unique example of irony is the allegory of Sin and Death which Addison and Dr. Johnson disapproved of but which modern readers seem to find very powerful. Part of the effect, especially of the first episode, is the further and direct revelation of the true character and associations of the "heroic" Satan. But the chief effect, as modern critics have seen, comes from Milton's making Satan, Sin, and Death

---

[1] E. H. Gardner (*MLN*, LXII [1947], 360) pointed out that the parallel was perhaps first recognized by K. Chetwood in translating Plutarch (1683). It was noted by R. C. Trench, *Plutarch* (2nd ed. [London, 1874], pp. 75–76), and, more recently, by F. L. Jones, *MLN*, XLIX [1934], 44–45), G. Ethel (*MLQ*, XVIII [1957], 295–302), and P. Turner (*NQ*, IV [1957], 10–11. Turner spoke of the irony in Milton's use of a passage referring to courage and divine favor. Others have cited other and much less close parallels. Arnold Stein has an analysis of the whole passage, without reference to sources, in *ELH*, XVI (1949), 120–34.

a monstrous counterpart of the Trinity, and this is done through a few
allusions—"thy only Son" (II, 728), "one for all / My self expose"
(II, 827-28), and that climactic phrase which brings a special shock in
the final inverted adjective,

> where I shall Reign
> At thy right hand voluptuous . . . .
>   (II, 868-69; cf. III, 62-64)

In the continuation of the allegory in Book X, when Sin and Death
set about building a bridge from hell to earth, they

> Flew divers, & with Power (thir Power was great)
> Hovering upon the Waters,

and the last phrase is again a grisly parody, of both Genesis and the
exordium of the poem, where the creative spirit of God dove-like sat
brooding on the vast abyss. In this whole passage, where Satan, returning to hell to report his triumph, congratulates Sin and Death on
their bridge, the ironic parallel with the Trinity is carried on; the
exchanges between Sin and Satan are like what might have been said
by the Son and the Father after the Creation. The next incident (X,
504 ff.) involves no particular allusion but is a general reminder of
Ovid, though the grotesque irony outdoes anything Ovidian—the
wholesale metamorphosis of the triumphant Satan and his applauding
followers.

Another and special Ovidian item may be added here, a myth-
ological-topical allusion no less potent than obvious, and one which
transcends irony. That is, in the invocation to Book VII, the appeal to
Urania to

> drive farr off the barbarous dissonance
> Of *Bacchus* and his revellers . . . .

Part of the idea had just been presented in Milton's half-personal, half-
impersonal way:

> On evil dayes though fall'n, and evil tongues;
> In darkness, and with dangers compast round,
> And solitude; yet not alone . . . .

At once, in terms that recall the passage on Orpheus in "Lycidas,"
he stridently depicts the savage murder of the ideal poet; but he asserts at the same time the protective guidance of his own Heavenly
Muse. Through the mythological metaphor the blind John Milton in
the London of Charles II is generalized into the inspired poet-priest in
a world of corruption.

The irony that envelops Adam and Eve, like the irony that envelops Satan, arises from their ignorance of the future and of what is
at stake; partly also it goes along with the human weakness that
eventuates in sin like his. If Eden is a symbol of the poet's lifelong
vision of perfection, its perfection is brief. It is a master-stroke of
ironic presentation, as critics have amply recognized, that what
seems idyllic innocence and beatitude is from the start overshadowed
by Satan's presence. And if the finest of all Milton's similes, "Not
that faire field Of Enna," is a distillation of the beauty of Eden, it is
also a distillation of the pervasive irony, since, as every reader sees,
the reference to Proserpine and Dis is a clear though tacit anticipation of Satan's seduction of Eve. Although we think of Milton as an
exponent of moral choice, of conscious virtue, the impending ruin of
Adam and Eve evokes his nostalgic compassion for the simple innocence that is unaware of evil:

> Sleep on
> Blest pair; and O yet happiest if ye seek
> No happier state, and know to know no more. (IV, 773–75)

> thrice happie if they know
> Thir happiness, and persevere upright.   (VII, 631–32)

In both utterances Milton is recalling Virgil's eulogy of the simple
Italian farmers who shun ambition and are content with their humble
life (*Georgics*, II, 458–60):

> O fortunatos nimium, sua si bona norint,
> agricolas! quibus ipsa, procul discordibus armis,
> fundit humo facilem victum iustissima tellus.

We know that Eve is to succumb to Satan's appeal to her ambition
and the reminder of Virgil's peasants adds a note of human actuality
to the pathos of idyllic innocence. Just before the first of these two
extracts (IV, 772–73) we have:

> And on thir naked limbs the flourie roof
> Showrd Roses, which the Morn repair'd.

The last phrase may echo *Georgics*, II, 201–202, where Virgil says
that what the herds crop in the long days the cool dew will restore in
one short night: "exigua tantum gelidus ros nocte reponet." In Virgil
the idea is merely nature's quiet, perpetual renewal; in Milton it becomes ironical because the morning's repairs will not go on much
longer. Apropos of this second *Georgic*, we may remember Milton's

echo, in the invocation to Light, of Virgil's lines 475 ff.; along with what Dr. Tillyard has finely said (*Poetry Direct and Oblique* [1934], pp. 189–90), we may note that Virgil's contrast between poetry of the cosmos and that of the countryside becomes in Milton a contrast between his beloved classics and the higher themes of Sion.

There has been in recent years a good deal of debate over the artistic problem of Milton's keeping Adam and Eve innocent while yet preparing the way for their fall; clearly the fall would be unreal and meaningless, a piece of melodrama, if it came as a sudden and complete surprise. The first hints of the possibility of weakness—they are no more than that—are given in a single speech of Eve's (IV, 460 ff.) and given through veiled allusions to two Ovidian myths. Though the first is made unmistakably clear—Eve's admiring her own face in a pool, like Narcissus—it achieves a quite subtle result, since the faint trace of latent vanity and self-centeredness is not incompatible with the naïve innocence of the newly created Eve. The second allusion is shorter and less obvious but would be immediately recognized by readers who knew their Ovid. Eve goes on to recall how, seeing Adam, she had turned away from a being less attractive than "that smooth watry image," whereupon he had followed, crying:

> Return faire *Eve*,
> Whom fli'st thou? whom thou fli'st, of him thou art,
> His flesh, his bone; to give thee being I lent
> Out of my side to thee, neerest my heart
> Substantial Life, to have thee by my side
> Henceforth an individual solace dear;
> Part of my Soul I seek thee, and thee claim
> My other half. . . .

These partly biblical words are an innocent declaration of pure love and devotion, yet they register Adam's potential weakness as Eve had registered hers, and chiefly because the first words recall those of Apollo as he pursues Daphne (*Metamorphoses*, I, 504 ff., 514 ff.):

> nympha, precor, Penei, mane! non insequor hostis . . .
> . . . nescis, temeraria, nescis,
> quem fugias, ideoque fugis. . . .

(The last phrase George Sandys rendered as "From whom thou fly'st, thou know'st not.") Milton's brief but clear echo of Ovid contributes to making his lines the germ, no more, of the extravagant avowal of idolatry in VIII, 521–59, where Adam is on the way toward letting Eve usurp his own proper place and come between him and God; later still, just before he surrenders to Eve's persuasions, he twice echoes the rest of the lines quoted above (IX, 911 ff., 952 ff.). In that dialogue in Book VIII, when Adam's excessive veneration for Eve has drawn a rebuke from Raphael, Adam, "half abash't," offers some defense, and in the course of it affirms (VIII, 610–11):

> yet still free
> Approve the best, and follow what I approve.

We do not share his confidence, partly because we know the story, but partly also because he is twisting the famous and more realistic saying of Ovid's Medea (*Metamorphoses*, VII, 20–21):

> video meliora proboque,
> deteriora sequor.

(Sandys' rendering is: "I see the better, I approve it too: / The worse I follow.")

A few examples may be taken from the drama of the fall. When Satan, working with specious logic upon Eve, argues from his own enlarged faculties to hers and Adam's, he says (IX, 713–14):

> So ye shall die perhaps, by putting off
> Human, to put on Gods. . . .

Whether or not Milton intended it, we think of the ironic difference between this argument and St. Paul's pleas for Christian rebirth, "put off . . . the old man" and "put on the new man" (Eph. 4:22–24; Col. 3:9–10). When Adam reaffirms his resolution to share Eve's fate, she exclaims "O glorious trial of exceeding Love" (IX, 961). If we met this phrase by itself, we would of course take it as an allusion to Christ's sacrifice for man;[2] here it is a large and ironic contrast to Eve's wholly selfish love. Fifty lines later, when Adam has eaten the fruit and Nature has given a second groan, the pair reach the height of their hubristic delusions (IX. 1008 ff.):

> As with new Wine intoxicated both
> They swim in mirth, and fansie that they feel
> Divinitie within them breeding wings
> Wherewith to scorne the Earth.

In *Comus*, lines 374 ff., Milton had used the image of wings in its Platonic sense, probably with direct reference to *Phaedrus*, 246 ff.:

> And Wisdoms self
> Oft seeks to sweet retired Solitude,
> Where with her best nurse Contemplation
> She plumes her feathers, and lets grow her wings. . . .

---

[2] Milton had so used "exceeding love" long before in "Upon the Circumcision," ll. 15–16 (E. S. LeComte, *Yet Once More*, p. 65).

And he may have blended the Platonic image with that of Pegasus when he wrote to Diodati on 23 September [November?] 1637: "Growing my wings and practising flight. But my Pegasus still raises himself on very tender wings" (*Complete Prose Works*, I [1953], 327). At any rate the lines in *Paradise Lost* recall, by ironic contrast, the Platonic ascent to the Good. The same ironic note attends the words of Sin to Death after the fall (X, 243–45):

> Methinks I feel new strength within me rise,
> Wings growing, and Dominion giv'n me large
> Beyond this Deep.

To come back to Adam and Eve, their sense of divinity sinks quickly into subhuman lust, and Adam indulges in a speech of repellent and sensual levity which ends thus (IX, 1029 ff.):

> For never did thy Beautie since the day
> I saw thee first and wedded thee, adorn'd
> With all perfections, so enflame my sense
> With ardor to enjoy thee, fairer now
> Then ever, bountie of this vertuous Tree.

The words, especially the aggressive crudity of "enjoy thee" from one who had been a reverent adorer, even idolater, are sufficient to show what Adam has become. Yet the effect is heightened for those who recognize a clear echo of the pagan sensuality of Paris addressing Helen, and Zeus addressing Hera (*Iliad*, III, 442 ff.; XIV, 313 ff.). The parallel with the second Homeric scene is carried further in lines 1039 ff.:

> He led her nothing loath; Flours were the Couch,
> Pansies, and Violets, and Asphodel,
> And Hyacinth, Earths freshest softest lap.

There is a double parallel here, with the hilltop bed of Zeus and Hera (*Iliad*, XIV, 346 ff.) and with the bower and nuptial bed of Adam and Eve in their first purity (*P.L.*, IV, 689–719); and Milton's picture, though largely Homeric, suggests the further contrast between innocent nature and corrupted man.

These scattered examples are enough to register what, as I said at the start, is often thought of as a very modern device. While *Paradise Lost* is not *The Waste Land* or *Finnegan's Wake*, such ironic allusions are one element in the poem's manifold richness of texture and reverberation.

SOME NOTES ON MILTON'S *ACCEDENCE*
COMMENC'T GRAMMAR

J. Milton French, University of Texas

Milton's *Accedence Commenc't Grammar* (1669) is without much doubt his least read and least known book. Since the original edition it has never, to my knowledge, been reprinted except in complete editions of his works. Yet it possesses a certain interest of its own.[1]

In approaching it we remember *Of Education* (1644), Milton's sketch for his friend Samuel Hartlib of an educational utopia.[2] In this tiny pamphlet he sets down (p. 1) "that voluntary *Idea*, which hath long in silence presented it self to me, of a better Education, in extent and comprehension farre more large, and yet of time farre shorter, and of attainment farre more certain, then hath been yet in practice." *Of Education* was, as he calls it, "the burnishing of many studious and contemplative yeers altogether spent in the search of religious and civil knowledge . . . " (p. 1). With regard specifically to Latin grammar, which was to be the subject of his *Accedence*, he deplores "the many mistakes which have made learning generally so unpleasing and so unsuccessfull; first we do amisse to spend seven or eight yeers meerly in scraping together so much miserable Latin, and Greek, as might be learnt otherwise easily and delightfully in one yeer" (p. 2). In his own mind is the picture of a school offering "the right path of a vertuous and noble Education; laborious indeed at the first ascent, but else so smooth, so green, so full of goodly prospect, and melodious sounds on every side, that the harp of *Orpheus* was not more charming" (p. 3). To enter the study of Latin, the fortunate students "should begin with the chief and necessary rules of some good Grammar, either that now us'd, or any better . . . " (p. 3). Whether or

---

[1] For financial assistance in pursuing this and other studies I gratefully acknowledge grants from the Henry E. Huntington Library for a research fellowship and from the American Philosophical Society's Penrose Fund.

[2] Quotations in this paper from *Of Education* and from *Accedence* are based on the Huntington Library copies of the first editions of those works (call numbers respectively 105613 and 105677). *Of Education* is accurately reprinted in Milton's *Complete Prose Works*, ed. Don M. Wolfe, II (New Haven, 1959), 357–415, with excellent introduction and notes by Donald C. Dorian. The text of the *Accedence* in *The Works of John Milton*, ed. Frank L. Patterson, VI (New York, 1932), 285–353, is also excellent.

not he was hinting that he himself had already produced this "better" book we have no way of knowing, because we have no clue to the date of composition of the *Accedence*. But the probability is that he wrote it for use during about this period, when he was teaching his nephews and other boys. Professor Donald C. Dorian, who edited *Of Education* excellently for the Yale edition of the *Complete Prose Works* of Milton, notes cautiously but quite accurately (II, 382) that "There is no evidence to show whether Milton had planned or written his own *Accedence Commenc't Grammar* (1669) as early as 1644." Masson (*Life of Milton*, VI, 640) more optimistically thinks that there is "little doubt that the substance of the thing had been lying among Milton's manuscripts since the days of his pedagogy in Aldersgate Street and Barbican. . . . "

At any rate, the goal at which he aimed in *Of Education* is so close to that set in the preface to the *Accedence* that they might both have been described on the same day. A few lines from the latter (sigs. A2^r-A2^v) will show the parallelism:

> *It hath been long a general complaint, not without cause, in the bringing up of Youth, and still is, that the tenth part of mans life, ordinarily extended,*[3] *is taken up in learning, and that very scarcely,*[4] *the* Latin *Tongue. Which tardy proficience may be attributed to several causes: In particular, the making two labours of one, by learning first the* Accedence, *then the* Grammar *in Latin, ere the Language of those Rules be understood. The only remedy of this, was to joyn both Books into one, and in the* English *Tongue; whereby the long way is much abbreviated, and the labour of understanding much more easie: A work suppos'd not to have been done formerly; or if done, not without such difference here in brevity and alteration, as may be found of moment. . . . Account might be now givn what addition or alteration from other Grammars hath been here made, and for what reason. But he who would be short in teaching, must not be long in Prefacing: The Book it self follows, and will declare sufficiently to them who can discern.*

Milton is thus setting up his grammar in competition with the famous grammar bearing the name of William Lily, which during its approximately 100-year reign up to that time as the "authorized" textbook had gone through many editions, and which was to achieve an incalculable number during the next 200 years.[5] In the edition of

---

[3] I.e., one tenth of threescore years and seven, or seven; compare the "seven or eight yeers" quoted above.

[4] I.e., inadequately; quoted in the *OED* as the final example of this now obsolete meaning.

[5] In its most easily available form, as edited by Vincent J. Flynn in 1945 for Scholars' Facsimiles and Reprints, Lily's book is entitled (part I) *A Shorte Introdvction of Grammar* ("Excusum Londini apud Reginaldum Vuolsium," 1567) and (part II) *Brevissima Institutio sev Ratio Grammatices Cognoscende* (same imprint). A copy of the

1567, for example, which was much like the others, it consisted of two parts: (1) "A Shorte Introdvction of Grammar," written in English though of course with Latin quotations to illustrate the rules, and (2) an ironically entitled "Brevissima Institutio sev Ratio Grammatices Cognoscende," more than twice as long and written entirely in Latin, greatly enlarged and considerably more advanced, and containing the versified rules which generations and even centuries of schoolboys memorized. These were the famous "Propria quæ maribus" (about genders), the "Quæ genus" (about irregular declensions), and the "As in Præsenti" (about conjugations of verbs). The second part also included sections on what Milton calls (sigs. A2^r-A2^v) "*That of* Grammar, *touching Letters and Syllables,*" which he omits "*as learnt before, and little different from the* English *Spelling-book . . .*"; and a longish final section on figures of speech and prosody, most of which he omits. Of the part on figures, he says, "*what is usefull is digested into several Rules of* Syntaxis. . . .*" That on prosody, "*after this* Grammar *well learnt, will not need to be Englisht for him who hath a mind to read it.*"[6] The two parts of Lily follow the same general outline: the declensions of nouns and pronouns and adjectives, the conjugations of verbs, the functions of the other parts of speech, the principles of concord or agreement, and the constructions of the several parts of speech.[7]

---

edition of 1636 in the Huntington Library is substantially identical. Other grammars which will be mentioned later, and which Milton seems to have known, are (1) Peter Ramus's *Latine Grammar translated into English*, Cambridge, 1585; (2) John Bird's *Grounds of Grammar Penned and Published*, Oxford, 1639; (3) John Brinsley's *Posing of the Parts* (second edition, London, 1615); (4) Charles Butler's *Rhetoricæ Libri Duo*, Oxford, 1598; (5) Thomas Farnaby's *Systema Grammaticum*, London, 1641; and (6), probably in some earlier form, James Shirley's *Via ad Latinam Linguam Complanata*, London, 1649. Useful aids to the study of these and other Renaissance books on grammar may be found in C. G. Allen, "The Sources of 'Lily's Latin Grammar': A Review of the Facts and some Further Suggestions," *Library*, 5th ser., IX (1954), 85–100; T. W. Baldwin's detailed *William Shakspere's Small Latine and Lesse Greeke*, 2 vols. (Urbana, 1944); J. Howard Brown's *Elizabethan Schooldays* (Oxford, 1933), ch. 4; Harris Fletcher's brochure describing the impressive exhibit of Renaissance grammars at the University of Illinois Library some years ago; Vincent J. Flynn's introduction to the edition of Lily mentioned above; and Foster Watson's *The English Grammar Schools to 1660* (Cambridge, England, 1908), especially chs. 14–16.

[6] Milton gives a scant half-page to figures of speech on p. 40.

[7] In the midst of all the fun that has been made of Lily over the years it is easy to overlook the immense advance which he and his colleagues made over the older books. Grammars of the fifteenth and sometimes sixteenth centuries are apt to present solid pages with hardly any paragraphing, a most dismal prospect for even an adult, to say nothing of a little boy, to face. Lily, on the other hand, broke up the material into short paragraphs and added frequent section titles so that the reader would know where he was and where he was going. The type was also more readable.

Though Milton followed the same general order, he evidently considered his originality or contribution twofold: (1) the blending of the two parts into one, all in English, though with Latin quotations, and (2) a drastic shortening to about one quarter of the length of Lily. Sometimes his wording may be almost exactly like Lily's: "The Present Tense speaketh of the time that *now is*, as *Laudo* I praise" (Milton, p. 18); "The present tense speaketh of the time that now is: as Amo, I *loue*" (Lily, Part I, sig. B3ʳ; mostly in gothic type). On the other hand, his paragraph on the construction of participles (pp. 58–59) is very different from Lily's (Part I, sig D4ʳ; Part II, sig. F5ᵛ). In general, he weaves together the material from both parts of Lily, so that a diagram of the corresponding pages would look like a network. And he compresses the 180-odd fairly large pages of Lily into the 60-odd small pages of his own *Accedence*.[8]

By integrating Lily's two parts and by omitting the more intricate and abstruse details and by writing all the rules in English, Milton calculated that he could reduce the time needed for mastery of this subject to one year. Apparently he himself succeeded. John Aubrey, in fact, included in his manuscript a statement of Milton's achievement. A section which he apparently got Edward Phillips to write for him, and which stands in Phillips' hand, says of Milton's teaching of his nephews that he "in a years time made them capable of interpreting a Latin authour at sight."[9] In Phillips' printed biography of Milton he mentions "the many Authors both of the Latin and Greek, which through his excellent judgment and way of Teaching, far above the Pedantry of common publick Schools (where such Authors are scarce ever heard of) were run over within no greater compass of time, then from Ten to Fifteen or Sixteen Years of Age."[10] Vague though this latter extract is, both together seem to indicate that Milton's plan stood the supreme test: it worked.

To be sure, Milton was not alone in his impatience with the length of time required for education, and in the conviction that he had

[8] Milton frequently reduces the length of even the quotations in Lily; he seldom if ever extends them. For example, his "*Longam ire viam*" (p. 50) abbreviates Lily's "Vergilius.—*longam incomitata videtur Ire viam*" (part II, sig. F1ʳ). On the other hand, Milton's long salvo of extracts from Cicero (p. 61) has no precedent in Lily.

[9] Aubrey's notes, Bodleian MS Aubrey 8, fol. 64ᵛ; French, *The Life Records of John Milton* (New Brunswick, N. J., 1949–58), 11, 8. Helen Darbishire reproduces in photographic facsimile this section in Phillips' hand in *Early Lives of Milton* (London, 1932), facing p. 12.

[10] Milton, *Letters of State* (London, 1694), Introduction, p. xvii; French, *Life Records*, 11, 6.

found an easier and speedier way of getting his students off the ground. John Brinsley's *Consolation for our Grammar Schools* (1622), for example, was designed, as the title implies, to be more helpful to the student and to push him along more swiftly and easily than previous books had done. Charles Hoole's *Grammar* (1651 and later) was advertised in *A Perfect Diurnall* for 31 October–7 November 1653 as "short, easie, and plain, for the easie [*sic*] both of Master and Scholar, as any yet published." James Shirley's *Manuductio* (1660; first published in 1656 under the title *Rudiments of Grammar*) bore the subtitle "a leading of children by the hand to the Latin tongue," a goal which it accomplished in part, presumably, by presenting the grammatical rules in English verse. Joshua Poole's *Youth's Guide: or English Accedence* (1662) was advertised in *Mercurius Publicus* for 30 January–6 February 1661/2 as "a more short and easie way for the speedy attaining to the Latin Tongue. . . . " Finally, in what sounds like a surprisingly modern touch, *A Perfect Diurnall* for 23–30 December 1650 advertised "*Grammatical Cards*, In which are compendiously comprised all the Rules of Grammer. Made by *Baptist Pendleton*, sold at his house neer S. *Dunstans* in the East." But all of these titles except Brinsley's probably postdated Milton's work, and few of them adopted his simplifications despite their promising advertisements.

Though Lily provided much of the material for the *Accedence*, Milton seems to have used other texts also. It is impossible to be positive on this point, but we can at least say that some of the illustrative Latin phrases in Milton's book which do not occur in Lily do appear in certain other books. This does not happen with a large number, but at least a few can be found in John Brinsley's *Posing of the Parts* (2nd ed., 1615) and in Shirley's *Via ad Latinam* (1649; in which direction did the borrowing go?); and a fair number show up in Thomas Farnaby's *Systema Grammaticum* (1641), Milton's own copy of which is now in the Harvard College Library. Probably a painstaking search would reveal a few others.

Milton illustrates his rules, or observations about Latin usage, with some 530 Latin quotations. About 330 of these he took from Lily, or about 60 per cent. Of the remaining 40 per cent, or slightly over 200, we find some 13 in Farnaby, 8 in Ramus, and one each in Bird, Butler, and Shirley. If we add those which occur both in Lily and in one or more of these writers, we may find almost any possible combination. If we care to use mathematical symbols, we may say of a given quota-

tion before we actually look it up that it may occur in Lily ± Bird
± Butler ± Farnaby ± Ramus ± Shirley. Though all these writers
identify their sources some of the time, Farnaby is by far the most
helpful of all, since he gives not only the name of the author, but also
the book, section, or other means of finding the phrase.

At the present moment Milton seems to have contributed about
175 quotations not found in other books. Some are extremely brief,
others fairly extensive. The shortest are single words, which he uses
to illustrate unusual Latin inflectional forms, like *"Ænean"* (p. 5) as
the accusative form of the Greek name "Aeneas." Sometimes he gives
his source for even a lone word like this, as with "Eriphylam" (p. 5)
as the Latinized form of the accusative case "Eriphylen," for which
he refers the reader to Cicero. He seldom gives more than the name of
the author, and by no means always even that. But he does so more
often when he is adding an example not in Lily than otherwise. From
this shortest example of only one word the opposite extreme is a whole
line or even more, as in a sentence from Cicero (p. 61): *"Nullum est
Officium tam sanctum atq; solenne, quod non avaritia violare soleat."*

Some of his examples are openly designed to teach good manners
and virtuous behavior to students: *"Sum tibi natura parens, preceptor
consiliis"* (p. 45). Others carry a rebuke to the unresponsive: *"Preceptor prælegit, vos vero negligitis"* (p. 42). Others carry considerable
worldly wisdom, as *"Vir sapit, qui pauca loquitur"* (p. 42). Some provide practice in matter-of-fact daily activities: *"Viginti minis usus est
filio"* (p. 45), or *"Arbor lata tres digitos"* (p. 47). Some introduce the
student to names of persons and places important in history or literature: *"Horatius salutatur Poeta"* (p. 49). A few might even be useful
in the local cafeteria: *"Vescor pane"* (p. 54). Finally, though these
few samples of suggested purposes could be extended, some provide
a touch of drama: *"Accusas furti, an stupri, an utroque?"* (p. 52);
"Ferit eum gladio" (p. 54).

Though I have not succeeded in tracing all of Milton's illustrations to their original sources, I have pinned down a large majority. It
is not always safe to say of one of Milton's phrases that a specific
location in a classical author is *the* source, especially for simple phrases
like *"In urbe"* or *"Amo te."*[11] Yet the more one works with this book,

---

[11] For example, *"Quoad ejus fieri poterit"* (p. 60) would not seem to be an important
or unusual statement; yet both Ramus and Farnaby take pains to give its author as
Cicero and to give a fairly specific location—though one places it in his familiar letters
and the other in his letters to Atticus. Quotations containing English place-names like

the stronger becomes the impression that in the great majority of these illustrations Milton used a classical author even for the simplest phrases. Of a sizable sentence like that quoted from Cicero above, there can be no question. But when we find Milton himself actually attaching the name of an author to a brief phrase like *"Hunc tu non ames?"* (p. 63) or *"Procul muros"* (p. 64), we hesitate to say that he may not have had in mind some classical usage for *"Ne metuas"* (p. 61) or *"Sub noctem"* (p. 64). With these cautions in mind, I will report my tentative findings.

Of the 530-odd illustrations in the book, the author whom Milton drew on far more frequently than any other was Cicero, for a total of somewhat more than 128. (It is not safe to offer more definite figures until I have made a more exhaustive study of concordances and drawn more exhaustingly on my friends in classics than I have to date.) Terence comes next with 70-odd, Virgil third with 60-odd, Horace considerably farther behind with 30-odd, Ovid next with 20-odd, Plautus after him with just over 20, and Livy with somewhat under 20. Following them are a large number with scores of from 10 down to 1: Boethius, Caesar, Cato, Catullus, Celsus, Claudian, Columella, Cornelius Nepos, Ennius, Erasmus, Aulus Gellius, Justinian, Juvenal, Lucan, Lucretius, Macrobius, Martial, Nonius Marcellus, Phaedrus, Pliny the Younger, Quintilian, Sallust, Seneca, Sidonius, Silius Italicus, Statius, Suetonius, Valerius Maximus, Varro, and Velleius Paterculus. Still untraced are over 100, or about 20 per cent.

It is perhaps more interesting to examine the 200-odd examples in Milton which do not occur in Lily, because they may perhaps give a better clue to his interests or his prejudices. Cicero leads the field by a far wider margin than before: nearly 80. The nearest competitors, though far behind, are Virgil and Horace about neck and neck with just under 20, Terence with just over 10, Ovid and Livy with about 6, and a scattered field of Catullus, Celsus, Columella, Cornelius Nepos, Lucan, Lucretius, Martial, Phaedrus, Plautus, Silius, Suetonius, Valerius Maximus, Varro, and Velleius Paterculus. In this list Cicero has gained greatly, Terence has lost his second place, Horace has caught up with Virgil, though neither has more than about half of the proportion which he holds in the total list, and Ovid has dropped far back. It is clear that for Milton Cicero was the great gold mine for the maker of grammars, as well as for the student of Latin.

"Londini" and "Anglia" and comparatively modern foreign names like "Parisiis" are probably made-up examples. Even so, probably the only important change from the older phrases is the substitution of one place-name for another.

The difficulties of editing the *Accedence* are different from those involved in most of Milton's other works. With a few exceptions, one has little to do in explaining the meaning of the text, variant readings, the growth of the text, Milton's ideas, and so on. The chief work is to find the originals of the 530-odd quotations. Finding the corresponding passages even in the chief immediate source, Lily, is often baffling, because Milton moves around a good deal, changing the order of some details while at the same time retaining the main outline, and because he frequently takes a quotation out of one context and uses it to serve a different purpose. Since many of his quotations are not in Lily at all, one has to search with care when any given example or rule does not come to light at once. It may not be there at all, or it may be in a different place. One two-page spread of Milton, for example (pp. 43–44), has text and examples corresponding to some in Lily's Part I, sigs. C4^v, C5^r, C5^v, C6^v, and C8^v; and to some in Part II, sigs. E1^v, E3^v, E4^r, F6^r, G2^r, G2^v, and G3^r. But the search in Lily is comparatively easy. It is the Latin originals that try editors' souls.

When Milton mentions the name of his author (as he does perhaps 10 per cent of the time), *and* when the quotation is accurate, *and* when there is a good concordance to the work of that author, *and* when the quotation actually comes from that author (for there are a few exceptions, though very few)—a severely limiting set of qualifications —the going is fairly easy. One need only find and verify the quotation in the Loeb Classics edition, find it also in the seventeenth-century edition which Milton might most likely have used, check his accuracy, and write off one problem out of the 530-odd. If we have a reasonable number in one author, and if we allow for the time required to get all the books, a quotation may not require on the average more than fifteen to twenty minutes. But after the first hundred or so allusions, the concordances begin to deteriorate. That for Cicero, for example, is so enormous and so frustrating for this particular purpose, whatever its merits for other uses, that finding a quotation in it is a wearisome task. If Milton changes a few words even slightly, as he often does, especially in prose, the phrase may be irrecoverable. When the concordances give out completely, as they do after one finishes the major authors, one turns to the big Latin dictionaries—Harper's, the fragmentary *Thesaurus Linguae Latinae*, and the like. These furnish many additional locations, for which the process is then the same as for words found in concordances. When both dictionaries and concordances fail, but when Milton still offers the name of the author, one can, if possessed of monumental patience, search the works of that author from beginning to end for the few tiny needles in the huge stack of hay. But no one in his right mind would read through all of Livy or Silius Italicus for two or three, or even ten, phrases. And when, finally, Milton names no author, one has met a clear Stop sign. There is always the outside chance that one's friends may recognize a few stray quotations and be able to exclaim, "Why, of course, Velleius Paterculus, IV, 2; I was just reading that passage last night for fun." But not many friends are likely to be thus extraordinarily prepared to rescue the perishing. There is therefore sure to be a sizable package of passages lost forever. But with the large majority safely located, we can be reasonably well satisfied about Milton's procedures and his preferences.

One cares little about the loss of some of these orphans. Others have a certain appeal that makes one reluctant to give them up unfound. For instance, *"Omnia quœ curant senes meminerunt"* (p. 50), attributed to Plautus though I have not found it in his plays, is so wry a comment on the crankiness of the aging mind that one would like to know its context. *"Diluculo surgere saluberrimum est"* (p. 43) sounds as if it might have come out of Milton's youthful theme on early rising.[12] *"Accusas furti, an stupri, an utroque?"* (p. 52) must be from some sort of public expression of indignation, whether genuine or dramatic. *"Malo me divitem esse, quam haberi"* (p. 58) summarizes the division between real and imaginary wealth so neatly that it should appear in all the collections of proverbs—but it does not. *"Recto stat corpore, despicitque terras"* (p. 62) could easily find a place somewhere in *Paradise Lost*, but it is unlikely that Milton plagiarized his own English poetry—especially years before he had written it—for this book. And so on. One regrets to leave these morsels dangling.

What do we learn about Milton from this book? I believe we can see several qualities of his mind illustrated here. One is, of course, a wide and intimate knowledge of classical Latin authors, on which he could draw not only for support in ideas but also for illustration of grammar and usage. One may speculate whether he may have cut corners by using some phrase book or anthology for his quotations,

---

[12] Dogberry in *Twelfth Night* quotes—or rather misquotes—the first two words of this one, but neither the variorum editor of that play nor Morris Palmer Tilley, who includes it in his *Dictionary of the Proverbs in England* (Ann Arbor, Mich., 1950), no. B184, offers any source for it. Tilley does not mention its occurrence in Lily or in Milton.

but I have found none that offer any help, and I have concluded that his amplification of Lily comes from his own reading in the original writers. Another quality is his ingenuity, his desire to do something better than others had done it, and his conviction that he could do so. The same man who offered in *Paradise Lost* (I, 16) "Things unattempted yet in Prose or Rhyme" offered here *"A work suppos'd not to have been done formerly."* Another quality is economy of style, by which he made sure of getting the full mileage out of every single word. The condensation here is remarkable.

No one will claim that the *Accedence* is a work of art. It is a simple elementary textbook for young schoolboys, and Milton makes no pretension that it is anything else. But it is workman-like and creditable. For a blind man dependent on chance amanuenses it is surprising that the printed text does not contain more errors. Some quotations are inexact, as are some of Lily's. They sometimes give the effect of having been done by memory without verification, as was probably sometimes the case. But they are very seldom grammatically wrong, and probably most of the few errors that do occur are printers' slips. If there is little in the book to increase Milton's reputation, there is nothing to damage it. And elementary though it is, it is one more piece of evidence, like the rest of his prose, of his efforts to improve the world.

FORM AND MATTER IN *PARADISE LOST*, BOOK III

Allan Gilbert, Duke University, and Rutgers University, Newark

I. MILTON AND ROMANTIC POETRY

> . . . my Celestial Patroness . . .
> inspires
> Easie my unpremeditated Verse:
> Since first this Subject for Heroic Song
> Pleas'd me long choosing, and beginning late;
> Not sedulous by Nature to indite
> Warrs, hitherto the onely Argument
> Heroic deem'd, chief maistrie to dissect
> With long and tedious havoc fabl'd Knights
> In Battels feign'd; the better fortitude
> Of Patience and Heroic Martyrdom
> Unsung; or to describe Races and Games,
> Or tilting Furniture, emblazon'd Shields,
> Impreses quaint, Caparisons and Steeds;
> Bases and tinsel Trappings, gorgious Knights
> At Joust and Torneament; then marshal'd Feast
> Serv'd up in Hall with Sewers, and Seneshals;
> The skill of Artifice or Office mean,
> Not that which justly gives Heroic name
> To Person or to Poem.   (*P.L.*, IX, 21-41).[1]

We need not press the autobiographical quality of these lines. The dramatic speaker is not so much Milton as the Biblical poet generally, who performs "the office of a pulpit" as much as does the clergyman. The literal Milton did not reject the "vain, amatorious" romances of the chivalric poets. In his youth he read them with delight, as he says in the *Apology for Smectymnuus*. Nor was this delight merely youthful. Ariosto is all but named in *Paradise Lost*, III, 459, and that poem owes much to his *Orlando*. Even in *Paradise Regained* Milton pays tribute to Arthurian story:

> . . . Ladies of th' *Hesperides*, that seem'd
> Fairer than feign'd of old, or fabl'd since
> Of Fairy Damsels met in Forest wide
> By Knights of *Logres*, or of *Lyones*,
> *Lancelot* or *Pelleas*, or *Pellenore*.   (*P.R.*, II, 357-61)

---

[1] Milton's poems are quoted throughout from *Complete Poetical Works, Reproduced in Photographic Facsimile*, ed. Harris Francis Fletcher (Urbana, 1943), 4 vols.

In the same poem he remembers Boiardo's *Orlando Innamorato:*

> Such forces met not, nor so wide a camp,
> When *Agrican* with all his Northern powers
> Besieg'd *Albracca,* as Romances tell;
> The City of *Gallaphrone,* from thence to win
> The fairest of her Sex *Angelica*
> His daughter, sought by many Prowest Knights,
> Both *Paynim,* and the Peers of *Charlemane.*
>
> > (*P.R.,* III, 337–43)

Such passages come from one who delighted in the romances of chivalry to the end of his days.

When the youthful Milton attempted heroic verse he turned to Christ as

> Most perfect *Heroe,* try'd in heaviest plight
> Of labours huge and hard.   ("The Passion," ll. 13–14)

In "The Passion" he praises Vida's *Christiad,* a Biblical epic. But a long Christian poem is not primary in his early life. When in *Epitaphium Damonis* he imagines himself the ideal poet in search of an epic subject, he turns to King Arthur. When in *The Reason of Church-Government* he revealed his hopes less poetically, an epic theme is to be found in "our own ancient stories," Arthur or King Alfred in the role of Odysseus, as in the notes of poetical subjects in the Cambridge manuscript. For the long epic his models are Homer, Virgil, and Tasso. So wars, the theme or "Argument Heroic deem'd," would have been the theme of any poem then written. For tragedy he does not specify subjects; we may assume such as he noted in the Cambridge manuscript, both Biblical and political, of which we have in developed form only *Samson Agonistes.*

Did he ever write anything in furtherance of the plan for a long epic outlined in *The Reason of Church-Government?* Not even an assertion that he did has survived. Yet military passages more than are warranted by the disclaimer at the beginning of Book IX appear in both *Paradises.* As Addison said, the war in Heaven in *Paradise Lost,* VI, is Homeric; it also owes something to the Italian romantic epics. The muster roll of Satan's host in Hell has often been referred to sources in the military epics, from the *Iliad* to the *Gerusalemme Liberata. Paradise Regained* too presents the muster of the Parthian host illustrated with the gorgeous comparison from an epic of war and love, the *Orlando Innamorato,* quoted above. So well are these passages suited to their present contexts that they can hardly have been rescued from one of Milton's own manuscripts of a conventional epic, though their spirit avows the author's long-continued and fascinated preoccupation with epic and romance.

However exaggerated the Biblical or reflective poet's position in the lines initially quoted in this study, something autobiographical still inheres in them. They represent a poet attempting the military epic and not succeeding, then finding that Biblical verse flowed easily from his pen, though such ease is rather a poetic figure than a literal statement. It shows, however, a poet happy in finding the right thing to do. Thus we can easily believe that for years Milton clung to his theme of Alfred or Arthur, treated in Virgilian fashion, and that for years his efforts did not satisfy him.

Meanwhile he considered what he could do in tragedy, noting subjects and making outlines in the Cambridge manuscript and writing *Samson Agonistes*. These outlines witness to Milton's interest in the subject of *Paradise Lost*. According to Edward Phillips, part at least of a tragedy on the subject was written. Then Milton, as it appears, changed his plans. Abandoning the military and romantic epic, he turned to the Biblical epic, following in part his outline for a tragedy on the loss of Paradise and using and adapting whatever tragic verses he had written on the theme. Since the tragedy was confined to the Garden of Eden, scenes in Hell, Heaven, and Chaos had to be composed (I; II; X, 235 ff.; III, 56 ff.; etc.). Other parts were much expanded. Book VII was planned as a choric song in the tragedy, requiring perhaps a hundred lines; the war in Heaven—a book and a half long in the epic—was also planned as a choric song. Much of Books XI and XII become angelic narrative instead of a masque of allegorical figures in a nonclassical tragedy. Thus the drama of *Paradise Lost*, whether or not complete, gave way to an epic of perhaps thrice its contemplated length. If twice as long as *Samson Agonistes*, which is limited to classical proportions, the tragedy would have extended to 3500 lines, or one-third the length of the present epic.

As has often been remarked, the Satan of the later part of *Paradise Lost*, so far as he is derived from Milton's dramatic plan, is not the Satan of Books I and II, but is diminished in physical proportions and mental scope. Great size appears in his defiance of Gabriel and his return to Hell; in the first "his stature reacht the Skie" (IV, 988) and in the second he sat on a throne apparently as huge as earlier (I, 793; II, 1; X, 445), though the word *monstrous* (X, 514) does not always indicate size; perhaps after what had preceded on the smaller Satan,

Milton preferred not to be specific on magnitude. The Satan of a tragedy influenced by the stage could not much exceed human proportions, but stature exaggerating anything possessed by giants of earlier epics is necessary to fit the colossal exploit of Satan in crossing the desert of Chaos, to appear as in some sense a heroic rival of the Almighty.

Thus in shifting *Paradise Lost* from drama to epic Milton still retained much of the romantic and military spirit that he apparently rejected at the beginning of Book IX. At first the long theological passage in Book III appears opposed to the nature of epic. At least epic magnitude makes reasonable long passages impossible in drama. In the *Furioso*, Ariosto could pause to give the history of the French invasions of Italy by describing the pictures decorating a hall (Canto XXXIII). By including in his *Morgante* (XXV, 136–61, 232–44) passages on Christian doctrine, Pulci furnished Milton precedent for theology in a poem primarily active rather than resembling Lucretius' *De rerum natura*.

II. MILTON AS THEOLOGIAN

For using theology Milton was well equipped. In the introduction to his *De Doctrina Christiana* he tells of assiduous study begun in his youth and continued throughout his life, with all the aids of scholarship and with attention to the necessary languages. We may recall that until "church-outed by the prelates" he intended to enter the Church. His nephew Edward Phillips says that he and Milton's other pupils read the Pentateuch in Hebrew, made "a good entrance into the Targum or Chaldee paraphrase," and came "to understand several chapters of St. Matthew in the Syriac Testament." Still further the pupil reports:

The Sunday work was for the most part the reading each day a chapter of the Greek Testament and hearing his learned exposition upon the same. . . . The next work after this was the writing from his own dictation some part, from time to time, of a tractate which he thought fit to collect from the ablest of divines who had written of that subject: Amesius, Wollebius, etc., viz. *A Perfect System of Divinity*.

The two similar works by Ames and Wollebius are among the shorter systems of divinity referred to in the introduction to *De Doctrina Christiana*. When after years of labor that work was in some sense complete, it seemed to its author "a powerful aid," "a treasure house," his "best and most valuable possession." As becomes the cherished life work of an active intelligence, the treatise never was beyond revision.

The manuscript seems gradually to have become so corrected and interlined as to require copying before it could be given to a printer. If we believe Phillips, it was at first little unlike the similar works by Ames and Wollebius. As time went on, Milton drew farther and farther away from them. When Milton's work is compared with theirs, their outline is apparent, but the content of the sections is different. In the *De Doctrina* itself and in his other writings Milton mentions so many other theologians and commentators on Scripture that his reading must be thought considerable. His actual knowledge frequently is hidden. For example, passages in the *De Doctrina* evidently intended to overthrow parts of Calvin's *Institutes* make no mention of that work; indeed he who does not know Calvin must remain ignorant of *De Doctrina Christiana*.

III. MILTON'S "GREAT ARGUMENT," THE FALL

Perhaps not until he was about fifty years old did Milton, "long choosing," determine his epic subject. At any rate he abandoned the epic on Arthur or Alfred, though retaining much of the action and more of the spirit of both classical and romantic epics, the Homeric poems, the *Aeneid, Orlando Furioso, Gerusalemme Liberata*. His tragedy of *Paradise Lost* offered its "great Argument" or theme, the Fall of Adam and Eve. To the seventeenth century that story was less personal and of wider significance than at present. Like the temptation of Job as Gregory the Great presented it in his *Moralia*, it personified the age-long conflict of light and darkness. More than that, it decided man's fate; had our first parents successfully resisted Satan, man's future happiness would have been assured. It was, partly for that reason, one of the best known of Biblical narratives. Thus to a seventeenth-century poet seeking to free himself from Ariosto's theme of knights in combat it could hardly be surpassed. It went far toward furnishing the "moral equivalent of war." If less evidently pertinent in our day, it illustrates how we must study to prepare for artistic appreciation that came easily and directly to Milton's first readers. The argument of the Fall in Genesis 3 is presented as a narrative. Thus Milton's

> That to the highth of this great Argument
> I may assert Eternal Providence,
> And justifie the wayes of God to men   (I, 24–26)

may be simply interpreted: That so far as my story permits I may express my belief that God rules the world and that his government is just. Milton knew that without story there could be no epic; he also knew that the possibilities of story limited his opportunity to present ideas, however willing he might be that his method, like Dante's, should be "digressive." Hence the "highth" of his argument is the utmost that his story allows.

In his day his subject or argument was able to bear great weight. Much theology, especially the Calvinistic theology that so influenced Milton, whether accepting or rejecting, may almost be summed up in the Apostle Paul's words: "As in Adam all die, so in Christ shall all be made alive" (I Cor. 15:22). No narrative in Scripture, not even in the Gospels, was more important for the theologian than the account of the Fall in Genesis 3. Here were found expressed man's weakness on earth and his need for redemption. Here was the root of the world's evil and suffering. To the first three chapters of Genesis one of Milton's favorite commentators, David Paraeus, devoted almost a hundred folio pages of finely printed exegesis. If we are to suppose that a poet can be most poetical on what most interests him and has most occupied his mind for years, and also harmonizes with the thought and feeling of his age, Milton, a life-long student of theology and an observer of man as a moral being, could choose no more suitable argument than the story of man's Fall—the most familiar of stories in a Biblical age and fundamental to prevailing belief.

IV. *PARADISE LOST*, BOOK III, EXAMINED

The chief overt statement of theological belief stands in *Paradise Lost*, III, 92–343, a passage of 251 lines, little enough in a poem of 10,565 lines. Long experience with epics had taught Milton that their chief components are action, dramatic dialogue, and description. To dramatic action he adapts the theology of Book III. Let us examine the passage.

What is its setting? At the end of Book II the revengeful Satan, escaped from Hell, has been described as flying through Chaos toward the World, where he hopes to thwart God by destroying man. Early in Book III the narrative is resumed. The Almighty Father, enthroned in Heaven, looks down upon the Garden of Eden, where he sees Adam and Eve

> Reaping immortal fruits of joy and love,
> Uninterrupted joy, unrivald love.   (III, 67–68)

He then surveys Chaos

> and *Satan* there
> Coasting the wall of Heav'n on this side Night

> In the dun Air sublime, and ready now
> To stoop . . .
> On the bare outside of this World.   (III, 70–74)

In an independence that for the time seems freedom, Satan is moving toward the Earth, where he is to achieve success in his immediate object, victory over mankind. But in Milton's theology Satan does not win an ultimate victory; he merely carries out heavenly intention, even when securing the appearance of success. However clearly Milton sees the evil of the world, he is certain of the triumph of good, believing that there is justice in God's ways, inscrutable and baffling to man though they are. This conviction Milton strives to translate into epic action. Hence the dramatic situation of Satan confidently moving on to his exploit, not realizing that even before he sees his victims, the Almighty, fully aware, is making complete preparations for his defeat. The scene in Heaven in which Father and Son look down on Satan is thus placed for the sake of dramatic effect. The reader has in his mind's eye that as the two speak they observe Satan as he passes through Chaos and alights on the world's outside shell. Quite ignorant of such anticipation, the Adversary moves toward his goal, the dwelling of man,

> with purpose to assay
> If him by force he can destroy, or worse,
> By some false guile pervert; and shall pervert.
>
> (III, 90–92)

So the Father asserts. He then explains the situation according to Miltonic theology. Man will fall, yet the fault is his own, for God created him free, with power to resist all Satan's wiles. In such freedom there is the possibility of defeat, for man is not under compulsion to maintain the happiness with which he originally was dowered. Thus man, the free agent, ordains his own fall; yet since he was deceived he shall find mercy.

The Son answers, praising the Father for his mercy, for if man should be irrevocably lost Satan would return to Hell successful; the Almighty's purpose in creating man would have failed. Thus both his goodness and his power would properly be questioned.

Assenting, the Father explains that grace is offered to all men and that repentance will bring forgiveness. Yet since man has sinned, justice demands punishment, the punishment of death. Man must die unless some other will pay his forfeit by dying for him. Who in Heaven will do so?

The Son offers himself as man's substitute. On him Death shall wreak his rage, and mankind shall be freed from danger and shall at last enter Heaven with the Redeemer.

This offer the Father accepts as redeeming such men as repent. It shall be brought about through the Incarnation of the Son, who finally shall reign as universal king.

Even within the 251 lines of the passage not all the space is given to theology in the narrow sense. There is a brief poem on the Harrowing of Hell and the Ascension (III, 246–56) and one on the Last Judgment and the end of the world (III, 323–38). Throughout the passage the energy and movement of the language are fitted to the divine participants. Something of this effect of vitality comes from evident means, such as the omission of conjunctions, pronouns, and modal verbs. Modifying phrases are set at some distance from the words they modify. Inversions appear, as

Dye hee or Justice must;   (III, 210)

on mans behalf
Patron or Intercessor none appeerd.   (III, 218–19)

Generally the thought proceeds by short statements; the periodic sentence when it occurs is short, and there is an abundance of brief assertions. But though such indications—as Longinus knew—are worth observing, there is no formula for poetic energy; its springs are deep within the poet's mind.

Further contributing to this artistic force is a development of repetition of sound serving also to emphasize the important theological ideas of the section. Properly to show this, the entirety must be read aloud, for the separate speeches both move as units and are related as parts of the whole. Some short passages are here offered, though in isolation they suggest excessive emphasis by repeated sound.

I made him just and right,
Sufficient to have stood, though free to fall.
Such I created all th'Ethereal Powers
And Spirits, both them who stood and them who fell;[2]
Freely they stood who stood, and fell who fell.   (III, 98–102)

if I foreknew,
Foreknowledge had no influence on their fall,[3]
Which had no less prov'd certain unforeknown.   (III, 117–19)

[2] I change the normal reading, *faild*, to *fell*, to me obviously correct, though with no textual support. Cf. *fell* at the end of l. 129; *Fate* (113, 120); *Decree, decreed* (115, 116, 126).

[3] In the same way I correct *fault* to *fall*. Cf. ll. 95, 99, 128, ending in *fall*.

I will . . .
            soft'n stonie hearts
To pray, repent, and bring obedience due.
To Prayer, repentance, and obedience due,
Though but endevord with sincere intent,
Mine ear shall not be slow, mine eye not shut.   (III, 188–93)

Behold mee then, mee for him, life for life
I offer, on mee let thine anger fall;
Account mee man.   (III, 236–38)

. . . I shall rise Victorious, and subdue
My vanquisher, spoild of his vanted spoile;
Death his deaths wound shall then receive.   (III, 250–52)

In addition to these and others there are more remote echoes, as *free* and its derivatives from line 99 to line 128; *die, death, dead* in lines 209–59, resumed in lines 295–99. Thus the poetical ornament of the passage is internal, derived from the words expressing its ideas and from the rhetoric; there are no extended similes and metaphors, no names from Greek myth or Biblical history. Perhaps no passage in Milton is verbally more highly developed; in other words, no passage more depends for its effect on reading aloud.

V. DIVINITIES AS EPIC CHARACTERS

In this scene in the heavenly court the Almighty and the Son are anthropomorphic, even though Milton protests against *anthropopatheia* as a figure invented by the grammarians to excuse poetical fables about Jove (*De Doctrina Christiana*, Bk. I, ch. 2). Little else than human conduct is possible when divine beings become actors in epic poetry, as appears in the Homeric epics. Indeed part of Homer's humanization of the gods may result from epic demands rather than from the loss of faith in the Homeric age often given as a reason for the ungodly behavior of divinities. The creator and sustainer of the universe can hardly use human speech without suffering humanization; for such a creator the only poetry is the hymn of praise. The monotheism of the Old Testament, which Milton took over, suffers such danger. To identify the Lord God who walked in the Garden of Eden in the cool of the day after man's fall (Gen. 3:8) with the creator of Genesis 1 is not easy. Since the theologians of Milton's era, depending on the Bible, could not wholly reconcile the humanized and the creating and sustaining divinity, Milton the epic poet can hardly be expected to do so.

Of the difficulty Milton was not unaware. When Raphael is about

to describe to Adam the war in Heaven, he says dramatically what
can also be a warning to the reader:

> what surmounts the reach
> Of human sense, I shall delineate so,
> By lik'ning spiritual to corporal forms,
> As may express them best . . .   (V, 571–74)

In the *Christian Doctrine,* where Milton strove for scientific expression,
the Biblical literalist unites with the artist whose instinct tells him
that abstract expression cannot be long continued in effective poetry.
Milton writes:

It is safest for us to conceive that God is just what he shows himself to be in
the sacred writings and that he is as he there describes himself. Even though
we concede that God is always described and pictured not as he is but as
we can understand him, nevertheless we ought to form such an idea of him
as he wishes us to hold when he adapts himself to our minds. . . . If God
usually assigns to himself human limbs and appearance, why should we be
afraid of assigning to him what he assigns to himself? (*De Doctrina Christiana,*
Bk. I, ch. 2)

Yet in the same chapter Milton attributes to God infinity, omnipres-
ence, omnipotence, etc. So in adaptation to man's experience and to
the possibilities of art, the God of *Paradise Lost* conducts himself as an
earthly ruler. The Son is a prudent courtier, beginning with deference
his speech to the monarch (III, 144) and then endeavoring to persuade him not to go too far in his punishment of disloyal man. Satan
should not be allowed any reality of triumph. From such policy, the
Son warns the Father, it would follow that

> So should thy goodness and thy greatness both
> Be questiond and blaspheam'd without defence.
>   (III, 165–66)

This is less extreme than Charlemagne's argument in his prayer to the
Christian God, who should give the French victory if he does not
expect general defection to pagan worship (*Orlando Furioso,* XIV, 70).
It is more nearly in the tone of Milton's remark that Calvinists make
God the author of sin (*De Doctrina Christiana,* Bk. I, ch. 3; *True
Religion,* p. 6). The Almighty answers like a wise ruler. Even his lyrical
speech on the Last Judgment (III, 323–38) is that of a mortal poet,
such as Cynewulf in his *Christ,* rather than a creator. Milton does
what he can to erase the mundane effect of the dialogue between
Father and Son by an angelic hymn to the Creator—a lyric inserted
in the epic and yet echoing *De Doctrina Christiana,* Bk. I, ch. 2:

> Omnipotent,
> Immutable, Immortal, Infinite,
> Eternal King; thee Author of all being,
> Fountain of Light, thy self invisible
> Amidst the glorious brightness where thou sit'st
> Thron'd inaccessible . . .   (III, 372–77)

Yet still the total epic effect is—as it should be—that of a debate on royal policy or *ragione di stato*, placed where its dramatic effect is greatest, negating Satan's attempt at seduction before he even sees his intended victims in their happy garden.

VI. POETICAL THEOLOGY

In his poetical use of theology Milton gave it little trace of his individual unorthodoxy. Addison, in his paper on Book III of *Paradise Lost*, commended the excellence of Milton's statement of the central truths of Christian belief; John Wesley produced an edition of *Paradise Lost* with apparent acceptation of its theology. Both these men lived before the revelation of Milton's heterodoxy on the discovery of his long-lost *De Doctrina Christiana* in 1824. That until then he had been thought a pillar of orthodoxy affirms the excellent camouflage of strange doctrine in *Paradise Lost*. Even after the revelation of the poet's rejection of the Trinity in his treatise, Sister Miriam Joseph has affirmed that his poem is suitable reading for the intelligent devout.[4] In other words, Milton dealt primarily with the elements of Christian doctrine obvious to all "fit" readers in his time. His touches on the unorthodox are covered by the flow of his verse and by Biblical language. For example, in a passage that forms part of the frame for the doctrinal explication of Book III the Son is celebrated by the angelic hosts as

> of all Creation first,
> Begotten Son, Divine Similitude,
> In whose conspicuous count'nance, without cloud
> Made visible, th'Almighty Father shines,
> Whom else no Creature can behold; on thee
> Impresst the effulgence of his Glorie abides,
> Transfus'd on thee his ample Spirit rests.   (III, 383–89)

The passage suggests *De Doctrina Christiana*, Bk. I, chs. 5, 7 (Columbia ed., xiv, 182, 190; xv, 8), where Milton explains the Son as subsequent to the Father and created by him. In the poetry unorthodox possibilities are masked by the use of Colossians 1:15,

---

[4] *Laval Théologique et Philosophique*, viii (1952), 243 ff.

where the Son is the "firstborn of every creature," and of Revelation 3:14: "the beginning of the creation of God." By the orthodox reader all Scriptural echo in the poetry is necessarily interpreted as orthodox, yet in his treatise Milton gives anti-Trinitarian interpretation to these passages. Without *De Doctrina Christiana*, then, *Paradise Lost* appears to present through its Scriptural language generally acceptable doctrine. If poetry, it is the poetry of Milton's age generally, not the expression of his personal belief.

As an absolute and irresponsible ruler, Milton's God has not found favor with such men as Shelley, just as the Calvinistic God has generally fallen out of favor in the present century. For example, a Methodist hero, Borden P. Bowne, protested against the "rectoral" theory of God such as Calvinists and other theologians held. No one need insist that this tyrannical God, however inclined to some application of mercy, is attractive in theology or in *Paradise Lost*. What Shelley and Bowne wished was a kindly God, conforming to their notion of ethics, who made existence agreeable to mankind. That is, they wished a world in which man could live an uninterruptedly pleasant life, the Utopia of reformers of various eras, including the present. But however we may respect the reformer in his desire to benefit the human race, his imaginary perfect world is not the real one; in fact it results from his reaction against a world far from perfect. The Almighty of seventeenth-century theology, appearing in *Paradise Lost*, results from observation of the world as it is, not a place pleasantly adapted to man but one where he has a hard time and where he attains salvation, if he does so, by effort and with fear and trembling. As the expression of his age Milton's God could hardly be a pleasant one. Hence if poetry presents the spirit of its time, a benevolent and tolerant God—however satisfactory to romantic desires—could not in the sixteen hundreds be poetical. That a reader may not like Milton's God is thus entirely apart from that God's poetical quality. Does criticism require that Iago, Macbeth, Cleopatra, or Shylock be such as we would gladly number among our personal friends? Milton's God is subject to such a test only if *Paradise Lost* becomes a mere versified *Christian Doctrine* or literal statement of belief. God as a poetic character is not in the first instance an object for ethical judgment.

Something is here demanded of the reader. He must not be so affected by the theology, whether accepted or rejected, as to dissolve in darkness its instrumental function in the poem, as dramatically thwarting Satan's plans. Secondarily, too, the passage has poetical quality as an ideal view of man theologizing, loving systems, asking for a clearly explained universe, formulating schemes that will take uncertainty out of the world. Neither primarily or secondarily is the reader's rational acceptance of the system poetically demanded. Indeed the opportunity to see the whole as poetical is even enhanced in an untheological age; we can look with charity on the unpoetical view that caused the Catholic Alexander Pope in a Protestant England to speak of Milton's God as a "school divine" or professor of theology. For an untheological modern to be so prosaic is less pardonable, though he needs historical preparation to condition him for such unwonted epic material.

On Milton's use in his epic of the theology so important to him as a man, the all-inclusive question is: Has he made theology poetic? This question the individual reader had best answer for himself, but only after he has considered the doctrinal verses in the whole movement of the epic. Poetically the theological exposition is the strategy of dealing with Satan the invader. If on reading Book III along with the rest of the epic, reading it aloud, an individual decides in either way, his judgment may stand for himself, until again he approaches *Paradise Lost.* At least there is no reason to suppose that Milton would have written more poetically if he had chosen an earthly king, Arthur or Alfred. Spenser's decision to deal with Holiness and other virtues suggests his judgment that Tasso was the last of the epic poets of war and love. The theology of Book III is important to the critic now as it was to the poet as he composed, but it is important in the same way as is the military or romantic theme handled by Virgil or Ariosto. As Charlemagne in *Orlando Furioso* prepares to thwart the attack of the Saracens on Paris, so the Almighty of *Paradise Lost* plans to ruin Satan's expedition. If Milton's was an age in which theology had imaginative force, if he had more of the craftsman's power over such lore than over any other, that was the material for him, the matter to which he could best give the form demanded by art. In and for itself the modified thought of Calvin and many predecessors is neither better nor worse than any other poetic theme labored by the human spirit and accepted by many readers.

MILTON'S BEE-SIMILE

Davis P. Harding, Yale University

Milton's borrowings, even the seemingly quite innocent ones, cannot rightly be ignored, for they not only provide the critic with important insights into his poetic method but they also frequently serve to safeguard the critic from false or misleading interpretations. A case in point is the famous bee-simile in Book I of *Paradise Lost*. Milton compares the clustering of the winged angels about the gates, porches, and hall of Pandaemonium with the swarming of bees about their hive. The Fallen Angels

> Thick swarm'd, both on the ground and in the air,
> Brusht with the hiss of russling wings. As Bees
> In spring time, when the Sun with *Taurus* rides,
> Pour forth thir populous youth about the Hive
> In clusters; they among fresh dews and flowers
> Flie to and fro, or on the smoothed Plank
> The suburb of thir Straw-built Cittadel,
> New rub'd with Baum, expatiate and confer
> Thir State affairs. So thick the aerie crowd
> Swarm'd and were straitn'd . . . .[1]

This passage has been criticized on the grounds of the impropriety of comparing still-radiant angels, fallen though they are, with a swarm of bees.

Milton, of course, did not invent the bee-simile. Its history in epic literature stretches all the way back to Homer, who compares the Achaian warriors, flocking forth in bands from the Greek encampment to hear what decisions their chieftains have reached in council, to bees issuing in tribes from a hollow rock.

Even as when the tribes of thronging bees issue from some hollow rock, ever in fresh procession, and fly clustering among the flowers of spring, and some on this hand and some on that fly thick; even so from ships and huts before the low beach marched forth their many tribes by companies to the place of assembly.[2]

---

[1] I, 767–76. All quotations from *Paradise Lost* are taken from the University of Illinois edition of *John Milton's Complete Poetical Works*, 4 vols., a photographic facsimile, edited by Harris F. Fletcher (Urbana, 1943–48). The text of *Paradise Lost* is reproduced in Vol. III.

[2] The translation of these lines from the *Iliad* is that of Lang, Leaf, and Myers in the Modern Library edition (New York, n.d.), p. 21.

This passage probably gave Milton the idea for employing an imitative bee-simile to describe the manner in which the Fallen Angels throng toward Pandaemonium, *their* place of assembly. The general parallel is enforced in several particulars. Common to both similes are the clustering of bees, the flying to and fro, the spring flowers.[3] It does very little good to say that Milton could have derived all these details from natural observation. So he could have. But we know that Milton did not habitually work in that fashion. We are dealing here with the rhetorical stratagem known as *retractatio*, or rehandling. Milton wanted his readers to recognize the source of his allusion so that they could compare his version with the original and then judge for themselves how skillfully, and with what new creative insights, he had reworked it.

They would have seen at once that Milton's simile differs from Homer's in several ways. Milton's bees reproduce the movements of the Fallen Angels from the time they converge on Pandaemonium to the moment they are called to order. And the emphasis is not the same. The main point of the Homeric comparison is to express the numbers of the Greek warriors and the manner in which they advance. It is exclusively a visual image. On the other hand, although Milton is making the same point, his simile engages the ear fully as much as it does the eye. We *hear* the rustling of innumerable wings and the busy humming, which is like the low murmur of statesmen sharing their views in an antechamber before some high conference gets under way. The effect is heightened by the onomatopoeia, produced by the massed sibilants, to which Milton resorts to reinforce his literal meaning. There is a third difference. Unlike Milton's bees, Homer's are quite evidently wild bees; they live in rock clefts, and we are not aware, as they fly from flower-patch to flower-patch, that theirs is in any sense a patterned or disciplined activity.

By Virgil's time, bees had come to be admired for other reasons; and, when Virgil imitates Homer's simile, it is the ordered, laborious, and constructive energies of the bees that receive the major emphasis. Virgil likens the Tyrians, Queen Dido's subjects, who are hard at work in diverse portions of the city, digging harbors, building houses, here laying a foundation for a theater, there rearing a citadel (*arx;* cf. Milton's "Straw-built Cittadel") to bees plying their separate tasks under the early-summer sun.

[3] Milton's great eighteenth-century editor, Bishop Newton, in a note to *P.L.,* I, 768, remarks that Milton's phrase, "In clusters," renders perfectly the force of the Greek *botrudon.*

qualis apes aestate nova per florea rura
exercet sub sole labor, cum gentis adultos
educunt fetus, aut cum liquentia mella
stipant et dulci distendunt nectare cellas,
aut onera accipiunt venientum, aut agmine facto
ignavum fucos pecus a praeseptibus arcent;
fervet opus redolentque thymo fragrantia mella. (ll. 430–36)[4]

Milton's rehandling of Homer's simile has obviously been influenced by the Virgilian imitation. Both the later poets introduce the
sun into the comparison, a detail missing from the simile in the *Iliad*.
Also Milton's "Pour forth thir populous youth" (l. 770) virtually
translates Virgil's *gentis adultos / educunt fetus* ("they lead forth their
nation's grown brood"). Both poets lend emphasis to their verbs by
putting them at the head of their lines. True, Virgil's simile has no
auditory function. But, if a literary precedent is insisted upon, one
may find it easily enough by turning to the sixth book of the *Aeneid*.
There the voices of the damned hovering about the river Lethe are
likened to the murmuring of bees in summer meadows (ll. 707–709).

Milton's indebtedness to Virgil's fine simile comparing the bees to
the Tyrians in the act of building Carthage is provocative. Coming
where it does, Milton's bee-simile heavily underscores the structural
parallel between the building of Pandaemonium in the first book of
Paradise Lost and the building of Carthage in the first book of the
Aeneid. This is one of the first of many structural correspondences
between the two poems.

But, for all this, the most significant influence on Milton's simile
is neither the *Iliad* nor the *Aeneid*. It is a hitherto unacknowledged
source, the fourth book of Virgil's *Georgics*. As the poem informs us,
the purpose of Book IV is to unfold "the wondrous show of a tiny
state"—the kingdom of the bees—embellished with a description of
its social and domestic structure, its mores and its works, its politics
and its leadership, how it conducts itself in war and peace. From
first to last, with a grave and affectionate irony, Virgil cultivates the
epic style and manner. What mighty warriors the bees are! All the
heroic virtues—and in good measure, too—are resident in them. No
wonder that their hearts beat fast when they hear the challenging
notes of the war-trumpets! Nevertheless,

---

[4] Latin citations from the *Aeneid* are taken from J. W. Mackail's edition (Oxford,
1930).

Hi motus animorum atque haec certamina tanta
pulveris exigui iactu compressa quiescunt.   (ll. 86–87)[5]

Consistently, through the *Fourth Georgic*, Virgil describes the bees in human terms. Verbal parallels make it certain that Milton had at least part of this description in mind. At eventide, says Virgil, the bees, wearied with the labors of the day, return to their hives, where, after refreshing their bodies (or as Milton has it, "New rub'd with Baum"), they hum around the edges of the doorway (*mussantque oras et limina circum*) before they enter their cells for the night (ll. 185–90). So

on the smoothed Plank
The suburb of thir Straw-built Cittadel,

Milton's bees "confer / Thir State affairs" until they are "straitn'd" and the Council begins.

Clearly we are meant to recall the *Fourth Georgic* when we encounter Milton's bee-simile. Milton compares the Fallen Angels with a swarm of bees. Now these same Angels had been previously linked— and not merely once but several times—with the insurgent mythological giants who sought to overthrow the Olympians.[6] It is, therefore, of more than passing interest that one of the key similes in the *Fourth Georgic* should involve a satirical comparison between the bees and Cyclops, the impious giants who (in the version of the legend Virgil followed) were punished by being compelled to do slave-labor in the boiling furnaces below Mount Etna:

Ac veluti lentis Cyclopes fulmina massis
cum properant, alii taurinis follibus auras
accipiunt redduntque, alii stridentia tingunt
aera lacu; gemit impositis incudibus Aetna;
ille inter sese magna vi brachia tollunt
in numerum, versantque tenaci forcipe ferrum:
non aliter, si parva licet componere magnis,
Cecropias innatus apes amor urget habendi
munere quamque suo.   (ll. 170–78)

---

[5] All quotations from the *Georgica* are taken from the text of Papillon and Haigh (Oxford, n.d.).

[6] For example, cf. the note of Merritt Y. Hughes to *P.L.*, I, 197, which I quote in part: "Both Titans and Giants were earth-born and were confused in the later accounts of the attack upon the Olympian gods. Milton's interest in the myth as well as his contempt for it may have sprung from his sympathy with the theory by which Sir Walter Raleigh was influenced in his *History of the World* (I, vi, 8) that the gentile myths were perversions but also corroborations of the Mosaic records."

The main purpose of Virgil's simile is to illustrate the division of labor among the bees. The Cyclops are specialists; each has his special task to perform. Now, as Milton's editors have remarked, the hill to which the Fallen Angels repair to excavate the materials for the building of Pandaemonium bears a close resemblance to Mount Etna as Virgil had described it in the third book of the *Aeneid:*

> Portus ab accessu ventorum immotu et ingens
> ipse: sed horrificis iuxta tonat Aetna ruinis,
> interdumque atram prorumpit ad aethere nubem
> turbine fumantem piceo et candente favilla,
> attolitque globos flammarum et sidera lambit,
> interdum scopulos avulsaque viscera montis
> erigit eructans, liquefactaque saxa sub auras
> cum gemitu glomerat, fundoque exaestuat imo.   (ll. 570–77)

In the passage of years, the burning interior of Mount Etna had been identified, by Christian mythographers, as a type of Hell. So it is not surprising to find Milton in his description of Hell in the first book of *Paradise Lost* comparing its acrid soil to the "singed bottom" of Mount Etna:

> And such appear'd in hue, as when the force
> Of subterranean wind transports a Hill
> Torn from *Pelorus*, or the shatter'd side
> Of thundring *Ætna*, whose combustible
> And fewel'd entrals thence conceiving Fire,
> Sublim'd with Mineral fury, aid the Winds,
> And leave a singed bottom all involv'd
> With stench and smoak . . . .   (ll. 230–37)

There is a general similarity between the two passages in the working out of the imagery of violence, and some similarity in detail. We may, for example, compare the use of the same metaphor by both poets to describe the interior of the mountain, Milton's "fewel'd entrals" almost exactly rendering the sense of Virgil's "torn entrails" (*avulsa . . . viscera*).

The analogy, however, does not stop at this point. Mammon leads his followers to a "Hill not far,"

> whose griesly top
> Belch'd fire and rowling smoak; the rest entire
> Shon with a glossie scurff, undoubted sign
> That in his womb was hid metallic Ore,
> The work of Sulphur.   (ll. 670–74)

Here the Fallen Angels, under Mammon's direction, begin their excavations. What is interesting is the way in which the several labor-groups are organized. Like Virgil's Cyclops and bees, the Fallen Angels are specialists: one group mines the metallic ore; another group melts it; a third builds the forms into which the molten metal is poured (see ll. 700–709). This tripartite division of labor is described in terms so close to Virgil's description of the labors of the Cyclops in the *Fourth Georgic* that the probability of coincidence can be eliminated. Thus, the bee-simile opens out into one more oblique allusion to the Giants who warred on Jove.

The *Fourth Georgic*, which contributed so significantly to the development of Milton's simile, also helps to define its meaning. Until the bee-simile occurs, the Fallen Angels have had pretty much the best of it. We have listened to the majestic, thunderous speeches of their leaders and have been impressed. We have watched them respond with alacrity, and out of a genuine loyalty and courage, to the inspiring words of Satan, and we have been impressed. We have witnessed the miraculous building of Pandaemonium, and that too was impressive. Confronted by this awesome display of heroic energy, the unreflective reader may succumb to the fallacy of seeing the Fallen Angels as they see themselves.

Elsewhere Milton has dealt with this danger by interpolating reassuring moral comments *in propria persona*, as when, after Satan had extricated himself from the Burning Lake, Milton reminds the reader that he could not have done so without God's permission. The bee-simile does the same work in a far less obtrusive fashion. Any tendency the reader may have had to exaggerate the importance of the heroic virtues displayed by the Fallen Angels should be sternly checked by the sobering reflection that Virgil's bees exhibit the same virtues. They too are valorous in battle, resolute in defeat, and fanatically loyal to their leader. In addition, as we have seen, they were celebrated for their skill in building and architecture.

The influence of the *Fourth Georgic* also crystallizes more clearly the situation of the Fallen Angels in the total scheme of Milton's universe. Despite all their energy, they are as helpless before God as Virgil's bees are before the bee-keeper. We know that God has only to stretch forth his omnipotent hand and all this heroic activity will cease. Or as Gabriel reminds Satan, God

> with solitarie hand
> Reaching beyond all limit at one blow
> Unaided could have finisht thee, and whelmd
> Thy Legions under darkness . . . .   (VI, 139–42)

SOME ILLUSTRATORS OF MILTON: THE EXPULSION
FROM PARADISE

Merritt Y. Hughes, University of Wisconsin

In a recent article Professor Kester Svendsen[1] has reproduced John Martin's treatment of the expulsion of Adam and Eve from Eden together with Fuseli's painting of "the beauty and gorgeous nudity of Adam and Eve [to] imply, as does their posture, a relation physically and spiritually that of lovers, not leavers." The purpose is to give Martin's handling of the scene the rank that it deserves among romantic depictions of the closing scene in *Paradise Lost*. His dark landscape with the distant dinosaur, the deep perspective of a river flowing away from the crags which the handfasted couple are descending, and the stag and the lion which represent "the solitude and the violence that await in the world," are described by Svendsen as both symbolizing humanity's future scientific conquests and perpetuating a symbolism traditional among Milton's illustrators. The serpent sliding away from Eve as she looks back toward the vague radiance behind her is mentioned, though the dog looking up at Adam is not; and in the writhing limbs of the dead trees in the lowest foreground Svendsen sees a symbol both of "arms agonized in supplication, the coils of the serpent, and by an inescapable association, the tree of redemption."[2] Though, if they could read Svendsen's explication of the painting, both Milton and Martin might be surprised by the triple symbolism which he sees in the writhen tree; they might well be happy in Svendsen's recognition of the painter's creation of a new myth emergent from the old one in the poem.

The case for the illustrator as a catalyst in the precipitation of a traditional myth in whose development the poem behind his illustration may be but a stage, can be made very strong. Indeed, the case may be defended as a reasonable extension of T. S. Eliot's critical doctrine and practice. In Svendsen's hands it becomes a touchstone to identify the few great illustrators of Milton among the many who have been recognized by Collins Baker.[3] In the list which ends at

[1] "John Martin and the Expulsion Scene in *Paradise Lost*," *Studies in English Literature, 1500–1900*, I (1961), 63–74.

[2] "John Martin and the Expulsion Scene," p. 71.

[3] C. H. Collins Baker, "Some Illustrators of Milton's *Paradise Lost* (1688–1850)," *Library*, 5th ser., III (1948), 1–21, 101–19.

1850 Svendsen finds only three whose interpretations of the Expulsion from Eden deserve reproduction in his article, and of the three he seems to regard Blake's as the finest, if not the most interesting. Its stylization of the lightning, the fig leaves, the thorns and thistles seems to him to enhance the mystery in the brooding eyes of Blake's mounted cherubim. Though Michael's foot is not quite on the head of the serpent, the uplifted faces of Adam and Eve are full of sweetness and of something like chastened confidence. The ambivalence in the conception seems to Svendsen to express the personal view of the Fall which Blake declared in *Milton* and the *Four Zoas*, and yet "his Expulsion Scene is faithful in fact (the clasped hands) as it is creatively free."[4] Full of symbolism though the packed canvas is, it is true to the moment imagined by Milton when

> In either hand the hast'ning Angel caught
> Our ling'ring Parents, and to th'Eastern Gate
> Led them direct, and down the cliff as fast
> To the subjected Plain.[5]

The ambivalence in Milton's closing scene has been magnificently shown by Svendsen elsewhere[6] in a study which lays great stress upon the final distich of the poem:

> They hand in hand with wand'ring steps and slow,
> Through *Eden* took thir solitary way.

In most of the happy scenes in the Garden of Eden their hands were clasped—at their first appearance in the story, when Satan sees them "hand in hand,"

> the loveliest pair
> That ever since in love's imbraces met"—[7]

and even in their dispute before the Fall, which ends when, as Eve turns away, "from her Husbands hand her hand / Soft she withdrew."[8] Their departure from Eden is a final confirmation of their original handfasting. If Bentley was right in taking "solitary" to indicate simply that Michael has finally left them alone together, their isolation is perhaps more than compensated by their re-established confidence and communion. If Bentley's reading is accepted,

---

[4] "John Martin and the Expulsion Scene," p. 70.
[5] *P.L.*, XII, 637–40.
[6] *Milton and Science* (Cambridge, Mass., 1956), pp. 107–13. Cf. Stanley B. Greenfield's note on *Paradise Lost*, XII, 629–32 in *Expl.*, XII (1961), item 57.
[7] *P.L.*, IV, 321–22.
[8] *P.L.*, IX, 385–86.

their solitude, which consists in the absence of their visible angel escort, is unreal, for they know what we are told in the preceding distich:

> The World was all before them, where to choose
> Thir place of rest, and Providence thir guide.

The tone of the four closing lines of the poem can be variously heard by readers of different temperaments and backgrounds. It can vary with the multiple meanings which can be given to the word *solitary*. For a theologically knowledgeable and concerned reader, the word will imply the end of direct intercourse between the banished couple and God. A flippant commentator may read the lines as meaning that the exiles are to be congratulated—now that their stern escort has vanished—upon being "alone at last." A sanguine optimist may regard their solitude as an invitation to their hearts to vibrate to the iron string of self-confidence. A non-Christian Existentialist may regard it as a statement of the perennial challenge of life to realistic analysis and intelligent assumption of responsibility. A Christian Existentialist may—like Professor Frye[9]—read the entire movement toward the climax of the poem as a fulfillment of God's declaration in Book III, 196–97:

> Light after light well us'd they shall attain,
> And to the end persisting, safe arrive.

The ambivalence in the final paragraph of *Paradise Lost* depends— as Svendsen says[10]—upon the view that the individual reader takes of the *felix culpa*,[11] and of Adam's response to Michael's declaration

[9] Roland Mushat Frye, *God, Man, and Satan: Patterns of Christian Thought and Life in Paradise Lost, Pilgrim's Progress, and the Great Theologians* (Princeton, 1960), p. 113.

[10] *Milton and Science*, p. 106.

[11] In *"Paradise Lost: Felix Culpa* and the Problem of Structure," *MLN*, LXXVI (1961), 15–20, William H. Marshall lists previous treatments as follows (p. 16): John Erskine, "The Theme of Death in *Paradise Lost*," *PMLA*, XXXII (1917), 573–82; Cecil A. Moore, "The Conclusion of *Paradise Lost*," *PMLA*, XXXVI (1921), 1–34; Allan H. Gilbert, "The Problem of Evil in *Paradise Lost*," *JEGP*, XXII (1923), 175–94; Denis Saurat, *Milton: Man and Thinker* (1925), p. 131; John S. Diekhoff, *Milton's "Paradise Lost": A Commentary on the Argument* (New York, 1946), p. 131; B. Rajan, *Paradise Lost & the Seventeenth Century Reader* (London, 1947), p. 45; Millicent Bell, "The Fallacy of the Fall in *Paradise Lost*," *PMLA*, LXVIII (1953), 863–83, and LXX (1955), 1187–97; Wayne Shumaker, "The Fallacy of the Fall in *Paradise Lost*," *PMLA*, LXX (1955), 1185–87, 1197–1202; H. S. V. Ogden, "The Crisis of *Paradise Lost* Reconsidered," *PQ*, XXXVI (1957), 1–19; William G. Madsen, "The Fortunate Fall in *Paradise Lost*," *MLN*, LXXIV (1959), 103–105. To this list must be added the study by Dick Taylor, Jr., "Milton and the Paradox of the Fortunate Fall Once More," *Tulane Studies in English*, IX (1959), 35–52, and the discussions of the Fortunate Fall by

Medina's illustration of the Expulsion from The Earthly Paradise,
for Tonson's edition of *Paradise Lost*, 1688.

(Ed.ⁿᵉ Alinari) P.ᵉ 2.ᵃ N.º 7768. ROMA—Vaticano, Loggie di Raffaello.
Adamo ed Eva scacciati dal Paradiso Terrestre. (Raffaello e Guilio Romano.)
Alinari Photo.

(Ed.ⁿᵉ Alinari) N.º 3846.
FIRENZE—Chiesa del Car-
mine. Adamo ed Eva Scac-
ciati dal Paradiso terreste.
(Masaccio) Alinari Photo.

This illustration, from the 1613 edition of Andreini's *L'Adamo*, which Voltaire declared to have been the inspiration for *Paradise Lost*, confirms the conclusion that Milton's expulsion scene was a deliberate break with tradition.

that in the fullness of time "the Earth / Shall all be Paradise, far happier place / Than this of Eden":

> O goodness infinite, goodness immense!
> That all this good of evil shall produce,
> And evil turn to good; more wonderful
> Than that which by creation first brought forth
> Light out of darkness! full of doubt I stand,
> Whether I should repent me now of sin
> By mee done and occasion'd, or rejoice
> Much more . . . "[12]

Among the illustrators Blake stands out as most distinctly interpreting the Expulsion in terms of redemption and possible joy. In the stance and expressions of his Adam and Eve there is lyric feeling such as J. B. Broadbent denies[13] to the treatment of the theme of "the Fortunate Fall" by Michael in his essentially theological exposition of it to Adam. He even denies it (by implication) to Adam's outburst of praise to "goodness infinite." Actually, it is hard to sever theology from lyric feeling in the ballad stanzas which he quotes as the natural habitat of the doctrine, for even there it is on account of Adam's sin, "As clerkis fyndyn wretyn in here book," that "we mown syngyn, 'deo gracias.' " Broadbent represents a prevailing opinion which is made the basis of William H. Marshall's analysis[14] of *Paradise Lost* as "constructed upon two systems, one dramatic and the other intellectual," the former packing its "most obvious emotional force" in the movement leading up to Satan's triumph in Book IX, and the other emerging only in the ironies of his defeat in Book X and of Michael's prophecy of his ultimate downfall in Book XII.

The truth in Marshall's depreciation of the last two books of *Paradise Lost* need not blind us to their value either as theology or as dramatic epic. In the situation resulting from Michael's exposition of God's purpose

> to reward
> His faithful, and receive them into bliss,
> Whether in Heav'n or Earth, for then the Earth
> Shall all be Paradise, far happier place
> Than this of Eden, and far happier days—[15]

J. B. Broadbent in *Some Graver Subject: An Essay on Paradise Lost* (London, 1960), pp. 282–86, and by Frank Kermode, "Adam Unparadised," in *The Living Milton* (London, 1960), pp. 116–24.

[12] *P.L.*, XII, 469–76.
[13] *Some Graver Subject*, p. 282.
[14] "*Paradise Lost: Felix Culpa* and the Problem of Structure," pp. 18–19.
[15] *P.L.*, XII, 461–65.

as Ogden points out[16]—Adam's burst of praise for "goodness infinite" is a dramatically appropriate ebullition of relief, amazement, and love. It is more appropriate if we adopt William G. Madsen's suggestion[17] that "the Incarnation involves not the lowering of Christ's nature to the level of human nature, but the exaltation of human nature to mystical union with God." In the movement of the poem as a whole Adam's outburst is still more appropriate if we accept John M. Steadman's view[18] that a deliberate and powerful Aristotelian epic recognition is involved in his last speech ending in his confession of faith

> that suffering for Truth's sake
> Is fortitude to highest victory
> And to the faithful Death the Gate of Life;
> Taught this by his example whom I now
> Acknowledge my Redeemer ever blest.[19]

To Christian readers—at least to those familiar with the epic theory of the seventeenth century—the Fall might indeed seem fortunate enough to inspire an illustration even more solemnly symbolic of redemptive joy than Blake's drawing. To those readers Addison might well have seemed justified in his inclination to drop the two last lines of the poem on the ground that they "renew in the mind of the reader that anguish which was pretty well laid by" the promise in the distich just preceding that Providence would be their guide as they sought rest in a world which was "all before them where to choose." In the climate of religious feeling which prevailed when Bentley published his edition of *Paradise Lost* in 1732 there may have been many assenters to his view[20] that the closing distich "contradicts the poet's own scheme" because he has told us "That Adam, upon hearing Michael's predictions, was even 'surcharged with joy,' ver. 372; was 'replete with joy and wonder,' ver. 468; was in doubt, whether he should 'repent of' or 'rejoice in his fall,' ver. 475; was 'in great peace of thought,' ver. 558; and Eve herself 'not sad,' but 'full of consolation,' ver. 620." Though Pearce and Newton dissented vigorously from Addison and Bentley for literary reasons, the latter's reasons for regarding Milton's closing distich as inconsistent with

---

[16] "The Crisis of *Paradise Lost* Reconsidered," p. 18.

[17] "The Fortunate Fall in *Paradise Lost*," pp. 104–105.

[18] *Studia Neophilologica*, XXXI (1959), 159–73.

[19] *P.L.*, XII, 569–74.

[20] Bentley is quoted from Henry John Todd's variorum edition of *The Poetical Works of John Milton* (London, 1801), III, 465–66.

Adam's surcharge of joy seem valid now to Broadbent[21] and Frank Kermode.[22]

Yet in spite of knowing that Bentley was right, as Broadbent puts it, "in demonstrating that the dénouement [of the return of 'long wandered man / Safe to eternal Paradise of rest'] is not amenable to what precedes, cannot be drawn dramatically out of Book XII despite the theological bonds," both he and Kermode see the ambivalence of the Fortunate Fall as clearly as Svendsen does. *If*, says Kermode, "Milton's 'scheme' was simply to show that everything would come out right in the end, and that this should keenly please both Adam and ourselves, Bentley is not at all silly here; or, if he is, so are the modern commentators who, supported by all that is now known about the topic *felix culpa*, tend to read the poem in a rather similar way." But Kermode suspects that some modern commentators have gone astray.

Though he names no one, the heads which Kermode's cap best fits are John Erskine's and John Crowe Ransom's. From the suggestion[23] that "Adam is proud" and properly proud in response to what may seem to an obtuse reader to be the "demoralizing comfort" of Michael's revelation of God's purposes, Erskine went on to draw a picture of Adam and Eve "in excellent spirits," leaving a tiresome Paradise with "nothing but zest" for "the world as a scene of action" such as Milton's "renaissance spirit" admired. Or, as Ransom finds, God has set his clever and adventurous creatures in "an infinitely tangled wilderness of a world which would be far more seductive presently to them than their idyllic bower."[24] Erskine and Ransom differ from Bentley only in missing the inconsistency between his view of the Expulsion and the closing lines of *Paradise Lost* in their unmistakable correspondence with God's commission to Michael in Book XI (117):

> So send them forth, though sorrowing, yet in peace.

And Kermode points out[25] that Bentley also forgot[26] God's command

---

[21] *Some Graver Subject*, p. 286.

[22] *The Living Milton*, p. 102.

[23] John Erskine, "The Theme of Death in *Paradise Lost*," pp. 573–82. The quoted phrases are from pp. 578 and 581.

[24] John Crowe Ransom, "The Idea of a Literary Anthropologist and What He Might Say of the *Paradise Lost* of Milton," *Kenyon Review*, XXI (1959), 137.

[25] *The Living Milton*, p. 102.

[26] Ants Oras, in *Milton's Editors and Commentators from Patrick Hume to Henry John Todd (1695–1801)* (Dorpat, 1931), p. 51, agrees with J. W. Mackail that "Bentley's notes . . . prove that the task was carried out in a hurry, and that much of the work in its final form may have been dictated."

to Michael and its relevance to the mood of Adam and Eve as they leave Paradise.

About the rightness of that mood disagreement is no longer possible. It is the result of an evolution in culture and in poetry which Professor Kurth traces[27] through the literature leading up to *Paradise Lost* and through the poem itself to the confrontation of the Christian hero in the last two books by "the grim reality of evil . . . and suffering of human life." It is the expression of what Professor Gilbert has called[28] "the virtue developed by the contest with evil [which] justifies the presence of evil." If with C. M. Bowra[29] we prefer to look at it in simple human terms as "the confidence and courage in which men should set out on the undoubted perils of life," it is still the same, for it is the basis of what he calls the "inimitable close" of the poem. Whether Adam misunderstands the Fall is of no importance, for his mood would not change if he could know that in heaven God had solemnly declared to the angels that he would have been

> Happier, had it suffic'd him to have known
> Good by itself, and Evil not at all.[30]

Though Professor Taylor regards these words as an "explicit denial—coming from God, Milton's ultimate Spokesman in the poem—that the Fall was in any way a fortunate occurrence,"[31] we may be sure that Milton did not intend any *hybris* to be read into Adam's view of the event. With Professor Diekoff[32] we must remember that Adam's view of the fall is no less explicit when he says to Michael: "full of doubt I stand / Whether I should repent . . . or rejoice/ Much more. . . ."[33] Our speculations about the *felix culpa* in itself, or in Milton's view of it, or in Adam's, may all be subject to the limitation which A. J. A. Waldock[34] compared to Heisenberg's "Uncertainty principle" in physics—to something in the nature of the concept itself which makes it immensurable under scrutiny. What is important is that Adam's conception of it, and God's as interpreted to Adam by

[27] Burton O. Kurth, *Milton and Christian Heroism: Biblical Epic Themes and Forms in Seventeenth Century England* (Berkeley and Los Angeles, 1959), p. 127.

[28] "The Problem of Evil in *Paradise Lost*," p. 188.

[29] *From Virgil to Milton* (London, 1948), p. 210.

[30] *P.L.*, XI, 88–89.

[31] "Milton and the Paradox of the Fortunate Fall Once More," p. 51.

[32] *Milton's "Paradise Lost": A Commentary on the Argument*, p. 131.

[33] *P.L.*, XII, 473–75. The full passage is quoted above.

[34] *Paradise Lost and Its Critics* (Cambridge, Eng., 1947), pp. 145–46.

Michael, should have brought *Paradise Lost* to what Waldock could call its "inimitable close."

The rightness of the close no longer needs defense. Its importance as an artistic achievement and also as marking a long step forward in thought about man's proper attitude toward his situation in life, is best understood in the iconographical context. Milton's re-creation of the myth of the Fall and its consequences was an achievement greater than that which Svendsen sees in Martin's treatment of the Expulsion from Eden. The measure of Milton's accomplishment in the last three books of his epic, and especially in the closing scene of Book XII, can be taken by comparing its closing lines with the treatment of the scene by his first illustrator, John Baptist Medina. His story has been told by Miss Helen Gardner,[35] and his illustrations of Tonson's edition of *Paradise Lost* in 1688 have been described by her and assessed as a genuine attempt at interpretation of the poem which deserves some respect and attention. Her accounts of several of his illustrations for the first ten books of the poem justify her estimate of their value, but she acknowledges that his treatment of the Expulsion from Paradise is "a sad disappointment." Her explanation for the failure is the fact "that the subject was too familiar, and that Medina, instead of studying his author, was content with a bad imitation of Raphael's 'Expulsion' in the Loggia, itself derived from Masaccio's fresco in the Carmine in Florence." The lack of intrinsic value in both Medina's picture and that by Raphael (with the help of Julio Romano) marks their documentary importance as transcripts of a traditional conception of the woe becoming to the couple being evicted from Paradise—woe which is foreign to the mood of Milton's ending of his poem.

Woe is the theme of Masaccio's much better painting, and there is nothing in the pose or features of his Michael that clearly suggests anything like divine compassion. The uplifted sword in the angel's hand is a sword of justice, compelling obedience of a different kind from that which Milton's couple have learned to pay to their guide. Masaccio's Adam has a dignity which neither Raphael nor Medina seems to have thought of giving to their male figures. Masaccio's Eve's face is a study in pure anguish, but neither of his figures moves with the contemptible animal fright that makes the Eve disgusting in the paintings by Raphael and Medina. If Milton saw Raphael's

[35] "Milton's First Illustrator," *Essays and Studies*, new ser., IX (1956), 27–38.

picture in the Vatican (as he probably did not), it could hardly have interested him for more than a moment. Nor can he have been interested in the illustration of the Expulsion in Andreini's *L'Adamo* (in the lavishly illustrated first edition by Bordoni, Milan, 1613), which represents Michael as pursuing the terrified exiles with his flaming sword lifted and ready to strike. If during his visits in Florence he saw Masaccio's obscurely placed painting, he may have carried its memory away to react morally against it—partly because its artistic merit made it unforgettable.

It was a long time before illustrators of Milton's expulsion scene could treat Adam and Eve as anything but studies in anguish or despair fleeing from the archangel's sword. So they appear in the headpiece to the Twelfth Book of *Paradise Lost* in the beautiful edition of the poem which was "Printed for Jacob Tonson, at *Shakespear's Head* in the *Strand*," in 1720. So, in a rather languid way, they survive in Gustave Doré's engraving of the scene.[36] Blake was the first artist to conceive Milton's Expulsion with hope and love in the faces of Adam and Eve, and an unarmed Michael leading them by the hands, as Milton has him do.

In the twentieth century it might be expected that illustration of Milton's Expulsion scene would follow the course which John Martin first explored in 1827. With John Erskine's new Adam and Eve in his essay on "The Theme of Death in *Paradise Lost*" as models a painter might create two figures for whom the Fall would obviously be inconceivable in any terms but Fortune. But in perhaps the most expressive modern treatment of the Expulsion, that in the edition of *Paradise Lost. A Poem in Twelve Books* which was published in London by the Cresset Press in 1931, death and not Fortune or Power is the theme. The very dark woodcut shows Adam and Eve close-up, nude, with hands clasped, but with averted faces. Adam's expression is wretched, resentful, and baffled. He is twentieth-century man, miserable in a hostile universe. Nothing more remote from the physical grace and dignity of Masaccio's Adam could be imagined. Beside him Eve covers her face with her free left arm. Her gesture is sheer terror, for a skeleton thrusts his jaws over her shoulder in an effort to bite her cheek. The Miltonic warrant for her escort in the place of Michael—if any—may be found in speeches like Adam's rhetorical demand to know "Why is life giv'n / To be thus wrested from us?"

[36] *Milton's "Paradise Lost,"* illustrated by Gustave Doré (New York, 1885), plate 50, opp. p. 312.

After gathering several such passages of poignant protest against death to support his thesis, Kermode declares[37] that *"Paradise Lost is a poem about death, and about pleasure and its impairment."* Kermode is not appeased by Milton's treatment of death as a release "from the great wound the senses have suffered," nor by his gratification of the senses for a while with the flowers and fruits of the Earthly Paradise, or with the perfumes and ethereal light of heaven. For Kermode, the great paradox of *Paradise Lost* is not the Fall but "the paradox of Eve as destroyer and giver of life."[38] The poem can be so read, and in our time that reading may make Michael give way to the skeleton as escort for Adam and Eve when they leave Paradise to choose their place of rest with no thought that Providence can be their guide.

The spirit of the symbolism in the other *de luxe* edition of our time[39] is similar, but it goes further than the Cresset edition in stripping Adam and Eve of their supernatural guidance. The woodcut at the end of Book XII is a horizontal panel showing them with hands clasped, stumbling forward without escort of any kind. Between them is a child's version of a serpent. Beside Adam is a half-crouching dog. Around them and hemming them in are four colossal faces, two menacing and two averted, with horrent locks. Since a fragment of Milton's Biblical myth survives in the serpent, one wonders whether the four faces are modern versions of the "dreadful Faces" and "fiery Arms"[40] of the Biblical seraphim who guard the gate of Paradise and watch Milton's Adam and Eve as they retreat. Or are they a modern reminiscence of the four mounted angels in the background of Blake's Expulsion? Behind the four hostile or threatening faces a still more enormous face fixes its expressionless eyes on the backs of the harassed human couple. Its expression is obscured by two swords crossed in front of it. Cosmic violence and indifference usurp the place of the Providence under whose guidance Milton's Adam and Eve were left by Michael to pursue what once seemed like a "solitary way."

[37] *The Living Milton*, p. 121.
[38] *The Living Milton*, p. 120.
[39] *Paradise Lost. A Poem by John Milton. The Text of the First Edition Prepared for Press by J. Isaacs and Printed at the Golden Cockerel Press* ([London], 1937).
[40] *P.L.*, XII, 644.

MILTON'S ANNOTATIONS OF EURIPIDES

Maurice Kelley and Samuel D. Atkins, Princeton University

Although its existence has been known since 1694, Milton's annotated copy of Euripides has received scant modern attention. W. R. Parker's *Milton's Debt to Greek Drama in Samson Agonistes*[1] accords it only a belated four-line notice; and the editors of Volume XVIII of the Columbia Milton[2] print only 92 of the some 820 annotations present in Milton's copy. Space does not here permit detailed analysis of all these annotations; so we restrict our discussion, first, to a specific consideration of some 146 marks, corrections, and notes that do not, we believe, belong in the Milton canon, and, second, to a brief, general report on the time, nature, and competence of what seems Milton's own work.

I

Preserved in the Bodleian Library under the pressmarks Don. d. 27 and 28, Milton's Euripides is the two-volume Paulus Stephanus edition of 1602,[3] which in addition to the Greek text contains a Latin transla-

[1] (Baltimore, 1937), p. 245.

[2] Pp. 304-20, 566-68. An earlier list appears in *Museum Criticum; or, Cambridge Classical Researches*, I (1814), 283-91; but contrary to *Friends of the Bodleian Ninth Annual Report* ([1933-34], pp. 5, 18-19, Plates II-III), this list is neither a transcript nor complete. It is rather some 180 notes made by Porson in a Brubachius edition of Euripides on readings that interested him in the marginalia of Milton's two volumes. Other references to or notices of Milton's Euripides include R. P. Jodrell, *Illustrations of Euripides, on the Ion and the Bacchae* (London, 1781), pp. 34-35, 335-36; *Monthly Magazine*, XXXVII (1814), 397-99; *The British Critic*, n.s., I (1814), 436; Edward Hawkins, *Poetical Works of John Milton* (Oxford, 1824), I, ciii; H. J. Todd, *Poetical Works of John Milton* (London, 1842), I, 158; S. L. Sotheby, *Ramblings in the Elucidation of the Autograph of Milton* (London, 1861), pp. 108-10, Plate XV; David Masson, *The Life of Milton*, I (1881), 568; *Archivist*, VI (1893), 58-59; G. B. Hill, *Johnsonian Miscellanies* (Oxford, 1897), II, 70, *Lives of the English Poets* (Oxford, 1905), I, 154; *Milton Tercentenary 1908* (Cambridge, 1908), p. 91; J. E. Sandys, *A History of Classical Scholarship* (Cambridge, 1908), II, 347; *TLS*, I Dec. 1927, p. 910; *Library*, 4th ser., XV (1934-35), 337-39; *ELH*, IV (1937), 320; J. M. French, *Life Records of John Milton*, I (1949), 282.

[3] ΕΥΡΙΠΙΔΟΥ ΤΡΑΓΩ- / διον ὅσα σώζονται. / EVRIPIDIS TRAGOE- / diæ quæ extant. / *Cum Latina Gulielmi Canteri interpretatione.* / . . . / SCHOLIA doctorum virorum in septem EVRIPIDIS / tragœdias, ex antiquis exemplaribus ab ARSENIO / MONEMBASIÆ archiepiscopo collecta. / *Accesserunt doctæ* IOHANNIS BRODÆI, GVLIELMI / CANTERI, GASPARIS STIBLINI, ÆMILII / PORTI, *in* EVRIPIDEM *Annotationes*. / Cum indicibus necessariis. / . . . / EXCVDEBAT PAVLVS STEPHANVS. / *ANNO MDCII.* According to the B.M. Catalogue, the translation is "rather that of D. Camillus (i.e., R. Collinus), corrected by Æ. Portus?"

tion, scholia, commentaries by Brodaeus, Canterus, Portus, and Stiblinus, and a subject index. On the flyleaf preceding the title page, Milton has written his name, the price paid for the volume (now partially eaten away by ink erosion), and the year of purchase: "Jo[:] Milton / pre: [12^s 6^d] / 1634". Below, in an unidentified seventeenth-century hand, is a copy of Milton's inscription with a negative mark of pounds added, followed by the twice-written initials, "DS" (Daniel Skinner [?]); and below these is Thomas Birch's note concerning his purchase of the work in 1754.[4] The paper of the two volumes is poor in quality: uneven in thickness and sometimes taking the ink no better than blotting paper. Some of the annotations are consequently hard to decipher, and brown flecks in the paper may be mistaken for minute corrections. On other occasions, the annotations are so brief that positive attribution is not always possible. But in spite of such difficulties, four different hands are distinguishable in the marginalia: two non-Miltonic hands written in ink, one non-Miltonic hand written in pencil, and Milton's autograph, written in ink.

The first of these two non-Miltonic hands employing ink appears in some 66 entries, as we identify and count them, scattered through the two volumes.[5] These entries consist of miscellaneous marks, underlinings, corrections, annotations, and references to classical and later authors, such as Gataker, Plutarch, Schottus, Strabo, and Tzetzes. That Milton did not dictate these entries seems indicated by the reference to Milton in the note "f. μελλ. Milton." (II, "Brodaei . . .

[4] Printed in Jodrell, *Illustrations*, p. 336, n. 8.

[5] In this and other lists that follow, we cite first the volume and page number of Milton's copy, then play and line. The abbreviations for Euripides' plays are those used in Allen and Italie, *A Concordance to Euripides*. Where the annotation concerns the Latin translation, we add L to the line number. Annotations consisting solely of marks or underlining we indicate by the sigla X or U. For annotations of scholia or commentary, we give only page number. Since some of the annotations consist of mere marks or a few letters, our attribution of them to a particular scribe cannot always be offered with certainty. Such instances we have indicated with a question mark, usually preceded by the name of the other scribe to whom the annotation may actually belong, and the whole enclosed in parentheses.

Volume I: 21, *Hc* 201; 48, *Hc* 539L; 76, *Hc* 864; 83, *Hc* 939; 84, *Hc* 949, 102, *Hc* 1151 (Hierocles annotator or Milton?); 185, *Or* 706L; 201, illegible word only; preceding ὄχθον seems by Milton; 224, *Or* 1137; 233X; 254, *Or* 1510–13; 262, *Or* 1635; 265; 266, *Or* 1686; 268; 271; 278, *Pho* 91; 279, *Pho* 103; 284U?; 286, *Pho* 164; 289; 292; 293; 304, *Pho* 364U, 366U, 367U; 305U; 412; 413; 420; 421; 432, *Md* 401 (Milton?); 451X; 471, *Md* 1007; 498.

Volume II: 51, *Su* 928; 935; 250, *Rh* 342, 351; 256, *Rh* 458–64; 292, *Tr* 120, 121L; 296, *Tr* 204; 305, *Tr* 355; 312, *Tr* 500L; 434, *Cy* 39L, 53L; 544, *Hl* 363L; 554, *Hl* 566; 557, *Hl* 626; 728, *HF* 572L; 732, *HF* 645; 746, *HF* 902L; Brodaeus, pp, 4, 16, 25, 30, 38, 40, 49, 63, 70, 71; Index, sigs.)( )(.j. and)( )( )(.ij.; Stiblinus, p. 187.

Annot.," p. 25), which refers to Milton's note on *IT* 644; and further
investigation shows that they are the work of Joshua Barnes, Fellow of
Emmanuel College, Cambridge, and editor of a 1694 edition of Euripides.[6] In his edition, Barnes acknowledges his use of Milton's copy;[7]
and the handwriting and style of annotation found in the 66 entries
closely resemble the script in Barnes' correspondence[8] and notes in
Barnes' annotated copy of his own edition preserved in the Bodleian
Library.[9]

The second non-Miltonic hand employing ink appears in some 46
entries, as we identify and count them, running through Milton's
Euripides as far as *El*.[10] Written in two sizes of script, small and large,
they seem at first glance to be the work of two different scribes; but
closer study shows that all 46 belong to one individual, whom we call
the Hierocles annotator.[11] These entries include small marks at the
beginning or end of lines of the Greek text, corrections, emendations,
annotations, a list of lost plays of Euripides, and references to certain
classical and later authors, such as Apollodorus, Apollonius Rhodius,
Cicero, Ennius, Eustratius, Grotius, Hierocles, Lactantius, Phocylides,
Probus, Stephanus, Theocritus, and Vigerus. In citing works ex-
traneous to Milton's two volumes, these entries resemble more the
notes of Barnes than of Milton, who, except for one entry (*IA* 7),
derives his annotations entirely from his Stephanus edition. In four
instances,[12] furthermore, Barnes prints matter of the Hierocles annotator over his own signature. These facts suggest that this scribe

---

[6] *Euripidis Quæ Extant Omnia Tragoediæ nempe* XX . . . *Opera & Studio
Josuæ Barnes . . . Cantabrigiæ . . . MDCXCIV.*

[7] See, for instance, sig. [a3], "Nomina Doctorum Virorum, qui Nobis in hoc
Opere facem praetulerunt," Index Secundus, *s.n.* Milton, and numerous unindexed
uses, such as II, 188 (*Ba* 592), 209 (*Cy* 33), 246 (*Hr* 602), 317 *Io* 319), 414 (*El* 475).

[8] Bodleian MSS Ash. 1136, fol. 133; Rawl. C. 146, fols. 43–55; D. 400, fol. 5;
697, fol. 6.

[9] Pressmarked Auct. S. 1. 5.

[10] Volume I: ¶. iij; [A.j.]; 17; 21, *Hc* 208; 27, *Hc* 283; 29, *Hc* 306 and scholia below;
31, *Hc* 326; 55, *Hc* 623; 314, *Pho* 527; 405, *Md* 3; 476, *Md* 1078.

Volume II: 175, *IT* 423; 389, *Ba* 592, 593; 405, *Ba* 909; 433, *Cy* 33; 434, *Cy* 49;
444, *Cy* 247; 450, *Cy* 357; 501, *Hr* 602 (Milton?); 507, *Hr* 727 (Milton?); 620, *Io*
103X; 621, *Io* 109X; 624, *Io* 166X; 625, *Io* 190; 636, *Io* 416X; 637, *Io* 435; 638, *Io*
454X; 639, *Io* 463; 648, *Io* 639, 651; 651, *Io* 705; 660, *Io* 875 Ψ only (Milton?); 679,
Io 1247; 717, *HF* 347X; 719, *HF* 379X; 723, *HF* 464X; 757, *HF* 1119X, 1126X; 763,
HF 1238X; 767, *HF* 1315X; 769, *HF* 1354; 779, *El* 95; 783, *El* 187; 798, *El* 481X.

[11] Note, for instance, the close similarity in the two sizes of writing of the letters
A, C, H, m, n. p, the consistent use of colons in situations normally calling for periods,
and the citations of Apollonius Rhodius (I, ¶. iij., II, 175) and Hierocles (I, 29, 476).

[12] Compare the notes of Barnes and the Hierocles annotator on *Pho* 527, *Md* 3,
IT 422, *Io* 439. Without signature, Barnes uses materials of the Hierocles annotator in
his notes to *Hc* 299, 306, 326, *Cy* 49, *El* 95.

helped Barnes prepare his 1694 edition. But in four other instances,[13] Barnes attributes entries of the Hierocles annotator to Milton. Since this annotator twice cites an edition of Hierocles published in 1673[14]— the year before Milton's death—the likelihood of his having served as Milton's amanuensis seems small. We are thus left knowing little about the Hierocles annotator other than that he worked in Milton's Euripides some time between 1673 and 1694, and that if he did not work independently of both Barnes and Milton, the content of his notes and the lateness of their *terminus a quo* indicate that he may be more logically associated with Barnes than with Milton.

Even more uncertain is the status of the third non-Miltonic hand, which appears in pencil. Through the two volumes, this scribe has left some thirty marks[15]—perhaps to indicate lines that struck him as meriting further study—and four annotations, now very faded, in *Tr* and *Ba*. The first annotation offers an alternate translation of *Tr* 120–21; the second attempts a more accurate translation of μετανισόμεναι in *Tr* 131; the third proposes that in *Ba* 857 ἐν τέλει be construed with γνώσεται of the preceding line and the three words translated "tandem cognoscet"; and the fourth offers an inferior alternate translation of *Ba* 894. The first of these four notes concerns a passage that Barnes has underlined in Milton's copy; but the remaining three annotations and Barnes' edition offer no further indications of a connection between Barnes and this pencil scribe. His work seems that of a translator whose scholarship is noticeably inferior to Milton's; and since his script is not distinctly seventeenth-century, his entries may possibly be later than those of Barnes.[16]

---

[13] *Ba* 592, *Cy* 33, *Hr* 602, *Io* 190. These are brief annotations, and in three instances we may be wrong in assigning them to the Hierocles annotator. But in the fourth instance, *Cy* 33, our attribution seems certain. We consequently believe that in these four instances, Barnes has confused the small script of the Hierocles annotator with the small writing that Milton sometimes employed in his pre-1638 notes. Such would not be surprising in view of Barnes' generally careless handling of the MS notes in Milton's volume.

[14] *Hieroclis philosophi Commentarius in Aurea Pythagoreorum carmina: Joan. Cuterio interprete . . . London, Printed by J. R. for J. Williams and are to be sold by H. Dickinson of Cambridge, 1673*, cited, with page number, as "Cantab: editio," (I, 476), and again by page number only (I, 29).

[15] I, 70, 72, 124, 125, 159, 171, 293, 294; II, 292, 293, 296, 317, 403, 405, 474, 476, 481, 492, 505, 604, 617, 709. Since these marks are in pencil and thus easily distinguished from entries in ink, we have omitted play and line number.

[16] The script of this pencil scribe does not significantly resemble the handwriting of either Samuel Johnson or Richard Porson; and the four annotations do not appear in the *Illustrations* of Richard Jodrell, the third later scholar known to have had access to Milton's two volumes. The handwriting of Francis Hare, who owned the Euripides after Barnes, has not been available for comparison.

Milton's Euripides thus contains 66 annotations that do not belong to Milton, and 80 others that can be reasonably assigned to him
only by disregarding such significant matters as different content and
inferior scholarship. In the Columbia Milton, therefore, we should delete the Euripides marginalia numbered 3, 8a, 9, 10, 11, 12, 17a, 52, 76,
80, 80a, and 81, for they are the work of Joshua Barnes rather than of
Milton. We should also query the marginalia numbered 1, 2, 4, 5, 6, 7,
8, 13a, 16, 16a, 32a, 49a, 51, 53, 55a, 65, and 66, for they are the work of
the Hierocles annotator.[17] This scribe cannot be firmly connected with
Milton, and his notes should not be offered as Milton's work without
proper reservation.

II

Milton's annotations of Euripides should consequently be restricted to
the entries that appear in his own hand and to the eighteen years between 1634, when he purchased the two volumes, and 1652, the year
of his total blindness. Within these years, many of his annotations may
be dated as before or after 1638 according to whether the *e*'s in the
Latin comment show the pre-1638 Greek epsilon or the post-1638
Italian form, and whether the annotation mark is the pre-1638 aster-
isk or the post-1638 supralinear x.[18] This evidence indicates that
Milton went through his Euripides at least twice, once before and once
after 1638,[19] with the variations in color of ink, pen point employed,
and size of script further suggesting that within these two periods
Milton worked intermittently.

Except for a reference (*IA* 7) to "Scaliger in prooemio ad Ma-
nilium,"[20] Milton's notes fail to indicate that his study of Euripides

---

[17] In the *Museum Criticum* list, the notes on *Hc* 200, 939, 1151, *Or* 873, 1686,
Pho 91, 189, *Tr* 355, *Hl* 626, are by Barnes; the notes on *Hc* 208, 306, *Md* 1078, *Ba*
592, *Cy* 33 are by the Hierocles annotator. In the *Concordance* of Allen and Italie, the
reading attributed to Milton under ἄδην belongs to Barnes, that under λύεται to the
Hierocles annotator.

[18] For the rationale of this method of dating, see our "Milton's Annotations of
Aratus," *PMLA*, LXX (1955), 1090–1106. Additional entries may be also assigned to one
or the other of these two periods if we assume that small writing is a pre-1638 practice,
and that larger writing, use of the caret to indicate insertions, and the abbreviation
"f." for "fortasse" are post-1638 characteristics. The few entries showing both forms
of "e," such as *An* 179 and *Io* 1360, probably belong to the years close to 1638, when
Milton was shifting from the Greek to the Italian *e* (Helen Darbishire, "The Chronology
of Milton's Handwriting," *Library*, 4th ser., XIV [1933–34], 229–35).

[19] *Al* and *Hr* show clearly only pre-1638 annotations, *Tr* and *Danae* only post-1638
entries; but plays adjacent to these four were annotated both before and after 1638.

[20] Milton's notes on *Cy* 52, *Hl* 1606, and *Io* 1503, which cite Stephanus, Suidas, and
"alii," derive from the commentaries of Canterus and Brodaeus, printed in the latter
portion of volume II.

went beyond the covers of his two volumes; but within those volumes Milton gave close attention not only to the Greek text but also to the Latin translation, the scholia, and the commentaries. The Stephanus text is far from a model of typographical and editorial accuracy, and a good portion of Milton's labors was devoted to correcting it. For instance, in the first four plays, *He, Or, Pho*, and *Md*, over two-thirds of Milton's annotations correct misspellings, transpositions of letters, illogical punctuation, wrong or omitted assignments of speeches, etc. This work tempts one to assume that Milton was collating his Euripides with another edition; but there seems no conclusive evidence for such an assumption, and many of the errors are such as would be readily apparent to a person of Milton's competence in Greek who was reading, as Milton did, his Greek text in conjunction with the Latin translation and the scholia.[21] Milton also gave close attention to the commentaries, as over 100 entries indicate.[22] These are restricted, however, almost entirely to the plays in Volume II, where the commentaries are also printed, with only one acknowledged citation in Volume I,[23] and that belonging to the post-1638 period. In Volume II, however, Milton's use of the commentaries is heavy. Pre-1638 Brodaeus notes appear in *Su, IA, IT, Hr, Io*, and the commentary itself (p. 79, on *Hr* 822); post-1638 Brodaeus notes appear in *IT, Tr, Ba*, and *Hl*. Pre-1638 Canterus notes appear in *Rh, Hr, Io*, and the Brodaeus commentary (p. 79, on *Hr* 822); post-1638 Canterus notes appear in *IT, Rh, Tr, Cy, Hr, Hl, Io, HF*, and *El*. Pre-1638 Portus notes appear in *HF* and *El*; post-1638 notes in *IA, IT*, and *Hl*. Post-1638 Stiblinus notes appear in *El*[24] and in the commentary itself (p. 148, on *Rh* 29). These notes suggest that Milton made greatest use of Canterus, and gave closest attention to *Hl* and *El*.

Other annotations, however, show that Milton read his two volumes as a poet and critic as well as a student of Greek. Notes such as

[21] For corrections in these four plays closely connected with the Latin translation or scholia, see *Hc* 982, 1117, 1118; *Or* 143, 761, 930, 1131; *Pho* 334, 617, 629, 669, 1686, 1737; *Md* 839, 941, 1201.

[22] In 48 additional notes, Milton offers, without acknowledgement, readings that appear in the commentaries: Brodaeus, *Su* 1110; *IA* 419, 1170; *IT* 215, 747; *Tr* 188; *Cy* 482; *Hl* 729, 1686; *Io* 189, 236; *HF* 1224; Canterus, *Pho* 669, 1737; *Md* 941; *Al* 488; *An* 56, 81, 100; *IT* 58, 62, 1010, 1011; *Ba* 282, 819; *Cy* 52–53, 432; *Hr* 109; *Hl* 794, 809, 1283, 1686; *Io* 1097, 1187; *HF* 245, 474, 1370; *El* 180; Portus, *Pho* 501, *Md* 892; *IA* 419; *Tr* 156; *Ba* 865; *Cy* 421; *Io* 580, 823; Stiblinus, *Su* 138; *Rh* 271.

[23] Possible instances of Milton's unacknowledged use of the commentaries in Volume I are the Canterus and Portus notes to *Pho, Md, Al*, and *An* listed just above in footnote 22. Of these, *Md* 892 seems a pre-1638 entry; *Ph* 1737 post-1638.

[24] The editors of the Columbia Milton (XVIII, 320, item 78) transcribe this note incorrectly as "vide Scholium"; Milton wrote "vide Stiblinum."

"ὅ versui magis quadrat" (*Hl* 1703) and " . . . sic enim metrum erit integrum" (*Io* 1423) indicate that Milton scanned Euripides as he read.[25] His close concern with metrics is no better illustrated than by his minute correction of *Or* 305. Here he changes οἰχόμεθα of the printed text to οἰχόμεσθα. Both endings, -μεθα and -μεσθα, are permissible, and there is no semantic difference between them; but the meter requires the use of the second. Other notes show Milton also reading with an alert attention to dramatic values. In *Su* 754 ff., he would shift to Adrastus a series of speeches assigned in the printed text to the chorus because "haec videntur potius inter Adrastum et nuncium pro choro itaque ponend." On *Hr* 822 (Brodaeus, p. 79), he comments: "videtur tamen potiùs eo in loco βροτείων sumi pro βροτέντων hoc est cruentatis nam hominum immolationes apud Athenienses ad modum raras fuisse [constat *inserted and deleted*] et magnis de causis notum est, ideoque hic etiam tanto cum horrore auditur oraculum de Marcariâ diis mactanda, rex etiam planè recusavit, se vel ullum e civibus coacturum filiam suam interimere ne pro salute publicâ itaque non est verisimile post virginis voluntariam necem alias fuisse victimas humanas, si ita Brodaeus intellexerit, sed vide Cant. Versione."[26]

Milton's marginalia,[27] finally, speak well for his competence as a student of Greek. Introduced into the stream of Euripidean textual criticism by the Barnes edition of 1694, and supplemented by Porson's *Museum Criticum* list of 1814, his notes have commanded respectful

---

[25] For similar notes, see *Io* 408, 1360; *HF* 328.

[26] For similar remarks, see note on *Rh* 234 (Stiblinus, p. 148); *Cy* 202; *Hr* 321.

[27] In addition to Milton's some 560 annotations, the two volumes also contain about 115 marks, ranging from enclosures of lines and underlining to what appear to be testing of pens and purposeless doodles. In many cases, one cannot be certain as to who made them. Fairly certainly by Milton is the enclosure of *Su* 440–43 (compare the ink with that of Milton's entries at *Su* 388, 420); and as Evans has pointed out (*JEGP*, LXI [1960], 497), this passage includes the last two lines of *Su* 438–41, which Milton printed on the title page of *Areopagitica*. Other marked passages, if also by Milton, have possible biographical significance. For instance, *Or* 601–607, probably marked by Milton, and in the post-1638 period, concerns fortunate and unfortunate marriages. *Hi* 644–52 and 628–36 are less probably Milton's and less susceptible to dating; but 644–52 is part of Hippolytus' famous denunciation of women, and 628–36 has been translated as follows: "The very father that begot and nurtured a woman, to get rid of the mischief, gives her a dower and packs her off; while the husband who takes the noxious weed into his house, fondly decks his sorry idol in fine raiment and tricks her out in robes, squandering by degrees (unhappy fellow!) his house's wealth. For he is in this dilemma: say his marriage has brought him good connections, he is glad then to keep the wife he loathes; or, if he gets a good wife, but useless kin, he tries to stifle the bad luck with the good."

attention from later scholars, continental as well as British;[28] and two modern, standard editions have adopted three of his emendations. Both the Oxford and Budé editions accept Milton's substitution of ἐπαγγέλλειν for ἀπαγγέλλειν (*Hi* 998) and σῷ for ᾧ (*Hl* 627 = Oxf. 622), and in their apparatuses give him credit for the readings. The Oxford editor (the Budé volume has not yet been published) also accepts and credits Milton for his suggestion of ἡδέως for ἡδέων (*Ba* 188). Three other accepted readings, though attributed in Oxford and/or Budé to others, actually seem to originate in Milton. One of these three appears in *Hl* 1644 (= Oxf. 1628): ἀφίστασ' for ἀφίσταθ'. Oxford has this reading but does not designate it as a conjecture. Budé has the same reading, but attributes it to Porson.[29] In this emendation, however, Milton had anticipated Porson. Another of these three readings occurs in *Su* 852. Both Oxford and Budé have ἀγαθός. Oxford makes no acknowledgment; Budé credits Milton and Markland together. Milton's conjecture was ὤ 'γαθός. Presumably, Milton receives credit for the introduction of the article before ἀγαθός (with crasis), which corrects the metrical irregularity of the line; Markland receives credit for supplying the shape of the crasis which is correct for tragedy. In short, Milton prepared the way for Markland. The third reading appears in *Io* 408: μαντεύματ'. This conjecture, which corrects the meter, both Oxford and Budé credit to Barnes. Again, it really originates in Milton. Noticing the metrical irregularity of the line, he substituted μαντεύματ' for μάντευμ', but failed to notice the following rough breathing of ἕν and wrote a final τ' instead of θ. Barnes' contribution seems to have been the correction of Milton's oversight. A seventh conjecture, Νηρέως for νηρῆδος (*IA* 628), is recorded and credited to Milton in the Oxford apparatus as a variant reading.

Bentley is reputed to have offered over 700 conjectures to the text of Horace, of which only one or two have found general acceptance. If this story be true, then Milton has fared considerably better than the one-time Master of Trinity. And Dr. Johnson's declaration that he "found nothing remarkable" in Milton's notes on Euripides seems more a measure of Johnson's limitations than of Milton's attainments as a classical scholar.

[28] See, for instance, in the Glasgow, 1821, variorum edition of Euripides the notes written by Hoepfner, Seidler, Markland, Monk, and Musgrave on *Hi* 653; *Al* 152; *Pho* 969; *An* 6, 179, 284, 388; *IA* 626, 792, 812, 1151; *IT* 58, 645, 891; *Rh* 525, 526; *Tr* 817; *Ba* 1216, 1375; *Hr* 321; *Hl* 619; *Io* 188, 189; *HF* 1354; *El* 448, 475, 1046, 1350.

[29] See Glasgow, 1821, Variorum, I, clxxxii.

NOTES ON THE TEXT OF *SAMSON AGONISTES*

William Riley Parker, Indiana University

It can be argued that there is still need for a reliable but readable text of *Samson Agonistes*. Obviously it should be reliable in its faithfulness to Milton's sounds and sense, including respect for the rhythms he intended. But should it not also spare the modern reader the impression (never intended by the author) of quaintness or pedantry or inconsistency in spelling or punctuation? Preventing such an impression is not, however, a simple matter of modernizing the spelling and punctuation, although countless editors seem to have thought so.

Milton's punctuation, for example, is both more economical and more rhetorical than ours, often clarifying his prosody while leaving it free to do its work. Modernizing it, therefore, must be a matter, not of parsing Milton's sentences by modern notions of grammar, but rather of altering his punctuation only to clarify meaning. Thorough imposition of strictly grammatical punctuation (as in the editions by Masson and the many based on Masson's text) interferes with the intended rhythms of Milton's verse. On the other hand, an absolute minimum of modern punctuation could remove the seeming casualness or awkwardness of seventeenth-century punctuation, and the occasional ambiguities created by it for modern readers, without seriously disturbing the clarification of prosody which Milton's own punctuation attempts.

As for spelling, most editors modernize to such an extent that many of Milton's sounds and rhythms are altered. An example is the popular edition by Harris F. Fletcher (1941), in which strictly modernized spelling alters the rhythms of 100 lines (yet in which the old punctuation is largely preserved). At the other extreme are the few more or less successful attempts to reproduce the 1671 text: editions by John Mitford (1851), H. C. Beeching (1900), H. J. C. Grierson (1925), and Columbia (1931).[1] These have had value for students unable to

---

[1] In the Columbia Milton text of *Samson* there is an obvious typographical error in line 1291, and the following additional corrections are necessary: change to "carelesly" (118), a period instead of a comma after "pure" (548), "expresly" (578), "brest" (609), "e're" (824), "wish" (1096), and "numberd" (1478). Columbia does not notice certain variants which Fletcher discovered by collating many copies of the first edition, and therefore, in some cases, clearly does not have the corrected readings: the lines are 1033, 1078, 1086, 1093, 1176, 1183, and 1340. Incidentally, Columbia's notes should be deleted for lines 118, 548, 578, 1078, 1086, 1176, 1183, and 1340, for in each instance the second edition actually follows the first.

consult the first edition, now more accessible in the photographic facsimile published (1948) by Fletcher with collation of sixty copies of 1671, twenty-three of them accumulated at the University of Illinois. More recently Miss Helen Darbishire (1955) and B. A. Wright (1956), while basing their texts on the first edition, have produced quite different versions of what they suppose to have been Milton's preferred spelling of many words, Wright also making many changes in the punctuation. The results are two fascinating documents for anyone deeply interested in Milton's experiments in orthography, but hardly texts to facilitate reading. (The first edition's "some Magicians Art / Arm'd thee or charm'd thee" becomes "Armd thee or charmd thee" in Miss Darbishire and Wright's editions; the modern "some magician's art / Armed thee or charmed thee" produces no different sounds or rhythms.)[2]

Numerous inconsistencies of spelling in the 1671 edition argue the use of several amanuenses for the manuscript sent to the printer, and/or intervention of the compositor.[3] There are three different kinds of spelling inconsistency. Let us notice first the omission from the 1671 text of some of Milton's known or supposed preferences. Absent from it, for example, and therefore substituted by both Miss Darbishire and Wright, are such spellings as "autority" (868), "averr" (323), "childern" (352), "deferr" (474, 1557), "doctrin" (297), "engins" (1396), "Iles" (715), "immediatly" (1614), "moderat" (1464), "preferr" (1374), "privat" (868 etc.), "transferr" (241), and "furder" (2, 1499; but not in 520 by Miss Darbishire, nor in 520 and 1252 by Wright).[4] For the first edition's "enrol'd" (1224) and "enroll'd" (653, 1736) Miss Darbishire substitutes "inrould" and Wright "enrould" (note "roul" in 290). Miss Darbishire substitutes "onely" in fifteen instances, but not in line 1659, whereas Wright makes this substitution only in 1659 and four other instances.[5] (Cf. their differing substitutions of "ther" in 84, 295, 300, etc.)

---

[2] When the rhythm requires pronunciation of the final "-ed," an accent must be supplied, and this may give the line an archaic look. So be it; the pronunciation *is* archaic. But in all Milton's poetry there are only about 127 instances of this (only 61 in the three major poems), and this small amount of unfamiliar spelling in a modern text is surely preferable to countless instances of "charm'd" or "charmd."

[3] The observations in this article are based on a verbatim, all-inclusive concordance of *Samson Agonistes* compiled for the purpose of this and other analyses. A number of errors and omissions were found in both the Bradshaw *Concordance* and the Lockwood *Lexicon*. For some of my remarks about Milton's normal spelling or spelling preferences, I am indebted to my friend and former student, Professor John T. Shawcross.

[4] Note that the 1671 edition does have such spellings as "Conferr'd" (993), "Intestin" (1038), "Magazins" (1281), "degeneratly" (419), "Effeminatly" (562), etc.

[5] In manuscript Milton consistently (nine instances) spelled "only."

Miss Darbishire alone makes such substitutions as "blaspheamd" (442), "counterfet" (189), "farr" (five instances, but not in 527), "hauty" (1069), "hostil" (531, etc.) "insensat" (1685), "intimat" (223), "maisters" (1215, 1404), "uncompassionat" (818), "unfortunat" (747, but not 1743), "warr" (1278), "wrauth" (1683), and "yeild" (15 etc.). Wright alone makes such substitutions as "baum" (186, 651), "don" (478, 1104, 1594, but not 243 and 1128), "endevor" (766), "flowr" (five instances, but not 987), "goe" (1146, 1237, but not in seven other instances), "gon" (997, 1350, but not 1244), "leasure" (917), "misdon" (911), "pitty" (814) and "pittied" (568), "som" (sixteen instances, but not in fourteen others), and "towrs" (266). On the other hand, Wright regularly turns Milton's conjunctive "then" into "than" (Miss Darbishire has "than" only in 1592), and, for reasons explained (pp. viii–xi), he modernizes a number of spellings such as "asswage" (627, but cf. 184), "atchiev'd" (1492), "causless" (701), "chuse" (1478), "compleat" (558), "earst" (339, 1543), "falshood" (955, 979), "hainous" (493, 991), "hast" (for "haste": 1027, 1441, 1678), "houshold" (566), "loosly" (1022), "perswade" (586, 1495) and "perswasion" (658), "sourse" (64, 664), and "strait" (385).

The most obvious criticism of the Darbishire-Wright method of editing Milton is implicit in the analysis above: the most careful scholars will forever disagree on Milton's orthographical intentions,[6] especially those intentions in the period during which he was totally dependent on amanuenses. If one assumes that he seriously meant to continue his personal spelling practices of the period before blindness, one should go beyond Wright and Miss Darbishire, and introduce into the text of *Samson* such spellings as "beeing" (885), "beleef" (117, 1535), "citty" (1194 etc.; cf. Wright's "pitty"), "com" (twenty-four occurrences), "comming" (187, 1395, 1452), "cours" (670), "dayly" (6 etc.), "els" (6 etc.), "fals" (227 etc.), "feirce" (612 etc.), and so on. But, making all these changes, one may wonder what is gained in the process. *What matters are the sounds and rhythms Milton meant to be heard.*

A second kind of inconsistency of spelling is purely internal: there are about sixty words for which the 1671 text offers two different spellings, ignoring capitalization. This total does not include certain words for which an uncommon spelling *may* (some editors confidently say *does*) indicate either emphasis—"hee" (124, 178), "mee" (220, 252,

---

[6] Professor Shawcross, for example, is confident that Milton wrote "blaspheam'd," "yeeld," "balm," or "baulm," etc.

290, 291, 1125), "yee" (193)—or lack of emphasis, i.e., the eighty-four occurrences of "thir" in contrast to fourteen of "their." (Incidentally, Miss Darbishire changes the 1671 text's "their" to "thir" ten times, and its "thir" to "their" once, in line 1267. Wright's changes differ slightly.) Also excluded from the total of sixty are cases in which Milton's rhythmic intention is clearly responsible for the difference in spelling: armed/arm'd (1190, 1617; 20, 347, etc.). (Milton also wants the final "-ed" pronounced in lines 1283, 1568, 1634, 1693.) Not included, moreover, is the use of the apostrophe to indicate the possessive case with proper names such as "Abraham," "Israel" (except for 1527), and "Zora"—but not otherwise. In connection with Milton's use of proper names, B. A. Wright has noticed that in at least two instances out of fifteen (240, 1714) the meter would seem to require that "Israel" be pronounced with three distinct syllables, but the 1671 text does not have the warning dieresis that Wright thus introduces ("Israël"), as also in "Baäl-zebub" (1231) and "Jaël" (989).

A modern editor working from the text of the first edition must decide between "Anac" and "Anak" (528, 1080), "Ascalonite" and "Askalon" (138, 1187), "Palestin" and "Palestine" (144, 1099), even "Manoah" and "Manoa" (328, 1441, etc.).[7] "Philistines" occurs in the poem, "Philistins" in the Argument, and "Philistims" seems to have been Milton's preference. His own spelling seems to have been "anough" (455, 1468, 1592), but "enough" occurs twice (431, 1256). His own spelling was evidently the pronunciational "bin" (874, 1297), but "been" occurs nine times (to be changed to "bin" by Miss Darbishire and Wright only in lines 98 and 1440). A more provocative inconsistency in the 1671 text—perhaps a clue to the detection of different hands—is the spelling "eie" (459, 584, 636, 690, 726) along with "eye" (nineteen occurrences).[8] "Murtherer" (832, 1180) is followed closely by "murder" (1186). "Public" occurs six times, "publick" but once (1327, not regularized by Miss Darbishire), unless we count also its triple appearance in the Argument and list of Persons. Among other editorial choices to be made are: choises/choice (420; 3 etc.), boist'rous/boyst'rous (1273, 1164), brest/breast (609; 1722, 1739), chuse/chooses (1478, 513), die/dye (1706, 32), dispense/dispence

[7] More important, "Manoah" (328) seems to be uniquely trisyllabic; "Manoa," dissyllabic. The spelling "Manoa" occurs in *De Doctrina Christiana* (Columbia ed., XIV, 244).

[8] The spelling "eie" occurs twice in the 1645 and 1673 *Poems* ("Il Penseroso" 141, "Comus" 328), but does not seem to occur elsewhere in Milton's writings, manuscript or published.

(1377, 314), femal/female (711; 777 etc.), joyn/join (456, 1342; 265, 1037, 1368), praiers/prayers (520; 359, 392, 961), profan'd/prophane (377; 693, 1362), pursue/persues (1275, 1544), recompense/recompence (746, 910), roul/enroll'd-enrol'd (290; 653, 1736; 1224), scarse /scarce (1546; 7, 79, 1525), servile/servil (5, 1213; 412, 413, 574), shewn/shown (994, 1475), and trial/tryal (1175, 1288; 1643).

Many of the inconsistencies of spelling may, of course, be attributable to a compositor rather than to Milton or his amanuenses. There is evident uncertainty over the spelling of preterites and participial forms: for the same word the ending may be "-t"/"-'t" or "-'d" (136, 450; 1183, 1467; 37, 1335; 1451, 1096; 1005, 266; 643, 466). There is uncertainty as to whether an apostrophe is even needed for such endings (252, 1597; 794, 1719, 900, 939; 45, 1661; 246, 516, 390, 1253; 1658, 146, 1589; 235, 281, 562). A similar confusion is found in the following: know'st/knowst (850; 1081 etc.), took'st/tookst (1591, 838), would'st/wouldst (1105; 794 etc.), and wond'rous/wondrous (1440; 167 etc.). Should we spell "add" or "adde" (1121, 1357; 290), "bondslave" or "bondslave" (411, 38), "deceivable" or "deceiveable" (350, 942), "fiery" or "fierie" (27, 549; 1690), "naught" or "nought" (588, 779; 1215), "toward" or "towards" (682; 334 etc.), "warriors" or "warriour" (139; 542, 1166)? Probably only a fine sense of editorial consistency is disturbed by such differences as these, and the occasional use of "oh" (349, 1268, 1516) instead of "O" (twenty-eight occurrences) seems scarcely worth remarking.

When the rhythm of a line is affected, it is another matter, and the editor has a decision to make when confronted with inconsistencies. The 1671 text normally uses an apostrophe to mark elision and contraction when it is needed to insure a correct reading. Moreover, since syllabic "n" was commonly spelled with an apostrophe in place of the vowel to indicate that the vowel was only a semivowel ("Heav'n"), presumably an apostrophe should not appear when two or more syllables ("Heaven") are to be pronounced. The kind of distinction the meter requires is illustrated by "forbid'n" (555), which is a metrical dissyllable, and "forbidden" (1139, 1409), which is not. Either the compositor or Milton's amanuensis[9] did not, however, recognize this distinction when syllabic "n" was followed by a word beginning with a consonant, and thus the editor of *Samson* meets in

---

[9] It is possible that Milton himself did not make this distinction; he seems to prefer the "-'n" spelling regardless of the number of syllables (i.e., expecting his reader to recognize the difference according to the meter).

the 1671 text a number of instances in which an apostrophe creates an ambiguity, the meter calling for an unelided syllabic "n":

"begott'n" (1699) should be "begotten."
"giv'n" (378) should be "given" as in 121 (which is in error); the other five instances of "giv'n" are metrical monosyllables.
"Hast'n" (576) should be "Hasten."
"Heav'ns" (549) should probably be "Heavens," though the reading of this line offers problems.
"light'n" (744) should be "lighten."
"Oak'n" (1123) should be "Oaken."
"op'n" (1609) should be "open."
"silk'n" (730) should be "silken."

The distinction is perhaps less troublesome (though still puzzling to some readers) when in the word itself an unelided syllabic "n" is followed by a consonant: "disheartn'd" (563) and "heartn'd" (1317) pronounced "hearten'd"; "fastn'd" (1398) pronounced "fasten'd"; and similarly "hast'n'd" (958), "slack'n'd" (738), "Softn'd" (534), and "threatn'd" (852).

The opposite of this problem occurs in a number of spellings. Both a regular meter and Milton's normal usage would seem to require an apostrophe to indicate contraction (elimination of the vowel sound and its syllable) in the following:

"burdenous" (567) should probably be "burd'nous."
"countenance" (684) should probably be "count'nance."
"given" (121) should almost certainly be "giv'n," as in six other instances.
"Heaven" (23, 1134, 1438) should almost certainly be "Heav'n," as in eleven other instances.
"Heavenly" (373, 635, 1035) should probably be "Heav'nly."
"offering" (344, 1152) should almost certainly be "off'ring," as in 26 and 519.
"Prisoner" (7, 808) should almost certainly be "Pris'ner," as in 1308 and 1460.
"seven" (1017, 1122) should probably be "sev'n."
"sufferings" (445) should almost certainly be "suff'rings," as in 701.
"wavering" (732) should probably be "wav'ring."

Why "ev'ry" occurs once (1323) and "every" four times (93, 97, 204, 749) is puzzling.[10] Still another kind of problem is offered by "rememberd" (677), where the meter would at least allow "rememberèd." Finally, we may note two clear errors: "delivered" (1158)

---

[10] It would seem that Milton normally wrote "burdnous," "countnance," "offring," "Prisner," "suffrings." On the other hand, he seems always to have pronounced "every" (so spelled) as two syllables; the "ev'ry" (1323) is almost certainly a scribe's doing.

should be "deliver'd," as in 437 and 1184; and "cryed" (1639) should be "cry'd."

To achieve regular meter Milton used the apostrophe to mark elision with "the" followed by a word beginning with a vowel.[11] There are nineteen instances of this in *Samson Agonistes*, one of which (973) seems to be an error, since it mars the rhythm. A modern editor must decide whether or not to use the same device in such lines as 316, 361, 640, 672, 695, 696, 893, and 1241. A similar problem arises with the use of the apostrophe with "to" followed by a word beginning with a vowel; the 1671 text has this in line 727, but not in 994, 1095, 1460, 1547, and other places where the meter would permit it if not encourage it.

A third kind of inconsistency of spelling, also internal, involves capitalization. In addition to proper names, some 289 words used in *Samson Agonistes* are capitalized regularly or irregularly, and an editor must decide whether to retain none or all or some of them. He may even decide to add capitals; for example, pronouns referring to the Deity are not capitalized, nor are such words as "beauty" (1003), "nature" (595, 890, 1545), and "vertue" (eight occurrences). Analysis of capitalization in the *Samson* suggests, however, that several principles operated more or less consistently. A correction made during the process of printing distinguishes helpfully between "God" and "god" (1176). Moreover, most names belonging to certain broad categories are capitalized. This principle and its inconsistent application are illustrated by the following: Adders, Ass(es), Boars, Bulls, Dragon, Eagle, Goats, Hornets, *Hyaena* (italicized), Kid, Lion, Monster, Porcupines, Scorpions, Serpent, Weather (i.e., Wether); not capitalized: bird, dogs, snake, viper, worm.

Most military terms receive capitals: Ambushes, Ammunition, Armories, Army, Armies, Brigandine, Captains, Cataphracts, Conquer'd, Conquerours, Conquest, Cuirass, Engines, Gauntlet, Greves, Habergeon, Heroes, Host, Iron(s), Magazins, Rebellion, Revolter, Slingers, Souldiery, Troops, Trophies, Victor, War, Warriour(s); not capitalized: appellant, battel, mail, shield. Most religious terms also receive capitals: Altar, Angel(s), Angelic, Atheists, Consecrated, Doctrine, (our living) Dread, Feast, Godhead, Godlike, Heathen, Heaven, Holy One, Holy-days, Idol(s), Idol-worship, Idolatrous, Idolatry, Idolists, Image, Infidel, Priest(s), (Divine) Prediction, Prophecy, Religion, Religious, Rites, Sacrifice(s),

---

[11] Or even a consonant, on occasion; see, e.g., "Vacation Exercise" 38.

Sacrilegious, Saints, Sanctuary, Sea-Idol, Seal, Soul, Superstition, Temple(s), (thou great) Word, Worshippers. To this same category perhaps belong: Circumcis'd (but cf. "uncircumcis'd," 260, 640, 1364), Doctor, Grave, Sepulcher, Holocaust, Magic, Magicians. Inconsistent usage of certain other words that belong to the three categories listed above will be discussed later.

Also regularly capitalized are the following words, categories for which perhaps suggest themselves: Parents, Sire, Father(s), Son(s), Children (cf. the remarks below on "Daughters"), Patrimony, Matron, Concubine, Virgins, Bridal, Matrimonial (cf. "Marriage," below), Paranymph; Skie, Moon, Sun, Eclipse, Sun-rise, Eastern (ray), Vernal; Hill, Vale, Mount, Mountains (cf. "abyss," 501, "cave," 89), Isles, Shore; Plant, Laurel, Palm, Oak'n, Opium; Theatre, Assembly, Champion, Antagonist, Antics, Dancers, Gymnic Artists, Livery, Mimics, Mummers, Riders, Runners, Swordplayers, Wrestlers; Pipes, Timbrels, Trumpets; Preface, Parables, Lyric Song, Legend; Giant(s), Giant-brood, Giantship, Gigantic; Ship, Vessel, Helm, Pilot, Stears-mate; City, Edifice (cf. "roof," 1634, 1651), Towers, Bar, Post, Mill; Gaol, Bondage, Fetters (cf. "manacles," 1309), Murtherer, Robber, Parricide, Traytor, Traytress; Masters, Governours, Heads, Kings, Princes, Scepter, Lord(s), Lordly, Lordliest, Ladies (cf. "nobility," 1654), Magistrates, Councellors, Politician, Public Officer, Messenger; State, National (cf. "Nation," below), Tribe(s), Countreymen (cf. "Countrey," below). Note finally this small miscellany of words that are also capitalized: Amber, Author, Superscription, Barbers, Weavers, Crystalline, Rubie, Jaw, Nativity, Poor, Reprieve, Rivals, School, and Tormenters.

Whether through carelessness and indifference, or by design at which we can only guess, the remaining words that are capitalized (ninety-two) occur also without capitalization. In some cases capitalization may have been intended to mark recognizable distinctions; possible examples are: Reason/reason (322, 323; 1546, 1641), Sea/seas (710, 962; 961), Prowess/prowess (1098, 286), Patience/patience (654, 1296; 755, 1287), Pomp/pomp (436, 1312; 357, 449), Praises /praises (436; 175, 450). In other cases a word to be used many times may have been capitalized for emphasis on its first appearance only; possible examples are: Arms (131), Eyes (33), Blind (366; cf. 68), Gold (389), and Hair (59). "Locks" (327) is also capitalized on the first of six appearances, but it there refers to Manoa's hair whereas the other five refer to Samson's. The hypothesis of initial emphasis is further shaken by words which occur a number of times, are capitalized only once, but then not on a first appearance: (Samson's) Birth (1431, last of four occurrences), Wine (1670, last of six), Hope (1535, next to last of eleven), Sight (152, fourth of fourteen), Glorious (363, second of seven), Honour (412, second of ten). Inconsistency of practice seems as evident in these as in the following words, all regularly capitalized with a single exception: slaves (41, first of five occurrences), prison (1480, last of five; cf. 922), marriage (320, second of four), pillars (1630; cf. 1606, 1633, 1648), deliverer (1270, fifth of six), heroic (527, third of five; cf. 1710), nations (890, sixth of ten).

Whatever principles may have governed some of the capitalization in *Samson Agonistes*, inconsistency of result is as conspicuous in this as it is in other aspects of spelling. Take, for example, the following words that occur only twice in the poem, once capitalized and once not: Balm (186, 651), Bond-slave (411, 38), Brazen (35, 132), Deity (464, 899), Delivery (1575, 1505), Duty (853, 870), Fowl (1695, 694), Games (1312, 1602), Graces (360, 679), Helmet (1119, 141), League-breaker (1184, 1209), Renown'd (125, 341), Sores (184, 607), Spies (386, 1197), Tomb (1742, 986), Treason (391, 959), Triumph (1312, 426), and Truth (1276, 870). To this list, though perhaps not so conclusive as examples of inconsistency, might be added: Ages (765, 1707), Beam (83, 163), Belief (1535, 117), Captiv'd (33, 694), Festival(s) (1598, 983), Fort (278, 236), Gates (147, 1597), Monument (1734, 570), and Off'ring (26, 519). A few words are twice capitalized, but once not: Beast (37, 1403; 127), Camp (1436, 1497; 1087), Dungeon (156, 367; 69), Earth (174, 1272; 165), Land (257, 710; 99), and Nuptial (385, 1194; 1743; cf. 1023). A few others are once capitalized, but twice not: Bride (320; 1018, 1198), Consolation (183; 664, 1757), Daughters (1192; 221, 876), Heavenly (635; 373, 1035), Husband (940; 755, 883), Sex (1026; 711, 774), and Spells (1139; 1132, 1149). Consider also: Deliverance (225; 292, 603), Fame (1248; 1706, 1717), Prayers (359; 392, 520, 961), and Sacred (363; 428, 518, 1001).

"Wife" is three times capitalized (227, 725, 1193) and twice not (724, 885; cf. 957). Dalila is twice "Woman" (202, 236) and thrice "woman" (50, 379, 1114; cf. 749, 783, 844, 903, 1012). There is the same inconsistency in capitalizing "Women" (211, 983; 216, 957), "Spear(s)" (1121, 1619; 132, 284, 348), "Prisoner" (7, 1308; 808, 1460), "Fool" (203, 298; 77, 496, 907, 1338), "Hostile" (1210, 1561; 531, 692, 893), and "Liberty" (270, 949; 271, 803, 1454). Thrice capitalized are "Countrey" (238, 1208, 1213; but ten times not), "Friend(s)" (187, 202, 1415; but nine times not), and "Foes" (366, 423, 424; but twelve times not). "Enemy(-ies)" (Samson's) receives capitalization five times and lacks it fifteen times. The hero is "Captive" four times, twice "captive" (1474, 1603). Capitalization does not seem consistently to make any recognizable distinction (as it might) in the frequent appearances of "law(s)," "love(s)," "man" and "men." The list of words receiving irregular capitalization includes also: Acts, Air, Art(s), Faith, Proof, and Spirit(s).

Despite all the carelessness and confusion suggested by the foregoing observations, it should not be overlooked that the 1671 text contains a number of examples of what students have come to recognize as distinctively "Miltonic" spellings. For most of these the compositor could not have been solely responsible; they are present because the compositor was working with a manuscript that was either written by persons aware of *some* of the poet's orthographical preferences, or partly in the handwriting of the poet himself. The preponderance of "thir" over "their" (eighty-four times to fourteen) is impressive; it should be noticed that "thir" also appears in the Preface (along with "sowr," "distinguisht," "unfinisht," "hap'ning," "bin," and "fift") and twice in the Argument (along with "perswaded," "threatnings," and "Ebrew"). Among other spellings of the first edition which, together, bespeak its Miltonic origin are: "battel" (287, 583, 1131), "Ebrew(s)" (1308, 1319, 1540),[12] "highth" (384, 683, 1349),[13] "medcinal" (627), "perfet" (946), "surfet" (1562), "suttleties" (56), "threds" (261), "trechery" (1009, 1023), and "verdit" (324, 1228).

It remains to discuss in more detail the punctuation of *Samson Agonistes*. As B. A. Wright observes (p. xix), it is both lighter and more casual than in *Paradise Lost*. If we do not count parentheses,

---

[12] This spelling occurs also in parts of *Tetrachordon* and *Colasterion* (Columbia ed., IV, 110, 178, 225, 235, 258), both published in 1645. Elsewhere (*Paradise Regained*, IV, 336, "Psalm 136," line 50, and prose of the period 1641–59) the spelling "Hebrew," after classical Latin and Greek, occurs. For some reason, Milton in 1645 followed the medieval Latin and Middle English ("Ebreu") form of the word. Masson conjectures that Milton wrote "Hebrew" for the adjective, "Ebrew" for the substantive; but the prose does not support this theory. Hilaire Belloc, *Milton* (1935), p. 279, has a long comment on this spelling.

[13] Shawcross (see n. 3) doubts that this is Milton's preferred spelling, despite the evidence of the three major poems. "Height" occurs in manuscript and at least eight times in the published prose ("Heighth" twice in *Animadversions*, 1641). Cf. Milton's preference for "fift," "sixt," "autority," etc.

there are 313 lines with no punctuation at all. But Milton's punctuation in all his poetry is, like his spelling, of his century and yet individual: more rhetorical than grammatical, it conforms for the most part to his peculiar prosody and hence, to the extent that we understand it, helps us to read the verse aright. Commas are used more sparingly than in modern practice (about 1,429 in 1,758 lines) and then often where we would feel a period or at least a semicolon necessary; there are more than three dozen instances of this. Perhaps less disturbing to the modern reader is the occasional use of a purely rhetorical semicolon (for a longer pause) where grammatical punctuation would require only a comma (e.g., 32, 34, 140, 232, 391, 489, 653, 654, 1258). Semicolons are frequent in the 1671 text of *Samson;* there are 181 of them. Colons (70 of them) also occur more frequently than in modern punctuation, often where we would expect a semicolon or full stop. This poem of 1,758 lines uses only 292 periods, 25 exclamation marks, and 81 question marks.

A modern editor of *Samson Agonistes* must deal with a number of errors in punctuation: total absence of it where a colon, semicolon, or period is needed (191, 783); superfluous or misleading presence of a period (228, 405, 548, 742, 987, 1488); absence of a question mark (54, 567, 1061, 1092, 1512, 1544); the question mark used for the exclamation mark (820) and vice versa (1509). These offer no special problems, but the editor's work does not end with correcting them; he must decide to what extent he will modernize the remaining punctuation, and upon what principles. Even if he wishes to retain the original pointing as an important aid to understanding Milton's rhythms, he will soon discover that the original pointing (for whatever reason) sometimes obscures Milton's *sense.* Examples of passages where the exact meaning is unclear (and where one meaning or another emerges with changes in punctuation) are lines 516–20, 543–44, 652–59, 701–704, 982–84, 1156–57, 1443–44, 1468–71, 1616–19, 1623–24, 1646–52, 1663–68, 1697–1707, and 1711–12. Should the editor interpret with punctuation in such cases (running the risk of interpreting wrongly), or leave the individual reader to struggle with the ambiguities unaided?

In the judgment of this writer, an editor should act like an editor. Nearly accurate proofreading is no more "scholarly" than the use of critical intelligence to assist the reader in discovering the author's intention. If one fears he is "tampering" or "popularizing," he can always explain what he is doing—in a scholarly footnote.[14]

SATAN'S JOURNEY: DIRECTION IN *PARADISE LOST*

H. F. Robins, University of Illinois

In his recent book, *Milton's Ontology, Cosmogony, and Physics* (Lexington, 1957), Professor Walter Clyde Curry traces Satan's travels through the Miltonic cosmos so that "something . . . about mental and visual perspectives, directions, and distances in *Paradise Lost*" may be elucidated. Among his conclusions are these: Heaven is circular (p. 156); Heaven's gate is in the west wall (pp. 3, 148, 151, and ch. 6, *passim*); Satan is thrust out through a gap far to the north in that west wall (p. 148); he falls through Chaos and Hell-gate into the burning lake (p. 149); after the demonic council in Pandaemonium, having made his way through Chaos, he emerges in a place roughly below the breached west wall of Heaven (p. 151); his flight southward to the newly created universe parallels the west wall (p. 151); the bridge built by Sin and Death consists of a section reaching from the floor of Hell upward to the gate in its roof, another tunneling to the surface of Chaos, and a third, arching southward over Chaos to the outside shell of the World and paralleling the western side of Heaven (pp. 149–51, 153). A very well drawn diagram (p. 156) incorporates most of Professor Curry's putative discoveries. As a pictorial representation of the Miltonic cosmos, this is certainly superior to other attempts, Masson's, for instance; it is reproduced in Professor Merritt Hughes's excellent edition of Milton's poetry and prose (p. 180). Unfortunately, both the diagram and Curry's chapter upon which it is based contain, I think, a number of errors which, though unimportant individually, tend to blur and weaken that ideal picture of the cosmos which Milton labored with care to raise in the imagination of his readers. Furthermore, if Curry's scheme be admitted, some interesting correspondences among details of Heaven, the World, and Hell are entirely lost, as is Milton's consistently symbolic use of directions. By retracing Satan's journey I believe that I can show wherein Professor Curry is mistaken; moreover, I shall present several hitherto unnoticed aspects of Milton's cosmography, point up certain parallels between parts of his cosmos, and suggest meanings which seem to me implicit in these parallels.

I have long been convinced that the scattered cosmographical minutiae which embellish *Paradise Lost* are part of an integrated concept present always in Milton's mind, and I do not think that Milton ever stumbled over details of his imaginary landscape. The famous line describing Heaven as "In circuit, undetermind square or round" (II, 1948)[1] is a case in point; for it has often been read out of context and cited to show that Milton was undecided upon so important a matter as the shape of Heaven.

At the close of Book II, Satan, winging his way on the last stage of his journey from Hell to the newly created World,

> in the emptier waste, resembling Air,
> Weighs his spred wings, at leasure *to behold*
> *Farr off* th' Empyreal Heav'n, extended wide
> In circuit, undetermind square or round,
> With Opal Towrs and Battlements adornd
> Of living Saphire, *once his native Seat;*
> And fast by hanging in a gold'n Chain
> This pendant World, *in bigness as a Starr*
> Of smallest Magnitude *close by the Moon.*
>
> (II, 1045–53; my italics)

The passage describes not the actual shape of Heaven, but how it looked to Satan "at leasure to behold" it from "farr off." It was, after all, "once his native Seat," a place in which he had lived for ages, in which through merit he had achieved a high position in the heavenly hierarchy, in which he had ruled over "the quarters of the north." Surely Milton would not imply any doubt in Satan's mind about the actual shape of his homeland. As to a traveler returning by ship or plane the familiar country appears first a faint line upon the horizon, so to Satan at this particular moment Heaven is "undetermind square or round." But he knows and we should know that it is square. It is not Heaven's shape but the relative size of Heaven and the World which is the burden of the final lines of the quotation, the key words being, of course, "in bigness as."

The evidence that Heaven is square is really quite strong. Sin, Satan's daughter, speaks of God's dividing with Satan "His Quadrature, from thy Orbicular World" (X, 381). Chaos, the old Anarch, tells Satan that the World is "link'd in a golden Chain / To that side Heaven from whence your Legions fell" (II, 1005–6). Obviously, "that side" implies other sides. Judging from his diagram, Professor Curry considers Heaven circular, but he explains the anomaly by saying that "the expulsion point is situated in an arc of a circle so

---

[1] Quotations of *Paradise Lost* are taken from *The Poetical Works of John Milton*, ed. Helen Darbishire (London, 1958).

vast in circumference that one might question whether the segment is straight or curved" (p. 148). The problem, however, remains; and one is reminded of Alice's dilemma when assured that one side of the caterpillar's mushroom would make her taller and the other shorter; as it was perfectly round, she found it impossible to make out which were the two sides of it.

The argument which militates most tellingly against the assumption that Milton favors a circular Heaven is this: Christian tradition consistently makes Heaven square. "And the city lieth foursquare, and the length is as large as the breadth . . . " (Rev. 21:16). Biblical authority for such a detail, not an article of faith but merely part of the extended metaphor which *Paradise Lost* is, certainly would satisfy Milton. The whole question would be of no importance whatsoever if it were not that a circular Heaven confuses the issue of direction in Heaven; and Milton's use of direction, as I shall show, is symbolic.

All direction in *Paradise Lost*—outside the World—is related to God's position in Heaven. From the center of Heaven's plain rises the mount upon which, bathed in light, "High Thron'd above all highth," God is seated. Milton compares the place of the earth in the geocentric World to that of God in Heaven:

> As God in Heav'n
> Is center, yet extends to all, so thou
> Centring receav'st from all those Orbs.   (IX, 107–109)

At God's right is the place of the Son, and far to the north rises the Mountain of the Congregation and Lucifier's "Royal seat" (V, 755–66).

Among the writers of the Old Testament there was a relationship between the parts of the body and the cardinal points of the compass. Cruden's *Concordance* offers the following under the word "hand":

> The *right hand* commonly denotes the south, as the left hand denotes the north. For the *Hebrews* speak of the quarters of the world in respect of themselves, having their faces turned towards the east, their backs to the west, their *right hands* to the south, and their left to the north. Thus *Kedem*, which signifies *before*, stands also for the east; and *Achor*, which signifies *behind*, marks out the west; *Jamin*, the *right hand*, is the south; and *Shemol*, the left hand, is the north.

Smith's *Dictionary of the Bible* (New York, Chicago, Toronto, n.d.) expresses the doctrine succinctly under the word "East":

> . . . *kedem* properly means that which is *before* or *in front of* a person, and was applied to the east from the custom of turning in that direction when

describing the points of the compass, *before*, *behind*, the *right*, and the *left*, representing respectively E., W., S., and N.

A further ramification of this principle of direction immediately comes to mind. Among the Hebrews, as among the Greeks and Romans, right stands for good and left for evil. Our word "sinister" is, of course, the Latin for "left hand." Examples from both Old and New Testaments are legion, the most familiar being, perhaps, the description of the Last Judgment in Matthew.[2]

East and south, before God and at his right hand, are favorable directions; west and north, behind him and at his left, are unfavorable. Satan's rule over the north places his seat at God's left, which is as it should be, for the Son sits at his right. Therefore, God faces the east, traditionally the holiest of directions; and directly in front of him, in the center of the east wall, I contend, lies the great gate of Heaven. From the

> blazing Portals, led
> To Gods Eternal house direct the way,
> A broad and ample rode.   (VII, 575-77)

Professor Curry's location of the gate in Heaven's west wall is at odds with this directional symbolism. If the gate were in the west and God faced it, then Satan's seat would be at his right, as would the bridge from Hell to the World. If the gate were in the west and God faced east, then Satan's seat and the bridge would be appropriately at his left but Heaven's gate and the pendant World would lie at his back, and the golden road would come from the gate to the rear of his throne. Curry's reason for the placement of the gate in the west I shall discuss later. It influences his total conception of the cosmos, just as the positioning of the gate in the east influences mine.

In order to see why the gate must be in the east, let us first review the events leading up to Satan's expulsion from Heaven. Upon a great day such as Heaven's year brings forth, the angels assemble before God to hear the decree which elevates the Son to be their head. Proud Lucifer, "fraught / With envy against the Son of God," gathers his legions and in the night withdraws to his citadel in the limits of the north. There completing the seduction of his followers, he moves them as an army southward to encounter the good angels led by Michael. The hosts meet "in the mid way" (VI, 91), —not, as

---

[2] For the east as a favorable direction see Ezek. 43:2; Mat. 2:2; Isa. 27:8. For north as malign see Jer. 1:14, 6:22. For west as evil see Ps. 75:6; Isa. 59:19; Hos. 11:10.

Curry says (p. 4), "centering around Satan's stronghold"—where the first day's battle is fought, the evil angels retreating northward (VI, 413–15, 530, 533, 551). Upon the second day neither army changes position. The third day sees the Son ride northward in the chariot of paternal deity. With his right hand armed in thunder he drives the dark legions to the wall of Heaven. They, facing southward, give way to the inauspicious left and are therefore driven to the east wall, which

> op'ning wide,
> Rowld inward, and a spacious Gap disclos'd
> Into the wastful Deep.   (VI, 860–62)

As Satan learns from Chaos, the newly created World hangs from that same side of Heaven (II, 1005–1006); and since directly above the World opens the jeweled gate of Heaven (III, 501–507), it must lie in the east wall.

The breach in the wall is thus located approximately half-way between the northeast corner of Heaven and the centrally placed eastern gate. Satan and his followers are expelled through the wall rather than through the gate for good Biblical reason: according to many passages in Scripture, the gates of Heaven, and indeed the road also, are for the use of the righteous only.

> And the gates of it [the heavenly Jerusalem] shall not be shut at all by day: for there shall be no night there.
> And they shall bring the glory and honour of the nations into it.
> And there shall in no wise enter into it any thing that defileth, neither whatsoever worketh abomination, or maketh a lie: but they which are written in the Lamb's book of life. (Rev. 21:25–27)
> And an highway shall be there, and a way, and it shall be called the way of holiness, the unclean shall not pass over it. (Isa. 35:8. See also: Ps. 118:19–20; Isa. 26:1–2; Matt. 7:13–14; Luke 13:24–28)

Forced through the wall of Heaven, the apostate angels fall for nine days through Chaos until "Hell at last / Yawning receavd them whole" (VI, 874–75). It has not, I think, been noticed hitherto that the fallen angels enter Hell not through its gate but through a temporary opening in its fiery vault, expressly created for this purpose as the breach in Heaven's wall was expressly created for their expulsion. The parallel has no Biblical sanction, as far as I can ascertain; but it can be shown that the demons do not enter through Hell's gate. From Pandaemonium on the shore of the burning lake (I, 700), Satan "toward the Gates of Hell / *Explores* his solitary flight" (II, 630–31; my italics):

> . . . som times
> He scours the right hand coast, som times the left,
> Now shaves with level wing the Deep, then soares
> Up to the fiery Concave touring high.
> . . . at last apeer
> *Hell bounds high reaching to the horrid Roof.*
>
> (II, 632–44; my italics)[3]

From Pandaemonium Satan has traveled a considerable distance—
how far is perhaps made clearer upon his return to Hell's capitol after
man's fall:

> . . . through the Gate,
> Wide op'n and unguarded, *Satan* passd,
> And all about found desolate; for those
> Appointed to sit there, had left thir charge,
> Flown to the upper World; the rest were all
> Farr to th' in-land retir'd, about the walls
> Of *Pandaemonium*
> There kept thir Watch the Legions. . . .
> . . . these the late
> Heav'n-banisht Host, left desart utmost Hell
> Many a dark League, reduc't in careful Watch
> Round thir Metropolis. . . .   (X, 418–39)

It is evident from these passages that Satan does not find the gate
of Hell in the roof over the fiery sea, but rather "many a dark league"
away in a part of the underworld which has never been explored.
Hell's gate, when the adversary comes to it at last, is not in the roof
at all. Its "huge Porcullis" is worked vertically by Sin, the unholy
portress, who alone is able to draw it up (II, 874).

The three gateways in *Paradise Lost*, to Heaven, to Hell and to
the Garden of Eden, are designed with reference to the fate of man.
Heaven's gate, as we have seen, is not used by evil beings; and when
the Son and the angels pass through it, they are on missions of importance to mankind. The Son passes through the gate when he
creates the World for man, returning through it in triumph; he uses it
again when he descends to judge Adam and Eve after the fall; and he
will lead the Saints through it after the Judgment. Raphael and Gabriel come through it to warn and to educate our first parents. The
angelic guard of Eden returns through it upon the failure of their
mission. The eastern gate of the Garden remains open until Adam

---

[3] It is surely unnecessary to argue the point that if "Hell bounds" are discovered
"high reaching to the horrid Roof" they are not in the roof but in the wall of Hell—
see the lines which immediately follow this quotation.

and Eve are banished through it; Satan, Sin, and Death do not enter by this gate; and the heavenly messengers, though they alight near it, seem not to pass through it unless they accompany man.

All this is pertinent, I think, to the opening of Hell's gate by Sin for Satan upon the occasion of his exploratory journey. Not until Satan has explained his mission does she allow him egress. He goes, he says, to seek out a new world and its inhabitants, who will enable Sin and Death to be "fed and filld" (II, 843). The key with which Sin opens the gates is characterized as "Sad instrument of all our woe" (II, 872). Satan, Sin, Death, and the demons may now pass through in order to overcome frail man. In soliloquy in Eden Satan promises Adam and Eve

> Hell shall unfould,
> To entertain you two, her widest Gates,
> And send forth all her Kings; there will be room,
> Not like these narrow limits, to receive
> Your numerous ofspring.   (IV, 381–85)

I have argued that the infernal gate is in the wall rather than in the roof of Hell. Curry, who believes it to be in the roof, suggests that the broad road later built by Sin and Death passes through the gate and on down to the floor of Hell. He incorporates this detail into his diagram, citing *Paradise Lost*, X, 280–99, the relevant part of which is:

> broad as the Gate,
> Deep to the Roots of Hell the gatherd beach
> They fast'nd.

The word "beach" is significant; for since a beach by definition is land adjacent to a sea, this beach must separate Hell from Chaos and can hardly be supposed to extend from Hell's roof to its floor. When the gate of Hell is located in the wall, Curry's extension of the bridge within the underworld becomes an unnecessary adjunct to Milton's cosmography. The quoted lines surely mean only that the bridge is anchored as firmly to Hell as it is at its other end to the outside of the World.

From the mouth of Hell Satan struggles through Chaos upward to a position somewhere near the repaired gap in Heaven's wall. Here he flies southward paralleling the east wall of Heaven (not the west, as Curry says) until he alights upon the bare outside of the World, which hangs from its golden chain directly underneath Heaven's gate. The bridge later built by Sin and Death follows Satan's route. From Heaven the golden ladder descends to the World; near its foot lies an aperture leading down to earth.

Milton's description of this junction of three ways is the basis of Professor Curry's entire directional system. Curry writes (p. 155):

Satan, as he stands facing the battlements of Heaven, is able to observe all three of them at their junction, for

> now in little space
> The confines met of empyrean heaven
> And of this world, and on the left hand hell
> With long reach interposed; three several ways
> In sight, to each of these three places led
>   (X, 320-324).

The triumphant Prince of Darkness enthusiastically approves of the road which stretches, on his "left hand, with long reach interposed," down to Hell.

Unfortunately for his argument, Curry has here confused the chronological sequence of events in the poem. Milton's depiction of the tripartite junction ends with line 324 of Book X; Satan does not reach the spot and meet his kinsmen Sin and Death until line 349. It is not therefore, in reference to Satan's left hand that the bridge is located. Nor upon his meeting with Sin and Death is he described as "facing the battlements of Heaven" or anything else. When he stood upon the lowest rung of the golden stair some seven books earlier, he had his back toward Heaven:

> *Satan* from hence now on the lower stair
> That scal'd by steps of Gold to Heaven Gate
> Looks down with wonder at the sudden view
> Of all this World at once.   (III, 540-43)

At this moment, if Heaven's gate is set in the east wall as I suggest, Hell lies to the north and upon Satan's left, as indeed it should to be consonant with the directional principle followed in the Bible and by the ancients.

In any case Hell should not be situated in relationship to Satan. Plainly he cannot, as he travels through the cosmos, keep it always at his left hand; for then he would orbit forever in a counterclockwise path around the underworld. Besides, as we know, Hell is with him wherever he goes—"Myself am Hell." All the directions in *Paradise Lost* outside the World are derived from the august, central, steadfast, and eternal God, who remains upon his eastward-facing throne even when he accompanies the Son at the creation.

> The Filial Power arriv'd, and sate him down
> With his great Father, for he also went
> Invisible, yet staid (such priviledge
> Hath Omnipresence) and the work ordaind,
> Author and end of all things.   (VII, 587-91)

In religious literature and art Hell is always to God's left. Writers in the rabbinical tradition, Matthew, the early Fathers of the Christian Church, the famous painters (including Michelangelo, whose "Last Judgment" in the Sistine Chapel depicts Hell to the viewer's right but to the Judge's left), Dante, Thomas of Celano (probable author of the famous *Dies Irae*) consistently place it so. In medieval religious plays Hell's mouth was always stage left. I shall not further belabor the obvious.

Of Satan's wanderings and discoveries upon the stationary exterior of the World, I have written elsewhere.[4] I shall pass them by here and discuss instead the aperture leading to the interior of the World, a peculiarity of which has not, I believe, been remarked. In syntactically involved lines Milton describes this opening just after his mention of the golden stair,

> Direct against which op'nd from beneath,
> Just ore the blissful seat of Paradise,
> A passage down to th' Earth, a passage wide,
> Wider by farr then that of after-times
> Over Mount *Sion*, and, though that were large,
> Over the *Promisd Land* to God so dear,
> By which, to visit oft those happy Tribes,
> On high behests his Angels to and fro
> Passd frequent, and his eye with choice regard
> From *Paneas* the fount of *Jordans* flood
> To *Bëersaba*, where the *Holy Land*
> Borders on *Ægypt* and th' *Arabian* shoare;
> So wide the op'ning seemd, where bounds were set
> To darkness, such as bound the Ocean wave.
>
> (III, 526–39)

The purport of these lines is this: when Satan discovered the entry to the World, it was very large indeed; later, though still large, it was reduced to the size of the Promised Land, stretching from Dan in the north to "Bëersaba" bordering upon Egypt and Arabia in the south; and still later it was limited to the size of Mount Zion.

Though Satan first brings the aperture to our attention and though he is the first whom we see making use of it, primarily it is designed to benefit man. The creating Son and the angelic messengers "on high behests" pass through it; and man was optimistically expected to ascend through it to replace Heaven's lost angels. It was in the beginning "a passage down to th' Earth" inviting the world-

---

[4] "The Crystalline Sphere and the 'Waters Above' in *Paradise Lost, PMLA*, LXIX (1954), 903–14; "That Unnecessary Shell of Milton's World," *Studies in Honor of T. W. Baldwin*, ed. Don Cameron Allen (Urbana, 1958), pp. 211–19.

wide salvation of man. Later, when men remembered not their maker,
it shrank to a size which could accommodate the chosen people.
When these failed to follow righteousness, the passage further contracted to the size of Mount Zion, upon which stood the temple of
God. The bounds which were set to darkness are those which on
earth separate true believers from pagans; far above the earth they
also differentiate the light and order of the physical World from the
abandoned darkness of surrounding Chaos. The concept of the gradual
narrowing of the aperture should be taken, I think, as a preview or
forecast, symbolically expressed, of Gabriel's discourse to Adam concerning the future of man (XII, 508–41).

Returning now to Satan, who stands wonder-struck at the sudden
view "Of all this World at once," let us follow him down through the
"first Region" of the Universe, past worlds and worlds to the sun,
and from thence down to the earth, where he lands upon Mount
Niphates to the north of Eden (III, 742; IV, 569). Southward lies
the fortunate Garden, an earthly Paradise. "One Gate there onely
was, and that lookd East" (IV, 178) like the gate of Heaven above;
and like the greater gate, this one too is designed to allow only the
passage of the upright:

> in at this Gate none pass
> The vigilance here plac't, but such as come
> Well known from Heav'n.   (IV, 579–81)

Therefore Satan enters over the western wall—"On th' other side'
(IV, 179).

> Due entrance he disdaind, and in contempt,
> At one slight bound high overleap'd all bound
> Of Hill or highest Wall, and sheer within
> Lights on his feet.   (IV, 180–83)

From the evil west has come evil to mankind.

Uriel, who descends to warn Eden's angelic guard of Satan's arrival, comes from the westering sun, but he alights near the eastern
gate:

> the setting Sun
> Slowly descended, and with right aspect
> Against the eastern Gate of Paradise
> Leveld his eevning Rayes . . . .
> Betwixt these rockie Pillars *Gabriel* sat
> Chief of th' Angelic Guards . . . .
> Thither came Uriel, gliding through the Eeven
> On a Sun beam.   (IV, 540–56)

His news is grave; it justifies his western approach.

Acting upon Uriel's tidings, Gabriel divides his guard into three parts. While one circles the garden northward and another southward, a third inspects our first parents' bower, where Satan is discovered squat like a toad at Eve's ear. It is to the west wall, where the circling angels have again met, that Satan is escorted under guard (IV, 861–4). Judged and found wanting, Satan flees westward—"and with him fled the shades of night" (IV, 1015).

At another time, Raphael, descending to arm Adam and Eve against surprise by the fiend, alights "on the Eastern Cliff of Paradise" (V, 275). Adam sees him approaching and reports to Eve:

> behold
> Eastward among those Trees, what glorious shape
> Comes this way moving.   (V, 308–10)

When Satan re-enters the Garden to effect the actual temptation, he comes with perfect consistency from the north. He arrives, it will be recalled, "involv'd in rising Mist" (IX, 75) with the river which feeds the fountains of Eden from beneath, a river, we have been earlier told, which flows from the north.

> Southward through Eden went a River large,
> Nor chang'd his course, but through the shaggie hill
> Passd underneath ingulft.   (IV, 223–25)

The tempter brings death to man from beneath, the direction of Hell, and from the north, traditionally the most ominous of directions.

When Gabriel is sent down to educate Adam and bar him from Paradise, his mission is for man a sad one. He comes therefore from the west. Adam asks:

> why in the East
> Darkness ere Dayes mid-course, and Morning light
> More orient in yon Western Cloud that draws
> Ore the blew Firmament a radiant white,
> And slow descends, with something heav'nly fraught.
>   (XI, 203–207)

The advent of the dread angels and the expulsion of Adam and Eve are forecast when from the west an eagle drives "Two Birds of gayest plume" and when a lion pursues a hart and hind through the gate into the wilderness (XI, 185–90). Finally man and his wife are evicted from the Garden.

> They looking back, all th' Eastern side beheld
> Of Paradise, so late thir happie seat,
> Wav'd over by that flaming Brand, the Gate
> With dreadful Faces throngd and fierie Armes.
>
> (XII, 641–44)

They are at least allowed, as Satan is not, to pass out through the gate—perhaps because they may be redeemed, whereas Satan and his followers are irrevocably damned.

Eden is a metaphor of Heaven. Before his account of events leading to the creation, Raphael has suggested.

> what if Earth
> Be but the shaddow of Heav'n, and things therein
> Each to other like, more then on Earth is thought?
>
> (V, 574–76)

Insofar as the symbolism of directions is concerned in *Paradise Lost*, Heaven and earth are indeed "Each to other like."

The path that this study has followed will perhaps have seemed to the reader rather like a series of precarious stepping stones flung across a powerfully flowing stream. The facts adduced, however, if their validity be granted, surely are the result of conscious artistry on Milton's part; awareness of them, accordingly, may well increase our understanding of the epic as a whole.

The cosmographical details dealt with here have been linked together by the travels of Satan. In at least one sense Satan is the hero of *Paradise Lost:* he is the voyager. It is his adventures we follow, as we do those of Odysseus or Aeneas or Dante. With Satan we explore the four divisions of the Miltonic cosmos. But he, unlike those other heroes, attempts to disrupt a physical and metaphysical system not his own—he is the adversary and the outcast.

The most famous line in the poem, "And justifie the wayes of God to men," introduces its foci. Everyone recognizes that God is the metaphysical center of *Paradise Lost;* but it is also true that God serves as the physical center, that from him all directions outside the World originate. Satan, Sin, Death, the infernal bridge, the gates of Hell, and Hell itself are to his left in the north, the direction of greatest evil. On his right to the south the Son sits in glory. In front of God, in the most favored of directions, lie the starry road, Heaven's eastern gate, the golden stair, the shrinking aperture allowing entrance to the World, and, of course, the World itself. Inside the World, though geographical direction is no longer specifically related to God, the connotative or symbolic meanings of east and south, west and north are maintained.

If God is a focus of the poem, so also is man; for the action is centered upon him. For him the World was created; upon him the stars and planets shed their benefits. To Satan's disgust, angelic beings serve him on earth. Yet the sphere of man's influence—perhaps it would be more exact to say the sphere which influences him—is vastly larger than the World. As I have tried to show, the entire cosmos, even Heaven itself, was created for him; he is its heir. The size of the aperture at the top of the World is governed by his fate; the golden road to God and the dark bridge to the underworld are his; the gates of Heaven and Hell await him and will finally be shut behind him. The physical details that I have indicated—and many others—support the contention that the drama of *Paradise Lost* is not God's nor the Son's nor Satan's but man's.

SOURCES OF MILTON'S CATHARSIS:
A RECONSIDERATION

Paul R. Sellin, Roosevelt University

Milton's version of Aristotle's tragic catharsis in the preface to *Samson Agonistes*[1] has commonly been attributed to the critical theories of Antonio Minturno,[2] primarily because Milton uses an analogy between catharsis and homeopathy like the Italian's. Allan H. Gilbert, in *Literary Criticism: Plato to Dryden* ([New York, 1940], p. 517, nn. 15, 17), has shown that Giambattista Guarini[3] also foreshadows Milton's theory, since Guarini not only utilizes homeopathic similes but anticipates Milton in another respect as well. While the parallels between these theories of catharsis have been acknowledged by many commentators, it seems to me that the dissimilarities have been neglected and obscured, sometimes with distortion and misinterpretation of Milton's remarks. I wish, therefore, to re-examine the bases for these attributions and to suggest another possible source—Daniel Heinsius' *De tragoediae constitutione*.[4] And I hope, in the course of this essay, that some of Milton's statements on catharsis will take on a clearer and more precise meaning.

The association of Milton's catharsis with Minturno's has had an interesting history. The original title page of *Samson Agonistes* (1671 edition) carried a portion of the *Poetics*, ch. vi, in Greek,[5] fol-

[1] *The Works of John Milton*, ed. Frank Allen Patterson (New York, 1931–38)— hereafter cited as "Columbia Milton." The preface to *Samson Agonistes* is in Vol. 1, Pt. 2, pp. 330–33.

[2] *Antonii Sebastiani Minturni de poeta, ad Hectorem Pignatellum, Vibonensium ducem, libri sex* (Venice, 1559)—hereafter cited as *"De poeta"*; *L'arte poetica del Sig. Antonio Minturno* . . . (per Gio. Andrea Valvassori, 1563)—hereafter cited as *"L'arte poetica."*

[3] Giambattista Guarini, *Il Pastor Fido e il compendio della poesia tragicomica*, ed. Gioachino Brognoligo (Bari, 1914), cited hereafter as *"Il comp."*

[4] *Dan. Heinsii de tragoediae constitutione liber. In quo inter caetera tota de hac Aristotelis sententia dilucide explicatur. Editio auctior multo. Cui & Aristotelis de poetica libellus, cum eiusdem notis & interpretatione, accedit* (Leyden: ex Officina Elseviriana, 1643). This work initially appeared in 1611 (Leyden: apud Ioannem Balduinum [prostat in biliopolio Ludouici Elzevirij]) as *Aristotelis de poetica liber. Daniel Heinsius recensuit, ordini suo restituit, latine vertit, notas addidit. Accedit eiusdem de tragica constitutione liber. In quo praeter caetera, tota de hac Aristotelis sententia dilucide explicatur.* My references will be to the 1643 edition.

[5] τραγωδία [*sic*] μίμησις πράξεως σπουδαίας, &*c*. Since this phrase is (with the exception of the iota-subscript omitted from τραγῳδία) identical with the standard reading of

lowed by this Latin translation: *Tragœdia est imitatio actionis seriæ, &c. Per misericordiam & metum perficiens talium affectuum lustrationem;* then, in the first two sentences of his preface, Milton gave his English version of catharsis:

Tragedy, as it was antiently compos'd, hath been ever held the gravest, moralest, and most profitable of all other Poems: therefore said by *Aristotle* to be of power by raising pity and fear, or terror, to purge the mind of those and such like passions, that is to temper and reduce them to just measure with a kind of delight, stirr'd up by reading or seeing those passions well imitated. Nor is Nature wanting in her own effects to make good his assertion: for so in Physic things of melancholic hue and quality are us'd against melancholy, sowr against sowr, salt to remove salt humours.

It seems that Jacob Bernays (in his "Grundzüge der verlorenen Abhandlung des Aristoteles über Wirkung der Tragödie," *Zwei Abhandlungen über die Aristotelische Theorie des Drama* [Berlin, 1880], pp. 94–95) began the process by drawing attention to Milton's analogy between catharsis and the effects of nature. Bernays, arguing for an interpretation of catharsis more as an aesthetic term (pleasure accompanies the relief—which resembles a homeopathic treatment— of pity and fear)[6] than as a moral or religious one, praised Milton's independence in foreshadowing his (Bernays') own theory; contrasting Milton with Heinsius (who translated catharsis as *expiatio*), he asserted that the analogy between physic and tragedy shows how close Milton was to the right—i.e., Bernays'—interpretation. The *lustratio* on the title page (a translation closely allied to *expiatio*) runs counter to Bernays' statement about Milton, of course, and he conveniently disposed of it as being the fault of a third party to whom the blind poet had entrusted the preparation of the title page.[7] Bernays' arguments, it seems to me, leave several questionable impressions in the mind of the reader about Milton's version of catharsis. They are (1) that Heinsius and Milton differ very sharply; (2) that Milton was an extremely independent interpreter of the *Poetics;* and (3) that, in anticipating a modern theory of catharsis, Milton

---

ch. vi, whether Renaissance or modern, it gives no clue as to the particular source from which it was obtained.

    [6] See particularly, pp. 16 and 78.

    [7] Although he gives no basis for the remark, Bernays is most likely following Bentley's assertions in his preface to *Paradise Lost*. Samuel Johnson's evaluation of the assumption in his life of Milton ("A supposition rash and groundless, if he [Bentley] thought it true; and vile and pernicious, if, as is said, he in private allowed it to be false") can scarcely be improved upon (*Lives of the Poets*, ed. George Birkbeck Hill [Oxford, 1905], I, 181).

likewise does not conceive of catharsis as being primarily a moral effect.

It was Joel E. Spingarn's *A History of Literary Criticism in the Renaissance* (New York, 1898), pp. 79–81, which first speculated that Milton followed Minturno in explaining Aristotle's catharsis. The basis for his conclusion was the similarity of terms in their homeopathic analogies, for, in his *L'arte poetica*, Minturno had compared poets and physicians, remarking: "Nor will the physician have more efficacy in extinguishing, with venomous physic, the fiery poison of sickness which troubles the body; than the tragic poet in purging the mind of violent passions by the force of passions in charmingly expressed verses."[8] Spingarn's contribution did refute Bernays' assertion about Milton's independence by claiming that Milton was following the Italian commentators; the implication, however, that Milton was close to a modern catharsis was not questioned but strengthened by attributing the same accomplishment to Minturno (p. 81): "Like Milton, Minturno conceived of tragedy as having an ethical aim; but both Milton and Minturno clearly perceived that by *katharsis* Aristotle had reference not to a moral, but to an emotional, effect." And Spingarn added, of course, a new suggestion— Milton's theory of catharsis is just like Minturno's.

Ingram Bywater, who commented on Milton's catharsis soon after Spingarn, did not agree with Spingarn about Minturno as Milton's forerunner, but his reasons for diagreeing still coincided with the earlier assumptions about Milton's catharsis. In his article, "Milton and the Aristotelian Definition of Tragedy" (*Journal of Philology*, XXVII [1901], 265–75), Bywater subscribed to the implication that Milton viewed catharsis in a rather modern way and credited him with being a precursor of Bernays in giving a pathological interpretation of catharsis (pp. 267–68):

The great interest [Milton's analogical illustration of catharsis] has for us is in the evidence it supplies that in Milton's view the Aristotelian κάθαρσις παθημάτων was to be conceived as analogous to a bodily process, that the term was borrowed from medicine rather than religion, and that it meant "purgatio" in its medical sense, and not, as Heinsius and Goulston had supposed, in its ceremonial sense of "lustratio" or "expiatio"—in other words that a great poet found no difficulty in accepting the initial assumption of the pathological interpretation of κάθαρσισ, and did not regard it as unworthy of Aristotle or beneath the dignity of Tragedy.

[8] P. 77: "Nè più forza haurà il Physico di spengere il fervido veleno della infermità, che'l corpo afflige, con la velenosa medicina; che'l Tragico di purgar l'animo delle impetuose perturbationi con lo empito degli affetti in versi leggiadramente espressi."

In Bywater's view, Milton's interpretation did not come from any of the "ordinary" versions of or commentaries on the *Poetics* because (assuming that Milton gave the term a new meaning)

it is pretty clear that the early translators must have taken κάθαρσις to mean "purification"; that their usual rendering "purgatio" was intended to have that sense; and that "expiatio" [Bywater notes that Minturno used *expiet* in *De poeta* (p. 63)] and "lustratio" were nothing but verbal improvements, which did not involve anything of the nature of a new view of the meaning of the term. The same impression is left on one by the notes of the various commentators of this period; in spite of their differences and jealousies they all manage to come round to one and the same conclusion, that the passions, or certain of them, are in some way or other "purified" by Tragedy; they have apparently no notion of any other interpretation, or of any other possible justification of the existence of Tragedy.

Such notions are rather to be found among the interpreters of Aristotle's *Politics*, Book VIII (e.g., Antonio Scaino da Salo or Tarquino Galluzzi), who thus are more likely forerunners of Milton than Minturno; and Bywater concluded, rather weakly, that, since "the truth is that some such theory seems to have been long in the air in Italy," "the Bernaysian theory had been to a certain extent anticipated by more than one Italian scholar, and . . . Milton does not stand so completely alone among the precursors of Bernays as is usually supposed. His words in the preface to *Samson Agonistes* are no proof of his having broken ground for himself, or excogitated a new interpretation of the Aristotelian text."

It is evident that while Spingarn and Bywater agreed in their view of Milton's interpretation, they differed on the question of the Minturno-Milton relationship. Although his argument scarcely touches on the point, Bywater leaves the reader to conclude that Minturno remains in the main stream of Renaissance poetics while Milton does not, and the evidence for this conclusion is that Minturno used *expiet*—implying that he holds a theory which Milton rejected. It hardly needs to be pointed out that this implication, as developed in Bywater's article, depends upon word choice, not upon actual comparison of their theories of catharsis. This approach did not occasion the rejection of Minturno as the source for Milton's catharsis, naturally, and the expression of this relationship reached full development when J. H. Hanford bluntly stated that Milton's interpretation of catharsis "is identical with that of the Italian, Minturno" (*A Milton Handbook*, 4th ed. [New York, 1954], p. 280, n. 12).

Although there has been but little scepticism about Minturno's catharsis being very close to Milton's, the idea that Milton's interpretation—unlike his contemporaries'—approaches a modern view has encountered some divergence of opinion. Indeed, the translation of catharsis as *lustratio* on the title page of *Samson* seems to be excellent evidence that Milton considered catharsis as a statement of the ethical benefit resulting from tragedy—not an emotional effect such as pleasure, for example, afforded by the relief of pity and fear. Although Marvin T. Herrick (*The Poetics of Aristotle in England* [New Haven, 1930], pp. 49–50) notes that Milton shows "familiarity" with a pathological theory of catharsis, he nevertheless takes *lustratio* as a clear indication that Milton "fell in with" the prevailing concepts of "moral purification." As we have seen, Bernays removed this difficulty by attributing the title page to an unspecified third party; surprisingly, however, neither Spingarn (who apparently overlooked it) nor Bywater (who either overlooked it or, since he must have been familiar with Bernays' *Abhandlungen*, deliberately ignored it) mentioned it, much less accounted satisfactorily for it, and this omission gravely weakens their position.

Besides this difficulty, however, it seems to me that such a modernistic view of Milton's catharsis has to be focused so exclusively upon the homeopathic analogy that the rest of Milton's remarks on catharsis in his preface cannot be taken into account adequately. Indeed, it would seem that the analogy, rather than the preceding text, is sometimes taken as though it were Milton's explanation of what tragic catharsis is. This is a questionable procedure, for the analogy really is no more than an analogy. Milton himself tells us clearly that it is intended to support Aristotle's "assertion"; he does not say that the analogy is to explain what catharsis is or does. Milton's version of the "assertion," then, is the real explanation of catharsis, and it appears not in his analogy but in the second portion of the opening sentence of the preface. In itself, the statement represents a rather careful specification of what Milton thought τὴν τῶν τοιούτων παθημάτων κάθαρσιν means. The analogy, however, serves an entirely different purpose: it only bolsters the likelihood that the assertion is true; it is not used to explain the explanation.

Milton's formulation of Aristotle's assertion cannot be fully understood, however, unless several considerations which it entails are taken into account. In the first place, Milton treats it as a conditional statement. He says that Aristotle conceived of tragedy as effecting catharsis *because* tragedy (as constructed by the ancients) had always been considered the most serious, moral, and useful of poetic forms. Since he considers ancient opinion and practice to have been the condition of Aristotle's assertion, does not Milton imply, conversely, that if tragedy had *not* been so considered, Aristotle would not have made the statement? Milton must have believed, therefore, that Aristotle conceived of tragic catharsis as an essentially moral and useful effect.

Secondly, what did Milton think Aristotle's assertion actually meant? What is the nature of the cathartic process itself? Milton's idea is, in its most elemental form, that tragedy has the power to adjust certain passions in the mind to a desirable mean. Aristotle, as Milton thinks, intended catharsis to be understood as the reduction and tempering, by means of the passions pity and fear, of these and like passions to some norm. Since, presumably, the phrase "the mind" means the mind of the spectator, catharsis will thus produce beneficial effects on members of the audience. Such a process certainly seems oriented more toward the production of an ethical good than of an aesthetic good not simply because of Milton's phrasing but also because it serves an important purpose in his argument only if considered ethically. Any well-wrought tragedy, Milton probably recognizes, produces delight in an audience. The difficulty is that skillful imitations please indiscriminately—a tragedy which may attract an audience to vice, for example, can be just as effective as one which induces virtue. With reference to their ethical effects on an audience, however, they can be classed as desirable or undesirable, and the important problem for the poet to solve is how to create a tragedy that will be ethically beneficial. Since ancient tragedy, Milton thinks, was designed to effect an ethical end, the poet can do no better than follow classical rules and imitate classical models. In this passage of his preface, therefore, Milton is not insisting that ancient dramatic poetry is emotionally more effective than contemporary practice; ethically, however, it was designed to effect a desirable end, and it is this end which enables Milton to establish grounds for modeling *Samson Agonistes* on Greek tragedy and the rules of Aristotle as he conceived them.

Closely related to this consideration, thirdly, is the matter of delight which forms the concluding element of Milton's explanation of catharsis. His remarks certainly do not seem to indicate any foreshadowing of more recent interpretations of Aristotle's catharsis, for the concept that pleasure arises from the process of relieving the passions seems hardly reconcilable with Milton's text. The kind of delight which concerns Aristotle, he states specifically, has its origin in the viewing of an imitation of passions, and from this stipulation of the source of pleasure, therefore, it appears that Milton is referring not to a kind of delight which results from purgation of the passions but to the natural delight which, Aristotle said, accompanies every skillful imitation of an object, even if the object itself is unpleasant.[9] For Milton, pleasure cannot itself be the end of tragedy; it merely accompanies or perhaps enhances the means—namely, the reading of or beholding skillfully contrived imitations of men's actions—of accomplishing a useful and moral purgation.

It is at this point in the discussion, finally, that Milton inserts his analogy, and he does so in order to deal with a question that naturally follows from his previous remarks. For Milton, especially, it is not enough simply to know what Aristotle asserted; the key consideration is the validity of his statement. Is Aristotle *correct* in saying that tragedy can effect the reduction of the passions to a mean by the principle of like purging like? Yes, says Milton in employing his homeopathic analogy, because the same principle can be observed operating in nature. The analogy between things corporeal and things mental cannot be taken as a key to the operation of the mental process; it only serves to confirm Aristotle's supposed principle of like driving out like by noting a similar phenomenon in the practice of medicine.

I largely agree, therefore, with A. P. McMahon's statements ("Seven Questions on Aristotelian Definitions of Tragedy and Comedy," *Harvard Studies in Classical Philology*, XL [1929], 192–93) concerning Milton's relationship to Renaissance thought:

Milton did not deviate from the orthodox doctrine in his views which are due partly to classical sources but also to the Italian theorists. . . . Spingarn correctly notes that Milton's discussion points to a reading of Minturno, but he reads into Aristotle, Minturno, and Milton something that did not occur to many minds until several centuries later, when he adds: "both Milton and Minturno clearly perceived that by katharsis Aristotle had reference not to a moral, but to an emotional effect." Milton did perceive, in common with previous criticism, that the phrase in Aristotle is best adapted to purposes of defense against the enemies of the drama. He paraphrases the idea, saying of the emotions that katharsis is "to temper and reduce them to just measure."

Very much the same should be said about Bywater's modern view of Milton's idea of catharsis. Milton's catharsis cannot be separated

---

[9] S. H. Butcher, *Aristotle's Theory of Poetry and Fine Art with a Critical Text and Translation of the Poetics*, 4th ed. (Dover Publications, Inc., 1951), p. 15.

from Minturno's in Bywater's manner, for once his assumption about Milton is questioned, the distinction between their theories disappears. To establish the similarity of their theories, it is necessary to examine and compare the arguments of both critics on the subject. A superficial glance at Minturno's *L'arte poetica* or his *De poeta* quickly shows that Minturno and Milton do not differ in considering tragic catharsis morally beneficial. *De poeta* (p. 61) declares, for example, that the chief office of tragic poetry is "to raise pity and to terrify to this end: that it may purge and expiate the mind from the wicked concourse of the passions."[10] In *L'arte poetica* the definition of tragedy (pp. 74–75) presents an ethically useful catharsis;[11] and, a little further on (p. 76), we find that the purgation of the passions not only partly differentiates tragedy from comedy and satire but is no less than the end "to which everything directs itself."[12] But despite these similarities, is Minturno's catharsis essentially the same as Milton's?

Decidedly not. In the first place, Minturno differs considerably from Milton in translating the key phrase τοιούτων παθημάτων. Milton, as we have seen, translated τοιούτων as *talium* in Latin and carefully expressed it as "those [pity and fear] and such like" in English. Minturno translates the phrase as *simili passioni*, but, from the definition alone, one cannot be positive that he means, as *simili* implies, emotions kindred to but not identical with pity and fear. What the relationship between the purging passions and the passions being purged is becomes clearer in this passage from *De poeta* (p. 63):

Indeed, is there anything which crushes the onrush of anger, quenches the thirst for money, diminishes the longing for rewards, suppresses ambition to rule, curbs the lust for wicked pleasure, and restrains whatever fierce rage of the mind you like as much as both pity and fear? For is anyone so led by unbridled ardor either for vengeance, for ruling, or for owning that if he is roused to pity and terror by the calamities of others, it will not purge and expiate his mind of the perturbation which brought on that unhappy state?[13]

[10] "At, quod eius potissimum munus est, ad hunc finem misericordiam facit, atque perterret, ut animum purget, expietq́; à nefario perturbationum concursu."

[11] "Ella [tragedia] è imitatione di cose gravi, e notabili sotto una materia intera e perfetta . . . che sene desti pietâ, e spavento à purgar l'animo di simili passioni con diletto, e profitto di lui. . . ."

[12] "Già potete conoscere, che l'imitatione delle cose gravi e notabili, e la purgatione degli affetti fanno questa poesia dalla Comica e dalla Satyrica differēte: e, come le cose gravi e notabili sono materia di lei; così la purgatione degli affetti è quel fine, alquale tutta si dirrizza."

[13] "Quid est enim quod aequè atque vel misericordia, vel metus irae impetum frangat, pecuniae sitim [sic] extinguat, honorum cupiditatem imminuat, dominandi studium comprimat, nefariae libidinem voluptatis cohibeat, quem vis indomitum fur-

The enumeration of passions expiated by pity and fear in these lines—further confirmed by a corresponding section of *L'arte poetica*[14]—indicates that the passions Minturno thought Aristotle meant to purge are other than pity and fear. Rather, pity and fear are desirable passions which tragedy should not purge but arouse, for they are the means of counteracting unwholesome passions which, though similar to pity and fear, are nevertheless not identical with them. Minturno most likely considers the passions as similar to one another in that they all perturb and stir up the mind, but he probably would not accept *idem* or *ipse* as the equivalent of τοιούτων. We find, therefore, a significant difference between the pathological analogies which the two critics used. The purpose of Milton's analogy, as we have seen, was to "make good" Aristotle's assertion that tragedy purged passions by the principle of like purging like. In Minturno's scheme, since pity and fear purge different passions, the analogy rather illustrates the degree of effectiveness which the tragic poet has in purging undesirable passions, and the poet's capability is compared with the physician's. Only on a very superficial level can this analogy be taken to show similarity between Minturno's catharsis and Milton's, for we cannot find, as in Milton, any suggestion that like purges like.

There is yet another important difference between these two theories of catharsis. When Milton uses the phrase "to temper and reduce them to just measure," it is clear that he is advocating the restoration of a proper norm or mean of the passions and that he does not intend that they should be extirpated completely. Minturno's view, in contrast to this, seems to be that passions such as wrath, envy, or ambition are undesirable and should be removed. While it is not possible, I think, to determine exactly to what extent he wishes to eliminate the passions, it is nevertheless certain that he has no developed theory of the mean, such as Milton appears to

---

orem mentis coerceat? Nam quis ita effrenato vel ulciscendi, vel imperandi, vel habendi ardore ducitur, qui si alienae calamitatis, aut miseratione, aut terrore concitetur, non animum purget, expietq; ab ea perturbatione, quae infelicitatem illam invexit?"

[14] "Il medesimo [tragico] poeta . . . molto diletta. Nè cosa ci rappresenta, che non piaccia: nè senza diletto muove . Ma con empito di parole, e con grave peso di sentimento desta nell'animo passione, & inducelo à meraviglia, così spaventando, come à pietà movendo. Qual cosa è così Tragica, come il muover altrui? E che muove tanto, quanto il terribile, & miserabile, & inopinato avvenimento? . . . Ma con tutto ciò, questo spavēto, e questa pietâ di simili passioni dilettevolmente ci purga: perche nulla piú raffrena lo'ndomito furor della nostra mente."

have, but conceives of purgation as the driving out of the undesirable passions rather than the reduction of all passions to some norm. In view of these differences, then, Milton's theory of catharsis can be considered to be related to Minturno's only very indirectly. They differ considerably, and to assert that the two views are identical or very close to one another is erroneous and misleading.

Let us turn next to Gilbert's claim for Guarini (p. 517). The first likeness to Milton which Gilbert noted (p. 517, n. 15) appears in the phrasing of Guarini's remark that "these two passions [pity and fear], then, need to be purged—that is, reduced to a virtuous temperament—and tragedy does this,"[15] for it reminds one of Milton's "to temper and reduce them to just measure." A little further on Gilbert points out a second similarity (p. 517, n. 17). Guarini's text (as Gilbert translates it) states: "When then terror purges terror, it is not as though wrath were joined to wrath, but the terror acts like rhubarb, which, though it has an occult likeness to the humor that it purges, yet in respect to its end is wholly opposed, for one heals and the other corrupts." From this, Gilbert, pointing out Milton's "sour against sour," asserts that "Milton and Guarini hold a homeopathic theory." But even though Guarini utilizes a homeopathic analogy, and his phrasing of a theory of the mean in the passions suggests Milton's, it is not to be thought that their concepts of purgation are at all similar; after all, the preface to *Samson Agonistes* specifically rejects mixing the tragic and comic—the very tragicomic form, perhaps, for which Guarini's treatise argues.

Guarini, to be sure, takes a stand on the interpretation of τοιούτων παθημάτων which is exactly the opposite of Minturno's, but it is no closer to Milton's interpretation than Minturno's was. In Guarini's argument, τοιούτων is the key to his theory of catharsis and essential to his theory of tragicomedy. As the passages quoted above show, he takes it as equivalent of τούτων or *idem*, thus meaning that pity and fear purge pity and fear alone. The same passions are at once the agent and the object of purgation—an interpretation very different from Milton's "those, and such like." It is certain that Guarini means for the end of tragedy to be limited to purging only pity and fear, excluding other passions. The reason for this is that Guarini distinguishes tragicomedy from comedy and tragedy only on the basis of two things. They are, as he terms them, the instrumental end and

---

[15] *Il comp.*, p. 237: "Hanno dunque bisogno questi duo [*sic*] affetti d'esser purgati, cioè ridotti a vertuoso temperamento, e questo fa la tragedia."

the architectonic end of each of the poetic forms. For Guarini, the instrumental end "is that by means of which the artist, as he works, introduces into the matter which he has in hand the form that is the end of the work"; the architectonic end is "that for the good and utility of which he labors at the work."[16] Comic and tragic forms are differentiated, therefore, by specifying these two ends so precisely that, as Guarini says in the case of tragedy, "when the end is changed the form will also be changed."[17] By adhering inflexibly to these arbitrary specifications, he can bring forth tragicomedy as a legitimate form, giving it the instrumental end of tragedy and the architectonic end of comedy. The following diagram will, perhaps, illustrate his distinctions more clearly.

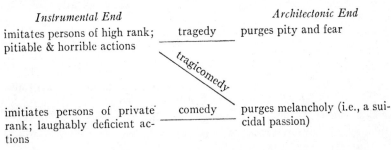

Instrumental End   *Architectonic End*
imitates persons of high rank;   tragedy   purges pity and fear
pitiable & horrible actions

imitiates persons of private   comedy   purges melancholy (i.e., a sui-
rank; laughably deficient ac-   cidal passion)
tions

Of these two ends, the architectonic is the most important in defining the poetic forms, for, unlike the instrumental, it cannot be varied and in part determines the nature of the instrumental end itself.[18] Since the architectonic end therefore largely determines tragic form, it is necessary for Guarini to explain very clearly what the exact meaning of catharsis is. For unless he can pinpoint rather

    [16] P. 234: "L'uno [fine], per cagion del quale operando, l'artefice introduce nella materia, ch'egli ha per mano, quella forma ch'è fin dell'opera; l'altro, per bene e uso del quale, la cosa, che vuol condurre a fine, viene operata."
    [17] P. 242: "Dunque dal terribile e dal miserabile, piú o meno purganti, nascono i gradi delle tragedie. Onde séguita che se, come s'è detto, l'esser tragico può ne'suoi gradi alterarsi, non ha dubbio che può anche corrompersi e dileguarsi, per modo che tragico non sia piú, ma passi in un'altra spezie. E però, se nelle sue alterazioni alcuna cosa riceverá che non repugni agli affetti del terribile e del miserabile, sará egli tragico sempre, ancora che piú meno. Ma, mescolandosi con qualitá repugnante e contraria ai soprannominati duo [sic] affetti, sí come è'l riso, converrá che si corrompa la spezie, e, mutandosi fine, si muti forma. . . . "
    [18] See p. 242. In tragicomedy the architectonic end is entirely different from that of tragedy and cannot be mixed with anything of the tragic. The instrumental end, however—though mainly like the tragic—changes because of the altered architectonic end and can be mixed somewhat with comic instrumental features.

precisely what effects tragedy is expected to produce, he cannot (which his whole argument endeavors to do) demonstrate how tragicomedy is a legitimate form differing from tragedy or why tragicomedy excels tragedy.

As should be expected, he devotes several pages (235–39) to this important subject. In considering τοιούτων as equivalent to τούτων, he immediately recognizes two problems which probably caused Minturno to reject this interpretation. One problem is that if tragedy purges men of pity and fear—particularly of pity—they will become cruel, pitiless, and inhuman. The second is, how can like purge like— would not like stimulate like instead? Guarini answers these objections by asserting that *purgare* has two meanings. In the first, *purgare* means to extirpate (*spegnere*); in the second it signifies purification or cleansing (*mondare, sgombrare*).[19] Guarini opens his argument by briefly disposing of the second alternative: "In the second meaning, the 'purgare' of tragedy ought to be taken as the physicians also take it, who . . . do not intend to blot out or wholly unroot [anger] . . . but to remove only that part of it which . . . corrupts the symmetry of life—from which sickness afterwards comes."[20] And he concludes this discussion by a short explanation of a theory of the mean which he expresses in phraseology similar, as Gilbert thought (see pp. 516–17), to Milton's: "the tragic poem, then, does not purge its passions in a stoic way, by driving them totally from our hearts, but by moderating and reducing them to that good temper which can be of service to virtuous habit."[21]

Having thus reviewed this idea, Guarini *rejects* it and turns back to the first alternative (extirpative catharsis) on which he prefers to

[19] Pp. 236–37: "Or queste sono le difficultá che ci bisogna prima risolvere, volendo bene intendere il modo con che il poema tragico purga. E, prima ch'altro s'intenda, è da sapere che la voce 'purgare' ha duo sensi: L'uno è 'di spegnere affatto.' . . . L'altro è di 'purificare e mondare,' e'n tale senso disse il Petrarca; . . . periciocché quivi non vuole spegnere il proprio ingegno, come il Boccaccio intendeva di spegnere le peccata, ma di sgombrarlo d'ogni viltá e farlo in sua natura perfetto."

[20] P. 237: "In questo secondo significato si dé'prendere il 'purgare' della tragedia, come altresí lo prendono i medici: i quali . . . non hanno intenzione di spegnerla [collera] o diradicarla affatto . . . ma di levarne sol quella parte, che . . . corrompe la simmetria della vita, onde poi nasce la'nfermitá." In connection with the phrase "In questo secondo significato si dé'prendere," Gilbert's translation (p. 516) seems to be misleading. Guarini builds his theory on the concept of eradication and he specifically rejects the interpretation of purgation as a reduction to a mean.

[21] P. 237: "Non purga dunque il poema tragico gli affetti suoi alla stoica, spiantandogli totalmente da'nostri cuori, ma moderandogli e riducendogli a quella buona temperie, che può servire all'abito vertuoso."

found his definition of tragedy. "If to purge is considered the effect of the thing purging," it is clear, he thinks, that complete extirpation is implied, "for good has its purpose to blot out and quite eradicate the bad."[22] The next step is to determine what the purging agent and purged object are, in order to explain how pity may purge pity and fear may purge fear—which he earlier specified as the architectonic effects of tragedy. Pity and fear are divided into good and bad classes: good pity purges bad pity and good fear purges bad fear—the bad being that pity and fear linked with the external or corporeal man, and the good pity and fear with the internal or intellectual man. It is in this context—wholly different from Milton's—that Guarini employs the homeopathic analogy which, Gilbert thinks, suggests Milton. Just as rhubarb purges a humor of the same nature, so the tragic representation excites good terror (fear of internal death which is the foundation of virtue) in order to drive out the bad (fear of corporeal death which can result in internal death, as when one prefers to exist rather than to avoid wickedness). And the same may be said of pity: compassion is likewise both good ("when we are sorrowful for someone who is afflicted in the mind because he has had too great pleasure in the body") and bad ("when we feel sorrowful for someone who injures his body that he may have peace in his mind");[23] the good pity, as in the case of good fear, purges bad pity just as medicine purges a noxious humor. As we can see, Guarini's analogy suggests no theory of the mean as Milton's did, but it is used rather to support the alternative principle of extirpation which Guarini preferred. It is evident, then, that these two analogies, though similarly worded, illustrate theories of catharsis which contrast very markedly.

Since Milton's catharsis, thus, is not the same as Guarini's and Minturno's, no single and undoubted source for Milton's catharsis— if he followed a single one—has been discovered hitherto. A theory of catharsis does exist, however, which resembles Milton's more closely than either of the two examined in this essay. This is the one put

[22] P. 237: "Ma, se il 'purgare' si considera come effetto della cosa purgante, diremo che questi affetto si purgano nel primiero significato, perciocché il buono intende di spegnere e diradicare affatto il cattivo."

[23] P. 240: "Ma questo male può essere in due maniere, o del corpo o dell'animo; onde nascon le due compassioni, buona e cattiva: perciocché la buona è quando noi ci attristiamo di chi s 'affligge nell'animo, perché troppo si sia compiaciuto nel corpo; e la cattiva è quando ci attristiamo di chi s'affligge nel corpo per aver pace con l'animo."

forward by Daniel Heinsius in his *De tragoediae constitutione liber.*[24] Two things should be kept in mind before considering this work as a possible source, however. First, Heinsius himself is clearly under the influence of the Italians, and it is not to be thought that his ideas are necessarily original. It is only in the sense of giving utterance to and elaborating on earlier ideas that he becomes significant. Secondly, Heinsius' theory of catharsis, like the two examined above, cannot be said to be identical with Milton's in all respects. Although the similarities are striking, there is one difference between them, as we shall see, and the only certain claim to be made is that the catharsis in Milton's preface is closer to *De tragoediae* than to the others.

The first point of similarity between the two theories involves the translation of κάθαρσις itself. As we have seen, Milton's title page translated it as *lustratio*—purification by sacrifice or rite. Heinsius' Latin text of the *Poetics* (p. 247) translates the term as *expiatio*, which means about the same as *lustratio*, and in *De tragoediae* it is adopted as the standard term for catharsis: "this Aristotle accordingly called the expiation of the passions (or perturbations), unless someone prefers purgation, the Pythagorean word taken from the school of the Italians, which—like many others—the Platonists later maintained."[25] When modern critics (e.g., Butcher, p. 245 n.) speak of the *lustratio* or *expiatio* interpretation of catharsis, they place so much emphasis upon the religious or ceremonial aspects of the terms that they obscure the real reason that Renaissance commentators and translators such as Heinsius preferred them to *purgatio*. As Guarini's statement of the theory of the mean may suggest, *expiatio* or *lustratio* do not imply complete extirpation of a passion, as *purgatio* might, but suggest rather the milder purification or reduction of excess passions without necessarily carrying ritual or ceremonial overtones. And here, as we have seen, there is a point of close similarity between Heinsius and Milton.

Furthermore, Milton's *lustratio* may itself be due directly to

---

[24] Cf. Milton's introduction to Book II of *The Reason of Church-Government Urg'd against Prelaty*, where his phrase "those Dramatick constitutions" offers an interesting parallel to Heinsius' title (*Complete Prose Works of John Milton*, ed. Don M. Wolfe, 1 [New Haven, 1953], 814).

[25] P. 10: "Quod affectum proinde expiationem, sive perturbationum, Aristotelis vocavit. nisi quis purgationem malit; voce Pythagorica, & è schola Italorum desumpta: quam deinde, ut alia non pauca, vindicarunt Platonici."

Heinsius. As Bywater indicates,[26] Milton could have picked up *lustratio* from Goulston's version of the *Poetics*,[27] but, if he did, the origin of the term is in Heinsius. Goulston, as his remarks on emendations of the Greek text show (p. 75), owes much to Heinsius, and correspondingly the main text of his edition rendered κάθαρσις (p. 12) thus: ". . . per Misericordiam, Metumque; *factis expressum*, [b] eiusmodi *vehementes animorum* Perturbationes undiquaque Purgans, *expiansque*.*" We do not find *lustratio* given as part of the main text but as a part of the marginal guide to matter discussed in the text. The superscript "b" preceding *eiusmodi* refers the reader to the left margin of the page where we find "Finis externus Tragici: Animor. lustratio." Obviously, *lustratio* is taken as the exact equivalent of *expiatio*, and, according to Bywater and others, Heinsius seems to be responsible for bringing *expiatio* as the Latin equivalent of κάθαρσις into seventeenth-century theory.

The second point of similarity is the strongest internal evidence indicating that Heinsius may have been Milton's immediate source. It is for the full development of catharsis as a process of reducing the passions to a virtuous mean that *De tragoediae* has been particularly known,[28] and here Milton could have found a most thorough development of such a theory. Heinsius, like most commentators of the Renaissance, viewed catharsis as the specification of the use and purpose of tragedy, and his thinking is that Aristotle meant to say that tragedy is morally profitable because it helps to form the virtuous state of mind, or habit. Tragedy could bring about this virtuous state because it effected the catharsis of certain passions—that is, the reduction of them to the proper mean. Heinsius explains catharsis this way: "Since this muse [the tragic] is engaged in moving the passions exeedingly, Aristotle thought that its end was to temper the passions themselves and again compose them. There are two passions proper to it, pity and horror. As tragedy excites these passions (thus moving themselves out little by little) in the mind it reduces them

[26] See Bywater's "Milton and the Aristotelian Definition of Tragedy," p. 268. His ΑΡΙΣΤΟΤΕΛΟΤΣ ΠΕΡΙ ΠΟΙΗΤΙΚΗΣ (Oxford, 1909), pp. 361–65, lists the more common translations into Latin of the catharsis clause. *Lustratio* appeared in Lambinus' version of the *Politics* (1567).

[27] *Aristotelis de poetica liber, Latine conversus, et analytica methodo illustratus* (London: Typis Thomas Snodhami, 1623).

[28] See Bywater's ΑΡΙΣΤΟΤΕΛΟΤΣ, pp. 158–61; Joseph E. Gillet's "The Catharsis-Clause in German Criticism Before Lessing," *Journal of Philology*, XXXV (1920), 100–101; and Edith G. Kern, *The Influence of Heinsius and Vossius upon French Dramatic Theory*, The Johns Hopkins Studies in Romance Literatures and Languages, Extra Vol. XXVI (Baltimore, 1949), pp. 60–61.

to the right measure [*quemadmodum oportet;* italics mine] and so brings them into line. This Aristotle called, accordingly, the expiation of the passions. . . ."[29]

Two things are remarkably similar to Milton's theory in this passage. In the development of Heinsius' theory, the phrase *quemadmodum oportet* occurs again and again, and Milton's "to temper and reduce them *to just measure*" echoes this phrase just as strikingly as it suggests Guarini's "ridotti a vertuoso temperamento." The use of *horror* further points toward a relationship. Milton rendered φόβος as "fear" and then specified "terror" as an alternative. Likewise Heinsius' translation uses *metus*, but, in *De tragoediae, metus* is discarded for *terror* (p. 19) and (most often) *horror* (e.g., p. 18). This substitution, again, can be explained in terms of reduction to the mean. In both theories, the excess of passions must be purged to regain the correct norm; since fear and terror, or horror, are synonyms for the same passion, the term implying the greatest degree of undesirable excess supports the theory best, and clearly *horror* or *terror* imply a greater and more uncontrollable degree of this passion than *metus.*

Heinsius goes on to develop his theory of the mean by describing what he thought Aristotle's concept of the passions to be (p. 11): Aristotle considered them to be neither virtuous nor vicious, since virtue (*virtus*) consists in keeping the passions under the control of reason. Tragic representation (p. 12) gives rise to such a virtuous habit because (by arousing passions not too excessively) it conditions men to bearing and controlling them. "The man who frequently sees miseries commiserates appropriately and to the proper measure; he who frequently looks on those things which move horror at last becomes less horrified, as is proper. Wherefore, also, those things need to be presented which are exhibited in the theatre—which is like a kind of training place for our passions—and it is indispensable that they (since they are not only useful in life but even necessary) be trained and relieved there."[30] For these reasons, thinks Heinsius, Aristotle must have judged tragedy not to be the fan of the passions, as Plato

[29] *De tragoediae,* p. 10: "In concitandis igitur affectibus cum maxime versetur haec Musa, finem ejus esse, hos ipsos ut temperet, iterumq; componat, Aristoteles existimat. Affectus proprii illius sunt duo: Misericordia, & Horror. Quos ut excitat in animo, ita sensim efferentes sese, deprimit, quemadmodum oportet, & in ordinem sic cogit. Quod affectuum proinde expiationem . . . Aristotelis vocavit."

[30] Pp. 12–13: "Ita qui miserias frequenter spectat, recte miseratur, & quemadmodum oportet. qui frequenter ea quae horrorem movent, intuetur; minus tandem horret, & ut decet. Quo & referenda sunt, quae in theatro exhibentur quod affectuum nostrorum quaedam quasi est palaestra. qui, cum non modo utiles in vita, verum etiam sint necessarii, praeparari ibi & oportet, & absolvi."

thought, but the norm by which they are brought back into service, and he exclaims (pp. 17–18) that "this is the end of it [tragedy], this is the utility which he [Aristotle] placed in the definition which has made so much trouble for the learned hitherto. This is the sense in which the greatest of men termed tragedy expiation, or purgation."[31] Thus, in Heinsius' formulation of Aristotle's definition of tragedy, it becomes very clear that the mean is the essential point of catharsis—so essential, in fact, that *De tragoediae* will even claim that remedying the deficiency as well as the excess of passions is the ethical end of tragedy (p. 19): "[the actions imitated in tragedy] lessen or appease these same passions in the human mind, and, if they are used correctly, they expiate and purge the excess and the deficiency of them also. They leave behind a mean—which is the primary aim in this matter."[32]

It is evident, then, that Milton could find in Heinsius an elaborate version of Aristotle's mean systematically applied to the *Poetics*. Furthermore, Milton and Heinsius resemble each other in their approach to considering the end of tragedy. In either case, Tragedy is *first* serious and moral: *then* follows the proposition that tragic catharsis contributes to this end—for, unquestionably, both of them hold that tragedy must be moral and useful. From this position Heinsius will maintain (as probably Milton would also) that there is no fundamental disagreement between Plato and Aristotle about what the *end* of tragedy ought to be. In Heinsius' eyes, Aristotle disagrees with Plato about the question of whether or not tragedy has the *capability* of effecting this end—not about the end itself. Plato, Heinsius maintains, held that tragedy excited the passions rather than allayed them; Aristotle (because he thought otherwise about the passions themselves), to the contrary, developed a formula which shows how and what sort of tragedy can effect this moral end. And Milton's opening statement in his preface ("Tragedy . . . hath been ever held the gravest, moralest, and most profitable of all other Poems: therefore said by *Aristotle* to be of power . . . ") seems to imply very much the same reasoning.

The last point about the catharsis of Milton and Heinsius concerns

---

[31] "Hunc illius [tragoediae] finem, hanc utilitatem esse, quam in definitione ponit. quae tot eruditis hactenus negotium facessit. Quo sensu expiationem aut purgationem, summus vir Tragoediam vocavit."

[32] "Quae eosdem in humano animo affectus mitigant aut sedant. & si recte adhibeantur, defectum quoque eorum atque excessum expiant ac purgant. mediocritatem vero, quod hic primum est, relinquunt."

their translation of τοιούτων παθημάτων. Although we find a similarity here, there is divergence too. Milton, as we have seen, specified τοιούτων as "those, and such like." Heinsius, on the other hand, does not face this problem squarely. He translated τοιούτων as *similium*, thus implying that he meant emotions similar to but not identical with pity and fear, and, in turning from his translation to *De tragoediae* one would expect him to hold that pity and fear purge other passions rather than themselves. Contrary to expectation,[33] this is not the case. As the passage quoted above (n. 29) shows, the first assertion Heinsius makes about the power of tragedy is that it greatly excites the passions. In this statement he is speaking of passions generically, and one assumes that he means tragedy can excite all sorts of passions. But, directly on the heels of this statement, he asserts that "the proper passions of it are two"—pity and fear. With this, several questions enter the reader's mind at once. Does tragedy properly excite pity and fear only? Apparently so. What passions, then, are these passions supposed to purge?—passions other than pity and fear?—pity and fear plus related passions?—or pity and fear and no other passions whatsoever? From the context of Heinsius' argument, it would appear that he intends that tragedy properly excite only pity and fear, and that these two emotions will expiate the excess only of pity and fear. Although in discussing Aristotle's opinions of the passions (p. 11) he speaks of joy, sorrow, commiseration and other passions as being reducible to habit, it seems that he intends only to recapitulate Aristotle's ideas on passions generally, not to elaborate on them specifically in relation to catharsis in tragedy; and, thus, we later find that pity and fear seem to be the only emotions involved in tragic purgation. For Heinsius' examples of expiation (e.g., p. 12) consistently involve only pity and horror; he formulates the end of tragedy in the definition only in terms of pity and fear (pp. 19–20); and, when he later discusses the types of plot and character best suited for tragedy, the criterion for approval is their ability to elicit pity and fear. Even so, Heinsius approaches Milton more closely than Guarini, for Guarini's distinction between the poetic forms depended on the rigid specification of their architectonic ends. Pity and fear are less

---

[33] A few commentators seem to have thought that he meant passions other than pity and fear. They probably follow his translation of the *Poetics* but have not compared it with his arguments in *De tragoediae*. Eugène Vinaver, in his edition of Racine's *Principes de la tragédie en marge de la Poétique d' Aristote* (Editions de l'Université de Manchester, 1944), pp. 59–61, seems to think that Racine rejected Heinsius by interpreting catharsis as the purgation of pity and fear alone rather than as *similis* passions.

integral to Heinsius' definition of these forms, however; Heinsius did differentiate tragedy from comedy, for instance, by the kind of action imitated (*seria* as opposed to *laeta*), and by elements in the plot (e.g., reversal of fortune) peculiar to tragedy. So far as the general proposition that tragedy excites passions in order to allay them by expiation is concerned, however, Heinsius does not differ from Milton, and, in principle, this theory is much much closer to Milton's than Guarini's was.

These, then, are the main internal resemblances between the catharses of Milton and Heinsius. There are other reasons, too, which suggest that Milton's catharsis could well have come from Heinsius rather than from Guarini or Minturno. Heinsius is closer in time to Milton, and he achieved his fame at Leyden just when it became a center of protestant learning. It is impossible, moreover, to believe that Milton was unfamiliar with Heinsius' work: Heinsius had twice opposed Salmasius long before the latter's quarrel with Milton, and the controversy—also associated with Salmasius—over Heinsius' *Herodes Infanticida* (1632) must have coincided with Milton's formulation of his dramatic plans.[34] Lastly, Milton apparently never referred either to Minturno or to Guarini,[35] whereas we find Heinsius mentioned in his marginalia (Columbia Milton, xviii, 289) for having written an oration on Pindar's Pythian Odes with a "full interpretation" of the first ode.[36] In view of these facts and the similarity of the interpretations of Milton and Heinsius concerning catharsis, Bernays' contrast of Milton and Heinsius seems particularly unfortunate. *De tragoediae constitutione* certainly ought to be considered as one of the likely sources of Milton's ideas on drama.

[34] The Columbia Milton, xviii, 511, cites Masson's dates of 1640–42 for these plans. It is interesting that two Herod plans figure among Milton's schemes for tragedy: the execution of John the Baptist ("Baptistes") and "Herod massacring" (Columbia Milton, xviii, 239–41).

[35] See Frank L. Patterson and French R. Fogle, *An Index to the Columbia Edition of the Works of John Milton* (New York, 1940), and J. Milton French, ed., *The Life Records of John Milton* (New Brunswick, N. J., 1949–58).

[36] Milton (incorrectly translated in the Columbia Milton, xviii, 290) refers to one of Heinsius' orations, entitled *Pindari Pythijs praemissa*, which appeared in the 1615 edition (Leyden: Lud. Elsevirium) of *Danielis Heinsii Orationes*, according to A. J. van der Aa, *Biographisch Woordenboek der Nederlanden*, Vol. viii, Pt. 1 (Haarlem, 1867), p. 424.

MACREADY'S *COMUS:* A PROMPT-BOOK STUDY

Charles H. Shattuck, University of Illinois

The first century of the stage history of *Comus* has been aptly described by Alwin Thaler, in his classic study called "Milton in the Theatre," as "a striking record of the shifty devices by which the managers capitalized the fame of a great poet."[1] In 1738 the Reverend John Dalton, of Queen's College, Oxford, transformed *Comus* into a three-act musical play for Drury Lane Theatre—a version which held the stage for over three decades and contained all the essential ingredients the theatre would need for the next hundred years.[2] Dalton pretty well anticipated Dr. Johnson's stricture that "as a drama it is deficient."[3] He cut Milton considerably, and, in spite of the modesty of his Prologue,[4] he added much more than he cut, so that the "play" is about a third part longer than the original masque. He shortened "tedious" speeches and broke them up with dialogue relief; invented a long scene in which the Brothers are tempted to "lawless pleasure" by a female bacchanalian; added several new characters, including a second Attendant Spirit named Philadel and a rollicking nymph named Euphrosyne, who sometimes rivaled the Lady as a starring role for actresses; increased the number of songs, with music by Thomas Arne, from four to about twenty. Most remarkably, he exploited every hint he could find to enliven the scene with "lickerish baits" and "lewdly-papered Luxury." Milton's "rout of Monsters, headed like sundry sorts of wild beasts" became "a rout of Men and Women dressed as Bacchanals"—which is to say, *un*dressed as Bacchanals within the limits of public decorum. The tone was no longer set by Milton's elevated discourses on temperance and chastity, but by tumultuous dances and by songs of the witty-fleshly school, calculated, says Thaler, to make "vice as seductive, and virtue as stupid, as possible."

[1] Alwin Thaler, "Milton in the Theatre," *SP,* XVII (1920), 269–307. The second half of Thaler's essay is devoted to *Comus.*

[2] *Comus, a Mask (Now adapted to the Stage) As Alter'd from Milton's Mask at Ludlow Castle* ... (London, 1738). This is John Dalton's adaptation; his name does not appear on the title page.

[3] Samuel Johnson, *Lives of the English Poets,* ed. George Birkbeck Hill, 3 vols. (Oxford, 1905), I, 168.

[4] "Small is our portion—and we wish 'twere none."

Thus lightened and brightened for the public stage, *Comus* became a perennial favorite, as Thaler's statistical table indicates; a later researcher has listed 214 performances of it in London alone, spread upon all but nine of the theatrical seasons between 1738 and 1800.[5] In the late 1760's Dalton's version fell out of favor, mainly because it carried too heavy a burden of Milton's "divine arguments," and because even Dalton's own dialogue additions were found too prolix. "When the cup of Comus is presented to the Brothers by a female of his train," said a later writer, "they are not contented with rejecting it, but proceed to argue with the cupbearer against pleasure with all the moral zeal of Mr. Wilberforce against the slave-trade."[6] In 1772, therefore, George Colman abridged Dalton's version to a two-act afterpiece:[7] he "expunged or contracted" the moral and descriptive passages, whether Miltonic or Daltonic, and retained most of Dalton's provocative lyrics and other inventions celebrating the "bowl's frolic joys" and the "raptures of love." In this form it held the stage for another three or four decades. Theatrical editors—out of respect for the classics, I suppose—continued from time to time to print the Dalton version but with inverted commas marking the lines "omitted in the Representation."[8] In 1815 Thomas Dibdin published a modification of Colman's text, with colorful scenic prescriptions based on the latest Covent Garden revival. At this time, too, music by Henry Bishop and Michael Kelly was added to Arne's old score.[9] And thus the afterpiece proceeded, though with somewhat diminishing popularity, into the 1830's.

The last major item in Thaler's survey is Madame Vestris' spectacular and quite "original" fantastication of *Comus*, produced at Covent Garden in March 1842.[10] It was much paragraphed for its scenic splendors by the reviewers of the day, and it is perhaps most often remembered in the glowing description of George Vandenhoff,

[5] Myrtle M. Carey, "London Stage Performances of Milton's *Comus* during the Eighteenth Century." Unpub. diss. (University of Illinois, 1939), pp. 49–59.

[6] Richard Cumberland, "Critique on Comus," *The British Drama* (London, 1817), II. Cumberland's critique appears to have been written in 1808.

[7] *Comus: A Masque altered from Milton. As Performed at the Theatre-Royal in Covent-Garden* . . . (London, 1772). Colman's name does not appear on the title page.

[8] See, e.g., *Bell's British Theatre* (London, 1777), XI, and *Bell's British Theatre* (London, 1797), I.

[9] *Milton's Comus: A Masque , in Two Acts, as revived at the Theatre-Royal, Covent-Garden, Friday, April 28, 1815* (London, 1815).

[10] *Songs, Duets, Choruses, Etc., in Milton's COMUS: a Masque in Two Acts, with Additions, from the Author's Poem, "L'Allegro," and from Dryden's Opera of KING ARTHUR* . . . (London, [1842]).

who called it "an honour to the theatre . . . breathing the divine philosophy of virtue in tones of highest poetry . . . truly a poetic realization of a poet's creation."[11] A contemporary writer for the *Spectator*, however, labelled it "the most disgraceful of all the revivals of *Comus*";[12] and Thaler concludes that "it is so very far from Milton that . . . if the poet had been at the performance he might have been seriously puzzled to recognize any part of it as his own." The plot seems mostly to have been omitted, and two strange innovations were the Will-o'-the-wisp Scene and the Frost Scene from Dryden's *King Arthur*!

Finally, Thaler notes that a season later William Charles Macready produced *Comus* at Drury Lane. Unable to find a copy of Macready's text, he can tell us nothing about it, but he speculates that "the chances are that it did not differ very much from that of Colman or Dibdin." This is unfortunate. Had he been able to study Macready's text he might have done an act of justice to the actor-manager's reputation, and at the same time brought his study to an especially interesting period. For here, for what it is worth, was the first genuine attempt to put a thoroughly Miltonic text of *Comus* upon the public stage.

Macready's *Comus* appeared at Drury Lane on 24 February 1843, as an afterpiece to *Much Ado About Nothing*. It was Macready's benefit night, and he acted both Benedick and Comus. Both plays were new productions, and both parts were new to Macready's repertory. He had advertised *Comus* and announced the cast a year earlier, in competition with Madame Vestris' production, but about ten days before the Vestris opening it was "deferred to a future season." It was now advertised as "adapted for presentation from the Poet's Text," with "Music, except One Air from the original Composer, HENRY LAWES, by HANDEL and ARNE." The supporting players were Priscilla Horton as Attendant Spirit, Helen Faucit as the Lady, James Anderson as Elder Brother, Miss Fortescue as Second Brother, Emma Romer as Sabrina, Henry Phillips as First Bacchanal, and Henry Allen as Second Bacchanal; the Chorus, never fully published, included Messrs. Sims Reeves, Redfearn, and S. Jones, Mrs. Thomas Serle, and the Misses Turpin, Gould, Webster, etc. It was performed fourteen times during the season (February 24,

[11] George Vandenhoff, *Leaves from an Actor's Notebook* . . . (London, 1860), pp. 59–61.

[12] *Spectator* (London), 4 March 1843.

28, March 4, 7, 11, 14, 18, 20, 23, 27, May 5, 8, 11, 13), variously combined with *Much Ado, Othello, The Lady of Lyons,* and the opera of *Acis and Galatea.* Macready played Comus only on the opening night and May 5, all the other performances being sustained by Samuel Phelps. Anderson was replaced by James Hudson on March 23 and 27. Miss Turpin was replaced by Mrs. Alfred Wigan on May 5, 8, 11, and 13.[13]

Almost nothing of the preparation of *Comus* is recorded in Macready's *Diaries:*[14] only that on February 1 he discussed it with his musical director, Thomas Cooke, on February 2 he completed his cutting, on February 7 he read it to the company in the green room. The scenery was apparently designed, and perhaps painted, by the famous scenic artist Clarkson Stanfield, who was a close adviser to Macready throughout this season. Stanfield brought Macready some sketches for *Comus* on February 8, and on May 5 Macready observed him at the theatre "refreshing the scene" for that night's performance. He made an easel painting from *Comus,* too, which Macready saw at his house on May 28. If he did create the scenery (rather than Charles Marshall, the regular Drury Lane scene painter) it is curious that the fact was not publicized, for his name was a "draw," and on other occasions, as of *Acis and Galatea* the year before, much was made of him in the playbills.

Macready's text of *Comus* was never printed, for in spite of the great pride he took in combating "corrupt editions" and championing textual purity in his productions of the classics (especially Shakespeare),[15] he was apparently disinclined to publish his acting versions.[16] Perhaps he was conscious that they were not "pure" enough. Perhaps, too, his artistic zeal prevented him from exhibiting the mysteries of his craft. "The real artist," he would say, "does not pre-engage your opinion by telling you what he is going to draw: if the tree, or rock, or man, or woman do not describe themselves on the canvas, the writing underneath will not persuade us of the resemblance." Such was his

[13] Drury Lane playbills of the 1841–43 seasons are in the Gabrielle Enthoven Collection at the Victoria and Albert Museum.

[14] *The Diaries of William Charles Macready, 1833–1851,* ed. William Toynbee, 2 vols. (London, 1912). The references are identifiable by dates of entry.

[15] *Macready's Reminiscences, and Selections from His Diaries and Letters,* ed. Sir Frederick Pollock (London, 1876), p. 652.

[16] For two of Macready's acting versions, see my forthcoming prompt-book studies of his *As You Like It (Beta Phi Mu Chapbooks,* Nos. 5 and 6) and *King John* (University of Illinois Press).

response when confronted with Charles Fechter's acting edition of *Othello*.[17] We know too that at times he was abnormally fearful that other actors would steal his ideas. When a young man, he sometimes wrote his playbook marginalia in Latin, apparently so that his fellow performers could not read them.[18] From the middle 1830's on, he was particularly afraid (and with reason) that his work would be pilfered by his hated younger rival, Charles Kean.[19]

It is a pretty irony, therefore, that the text of Macready's *Comus*—indeed, his whole prompt-book of the production—is extant, in what is probably a unique manuscript copy, simply because Charles Kean *did* pilfer it and preserve it. The whole story of Kean's nibbling at Macready's granary door has yet to be told. Suffice it here to mention that beginning in 1845, Kean being then in America, the Drury Lane prompter, George Ellis (formerly an under-prompter to Macready's company, later Kean's stage-manager at the Princess's) began sending Kean beautiful transcriptions of Macready's Drury Lane prompt-books. Kean used one of these to produce *King John* at the Park Theatre in New York in the fall of 1846, and he would have staged *Macbeth* and *Comus* next, had not *King John* and his Park engagement simultaneously failed.[20] The book of *Comus* is preserved with the rest of the Kean collection at the Folger Shakespeare Library.

It is a manuscript executed by two hands. The text was transcribed by *D. Home—Copyist & 2ᵈ Promʳ T.R.D.L. 1846;* the stage directions were inserted by *Geo Ellis T.R.D.L.* The pages, which measure $7\frac{1}{4} \times 8\frac{7}{8}$ inches, are stitched into a white cardboard cover, now tanned with age and dust. Ellis wrote on the title page # *Prompt Copy # Private Property, C Kean, Esqʳ.* and *Cut,—marked,—corrected, —&ᶜ—as acted at the Theatre Royal, Drury Lane by—George Ellis / Prompter / 1ˢᵗ Jany.—1846.* A cast list within gives the names of the principals of the 1843 production.

Two or three obvious facts appear from the most superficial scan-

---

[17] *Macready's Reminiscences*, pp. 719–20 (a letter to Mrs. Pollock, 31 October 1861).

[18] See, e.g., Macready's acting copy of *Richard III* in the Folger Shakespeare Library.

[19] John Colman, *Players and Playwrights I Have Known*, 2 vols. (London, 1888), I, 78–80. Colman tells of Kean's obtaining Macready's prompt-book of *Sardanapalus* in 1834. For Kean's unsuccessful attempt to secure Macready's *King Lear*, see Macready's *Diaries*, entry for 22 July 1841.

[20] *The Albion* (New York), 5 December 1846.

ning of the document. The text has been cut to less than half its original size (some 560 out of 1023 lines have been dropped). Both poetry and "philosophy" have vanished in such quantity as to scandalize the proper Miltonist. What remains is plainly the scenario for an afterpiece, of which the playing time, according to a note at the end, was *One Hour*. On the other hand, it is indeed, as the playbills quietly assert, "adapted from the Poet's Text"—purified of all non-Miltonic intrusions. There are six songs taken or adapted from other Milton poems, but no trace of Dalton-Colman remains to vulgarize or distract, and, in this sense at least, Milton's *Comus* is "restored." Finally, one would note, the stage directions, few but vivid, show us almost exactly how the play "worked" upon the gas-lighted, wing-and-shutter stage of the midcentury, both from the point of view of the spectator out front and from the prompter's station offstage left. In describing the production I shall quote these stage directions in fair completeness (excepting only anticipatory calls and warnings), reserving *italic type* to distinguish them from other necessary quotation. I shall not attempt in this description to account for the details of the textual arrangement; but a complete list of the cuts and emendations is appended below. To anyone interested in staging *Comus* (a pastime even nowadays not unheard of) I recommend that he mark a copy of the poem exactly as Macready's book was marked: cut to the bone. Then, proceeding very cautiously in the light of his own preferences, the skill of his performers, and the predictable tolerance of his audience, he should restore what needs to be restored. Even the most proper Miltonist, if he so faces up to the exigencies of stage performance, may be less scandalized than he was at first by Macready's ready knife.

At the head of the text there are two prompter's warnings in George Ellis' hand: # *All the Lights quite down!* and # # *Open^9 Symph^y before the Curtain rises.* According to the playbill, the overture music before *Comus* was Cherubini's Overture to *Anacreon;* but the "opening symphony" which Ellis refers to is rather, I think, the music for the first song of the play. This song is described as *Solo / Lady*, "*Gould*" / *and Chorus, / sung at back*, and it consisted of the thirteenth stanza of "On the Morning of Christ's Nativity," the first three lines altered as follows:

> Ring out ye crystal spheres
> And bless our raptured ears
> If ye have power to gladden Spirits so.

Why the Lady should be indicated as leading the Chorus of Spirits is not clear to me, but since it all went on behind the scenes and Miss Gould, a skilled vocalist, did the singing, it does not much matter.

\# \#

\# *As this Chorus comm^s behind Ring for Curtain to rise.* The curtain rises on *Scene 1st. The Abyss of Space*—evidently a skyscape of twinkling stars. A spectacular effect seems to have been intended whereby *A central Star enlarges, and, opening, forms a Glory around the Attendant Spirit;* but this effect was not realized and the words are lined out. Instead, at the sixth line of the song, "And let the bass of Heaven's deep organ blow," \# *Scene ascends, and discovers a Wood, / by bright moonlight / A Double for the Attend^t Spirit, flies down, from the borders, PS.—at back, to stage, in UE–OP.–,* and *Spirit / Entering UER / comes forw^d thro' Wood,–the instant his "double," descends out of sight of the audience.* These directions may be translated as follows. "Scene ascends" means that the sky-cloth of the Abyss of Space, which is hung far downstage, perhaps in front of the first grooves, is drawn up to reveal the enchanted wood. The wood is composed of wood-wings, and "cut flats" representing free-standing trees, and back flats showing a forest vista, set in the first, second, third, and fourth grooves. The doubling aerialist flies down on a wire from the overhead borders upstage left (P.S. = Prompt Side = stage left) to the floor at upstage right (U.E.O.P. = Upper Entrance Opposite Prompt), where the actress of the Attendant Spirit, Priscilla Horton, stands ready to emerge from the wings, come forward through the "cut flat" trees, and speak the opening lines. The beauty and mystery of this forest scene was vividly remembered over forty years later by Helen Faucit in her "Letter to John Ruskin":

The enchanted wood was admirably presented, with its dense, bewildering maze of trees, so easy to be lost in, so difficult to escape from, with the fitful moonlight casting deep shadows, and causing terrors to the lonely, bewildered girl, whose high trust and confidence in Supreme help alone keep her spirits from sinking under the wild "fantasies" that throng into her memory, "of calling shapes, and beckoning shadows dire." It seemed to me the very place the poet must have pictured to himself.[21]

The Attendant Spirit's prologue is reduced from 92 lines to an efficient 34. He (she!) mentions his heavenly mansion (5 lines), announces his errand, which is to guard the Peer's children (8 lines),

---

[21] Helena Faucit, Lady Martin, *On Some of Shakespeare's Female Characters* (London, 1885; 7th ed., 1904), pp. 329–31.

describes the danger from the sorcerer, "Of Bacchus and of Circe born, great Comus" (12 lines), restates his mission and indicates the disguise he will take (8 lines). At line 85 he hears *Distant Yells / &c at back L*, and with one line more *disappears OP*—that is, exits stage right.

$$\#$$

A note to the prompter after line 92 directs him to $\#$ $\#$ *Raise Lights in front but not the float*—that is, not the footlights. The copyist has transcribed Milton's description of the entrance of Comus and his rout of Monsters, and Ellis has entered a cue for *Music*. Then Ellis elaborates the entrance into exact stage directions: *The Rabble Rout of Monsters, enter, first, from L–1ˢᵗ, 2ⁿᵈ, and 3ʳᵈ Entˢ,— / preceding Comus. / —in wild sport, running from, and pursuing one another, across, from opposite corners of the stage, —looking back,—shrieking, and waving their torches, at particular notes,—catching each other's garments and hair,—whirling round with scream[s],—&c. &c—then Comus, in a Car, drawn by panthers,—and surrounded by others of the Rout, from L–2 Ent, round in front, up R—to C.—He holds a drinking glass, in one hand,—and a short charming-rod, in the other,—the Monsters carry Torches,—Thyrsisses,—Drinking Cups & Bunches of Grapes,— Cymbals,—and Tambourines.*

Comus spins off the invitation to revelry (ll. 92–110) without interruption except for bursts of laughter at the ends of lines 102, 103, 104, and 110. Then *A Bacchanal Monster* (H. Phillips) sings a six-line song mainly repeated from Comus' lines 102–106; the massed monsters repeat

> Braid your locks with rosy twine,
> Dropping odours, dropping wine

in chorus, keeping up *A slow dancing movement* the while and ending with *Loud laugh*. Comus speaks lines 111–18, then *reclines in his Car* while *All group around him, and sit*. The *2ⁿᵈ Bacch' Monster* (Allen) renders lines 119–26 as a song; the chorus of monsters repeats line 122 and *All drink*, line 126 and *All laugh again*. Comus speaks the invocation to Cotytto. At "Come, knit hands," Comus *Advances from Car,—which is taken off, immedʸ, L–2E.—All rise, quickly, and join hands, by threes and fours*. While they dance the "light fantastic round" they sing from "L'Allegro" the couplet

> Come and trip it as you go
> On the light fantastic toe.

At the command to "break off" *All go 2 paces a' X R & L,—putting out their torches, at the same time,* and the prompter is directed to put the # *Lights down.* Three lines later *Exeunt Omnes,— / except Comus, / —at every entrance, R & L,—but the 1ˢᵗ Ent R.H–* Comus announces in about 8 lines the coming of the Lady, and at line 168 *retires to disguise himself / thro' wood, R,–3 Ent'.* /

The Lady enters in the first entrance at stage right and describes her fright and her trust that "He, the supreme Good" will send a guardian—her 60-line soliloquy being cut to about 35 lines. The prompter has been instructed to be *Ready at Check, and Lights* (the "check" was a signaling device to communicate with stage-hands underneath the stage and above on the fly-gallery). At line 217 ("He, the supreme Good") the prompter effects a bit of scenic magic: # *Check above, to take up Gauze Cloud, and discover Moon,—then Raise Blue float grad^y,—and Put Lights down / in front.* / At "did a sable cloud Turn forth her silver lining" the direction is *Lower Cloth beh^d Wood,* so that somehow *The Wood appears transp^t.* During her soliloquy the Lady has worked across to stage left, and by line 229 she is at *L–IE,* so that the "Echo Song," sung in the wings by a substituting vocalist, Miss Romer, is identified as emanating from herself. A prescriptive note reads, *If the Lady who plays the "Lady" is not a Vocalist, she Exits L—after 1ˢᵗ line of the Song.* She does so.

Immediately after the song *Comus appears disguised as a Peasant— R 3 Ent* (upstage right), and speaks of the Lady's beauty. At "lap it in Elysium" *Lady Re-enters L,—but does not imm^y perceive Comus;* when he addresses her directly, at line 265, / *She starts* /, and Comus *advs R.* Their courteous dialogue proceeds without excessive cutting, as Comus assures her of his sympathy and wins her confidence. He indicates the probable whereabouts of her brothers by *pointing L,* and when he offers to conduct her to "a low But loyal cottage" he *Xes to L,* the Lady being at center. She thanks him, and prays to "Blest Providence": *As the Lady raises her eyes, as to Heaven, at "Eye me," &c Comus unobserved by her, beckons on his Rabble, who steal on at R–1ˢᵗ, 2ⁿᵈ, & 3ʳᵈ Ents & L 2ⁿᵈ & 3ʳᵈ Ents.* Immediately is heard # *1ˢᵗ Peal of Bells /L/ Very distant,* and # *2nd Peal of Bells /L/ a little nearer;* and *As he conducts her L a Distant Chorus is heard* from the left singing lines 93–96 of "L'Allegro" about the "merry bells," the "jocund rebecks," and "many a youth and many a maid Dancing in the checquer'd shade." *The followers of Comus steal softly after them as if enclosing the Lady in their toils—/ Exeunt, in a circle, at the various entrances, L /.*

The prompter's directive is # *When the Rout are off put Green & Blue Lights down, and*—/ *W.-* /—that is, blow his whistle to cause a scene change.

The next scene is labelled *Scene 2ᵈ—Another part of the Wood / 1G.* / It was effected very simply: from either side of the stage the carpenters thrust on in the first grooves, to meet at center, a pair of huge flats (each flat about 14 feet wide and 21 feet tall) which displayed a woodland scene. # *Stage quite dark!* The two Brothers entered from the first entrance at stage right. This scene of the Brothers and their following colloquy with the Attendant Spirit (disguised as their family shepherd, Thyrsis) may have been for Milton the heart of his poem, but its moralizing dialectics are of course theatrically impossible, and Macready reduced it to little more than a "carpenter's scene"—the term given a brief "front scene" used to cover the setting up of an elaborate and deep scene next to appear. The 328 lines are reduced to 109 (plus an inserted song), and here as elsewhere a reader like John Keats could feast for a lifetime on the "poetry" which is discarded. Not even the magic Haemony root is allowed, and the brothers are dispatched with little more than their "dauntless hardihood And brandished blade" with which to assault the dread necromancer. There are not even stage directions of any interest in this section. The Elder Brother advances to stage left; the Second Brother lingers at stage right. The Attendant Spirit "habited like a shepherd," bearing *Shepherd's Crook and Double Pipe*, is heard to *Halloo!* five times, *at back, L, A little nearer!*, and *Nearer!* during the dozen lines before his entrance, *LIE*, at line 492. The Elder Brother, of course, *draws his sword* for a moment until he recognizes the Attendant Spirit as "Thyrsis," and withdraws to center, leaving the stage left position for the Spirit. At the end of the scene, the Spirit sings at stage left a very slightly modified version of the second song from *Arcades*, "O'er the smooth enamell'd green . . . Follow me as I sing," and leads them off left to find the Lady "where she sets In beauty's splendour."

# #

/ *W.-* / and # *Raise all the Lights.* Here the prompter whistles and the carpenters draw away the front flats to reveal *Scene 3ᵈ*: Comus' "stately palace, set out with all manner of deliciousness," as Milton describes it. It is a deep scene, made up of wings in the 2ⁿᵈ, 3ʳᵈ grooves and back flats in the 4ᵗʰ *Gr.* There are two tables *R & L*; Comus is at the right, the Lady in an enchanted chair near the center.

Some of the rabble are *disc^d R & L* and *Several of the Rabble, Enter, R & L,–1st Ents,–at change of Scene,—and fill up, in front.* A chorus is sung, *All pointing to the Lady,* the words being the second stanza of the first song from *Arcades:* "Mark what radiant state she spreads . . . Sitting like a goddess bright In the centre of her light." At the end of the chorus *Lady attempts to rise—Comus prevents her / by presenting his charming-rod,—All the Rabble,—in action,—request her to sit.*

Helen Faucit remembered the staging of this scene, like that of the forest scene, as

The very place the poet must have pictured to himself . . . so far as I could see it from the enchanted chair, in which the Lady sits spellbound. It was a kind of Aladdin's garden, all aglow with light and colour. And then the rabble-rout, so gay, so variously clad, some like Hebes, some like hags; figures moving to and fro, some beautiful as Adonis, others like Fauns, and bearded Satyrs. Add to this the weird fascination of the music, the rich melody, the rampant joyousness, the tipsy jollity! All served to quicken in me the feeling with which the poet has inspired the lonely "Lady," when she sees herself without means of escape, surrounded by a rabble-rout full of wine and riot, and abandoned to shameless revelry. I lost myself in the reality of the situation, and found the poet's words flow from me as though they had sprung from my own heart.[22]

Just before Comus offers her his cup of "cordial julep," he *directs one of his Bacchantes or Bacchanals to sing to her. Song. / "H. Phillips." / L /*, the words being garnered from "L'Allegro":

Haste thee nymph and bring with thee,
Jest and youthful jollity,
Sport that wrinkled care derides,
And laughter holding both his sides.

The Chorus repeats the song, and when the cup is presented *All, in action, request her to drink.* Except for the musical expansions, the scene is of course severely cut (from 155 lines to 72), so that it hews to the hard line of theatrical action: temptation and resistance. Thus stripped down, the scene reminds one of a nineteenth-century Temperance melodrama. Will she or will she not let the villain persuade her to that first fatal glass? It is theatrically expectable, too, that in the cutting of lines the Lady should win the battle of words: of Comus' major temptation speech he speaks but 12 lines out of 50; the Lady resists with 28 lines out of 44. "I could never speak these lines,"

---

[22] Faucit, pp. 329–31.

says Helen Faucit, "without a thrill that seemed to dilate my whole frame, and to give an unwonted fulness and vibration to the tones of my voice." Bound as she was by the magician's spell, so that she could not move a muscle, yet "the revellers near my chair upon the stage told me, the morning after the first representation, that they were struck by awe; that my whole appearance seemed to become so completely transfigured under the influence of my emotion, that they would not have been amazed if the chair with the Lady in it had been swept upwards out of sight to some holier sphere." Even Dr. Johnson found this portion of the play "animated and affecting," and perhaps Macready's scissoring of the speeches provided enough of the "brisker reciprocation of objections and replies" which Johnson thought was wanting.[23]

After line 813, when "The Brothers rush in [from the left] with swords drawn, wrest his glass out of his hand, and break it against the ground," the prompter is ready to signal for several effects, *All done together!* These are to

> *# #*
> *# Work CRASHES and Iron braces R & L*
> *Double check &—/ W.–/*
> */ to sink tables, Scene &c /*
> *Put all the Lights down, Green mediums on*

As the resisting rout are driven off right and left, and just before the Attendant Spirit enters from the left, workers under the stage answer the "Check" by causing the two tables to sink out of sight, opening the "sliders" (a long trap across the back of the stage, probably in front of the fourth grooves), and thrusting up some sort of "ground row" to represent a river bank;[24] meanwhile those in the wings draw off the wings and flats that represent the "stately palace"; and those in the fly-gallery lower a landscape backdrop. Thus in an instant or two the scene is changed *To the Banks of the Severn.* The Lady, of course, *remains enchanted in her chair* in the center of the stage, and when the Spirit scolds the Brothers for not having seized the enchanter's wand, without which she must sit "In stony fetters fixed

---

[23] Johnson, I, 169.

[24] The prompt-book does not here mention the opening of the sliders or the raising of the ground row to create the river. A possible, or probable, alternative is that the river was presented farther upstage, in the space in front of the fifth grooves; in that case it would already have been set up, and would simply be "discovered" by the withdrawal of the fourth groove palace flats.

and motionless," the Brothers at stage right exhibit *Expression of grief, &c.*

The Spirit, at stage left, describes Sabrina, the nymph of the Severn, in a dozen lines, sings the "Sabrina fair" song, and in 10 lines invokes her to appear. Meanwhile all the chorus have gone aloft behind the scenes / *for Finale, in "flies"* /. At line 888, just before "Listen and save!" the prompter is to # *Check below, to raise Sabrina, and Water Nymphs / at back C* / . She rises up *in waters* bearing a conch shell, with six nymphs attending her. If music is supposed to cover this splendid event, it is not indicated in the prompt-book; and— quite unaccountably, for the Miss Romer who played Sabrina was a famous vocalist—the lovely song, "By the rushy-fringed bank," is deleted.[25] Sabrina *advˢ to front, L C.* as the Spirit implores her to set free the "true virgin here distressed." At this point the prompter orders # *White fires ready, R & L.* Sabrina's actions as she fulfills the office of disenchantment are as follows: at line 909 she *goes up to chair C;* at 910, *In action, sprinkles water, from a conch shell, which she brings on with her;* at 914, *touching the Lady's fingers & lips, 3ᶜᵉ, with the water;* at 917, *lays both her hands, on the sides of the chair.* At line 918, *The Lady leaves the chair, and goes to her brothers,–R— who embrace her.* The prompter is at once to # *Pull CHECK below, imm'y to sink chair;* and as Sabrina steps back upon her elevator platform in the middle of the river, he is to

Check above—to take up "Severn Cloth," very slow!—
  And
# #
 # *Check below, to lower her and the Water Nymphs*
  Then
 / W /

when they are down, for last Sc—and to send forward Slote, w̄ Glory, from back, for Spirit.

# #

As he whistles he is also to # *Raise border lights, a little!*

The last scene is not Milton's "Ludlow Town, and the President's Castle" (indeed, at line 946, the Spirit *points off L* to indicate "your Father's residence"); and the presentation of the children to their parents and the country dance that is called for are entirely omitted.

---

[25] This song had been omitted in the 1815 abridgment.

Apparently the scene is a night skyscape (reminiscent of the opening "Abyss of Space"), hanging behind the "Severn Cloth," with a Glory Arch—that is, a circle of illuminated clouds—hung in front of it. The Slote is a part of the Glory Arch—a cloud-festooned platform and frame sufficiently big for the Attendant Spirit to ride in, and so rigged that it could be detached from the Glory Arch and thrust forward toward the center of the stage.[26] At line 957, the Spirit *Gets on to the end of Slote*, and *The Lady and her Brothers, advance, hand-in-hand —to the C—and kneel to the Spirit,—their backs to the audience.* By way of epilogue the Spirit speaks lines 976–79 ("To the ocean . . . broad fields of the sky") and then lines 970–75 ("Heaven hath timely . . . O'er Folly and Intemperance"), and sings the last six lines of the poem ("Mortals, that would follow me . . . Heaven itself would stoop to her"). *As the Spirit comm⁸ Song, Work Slote / with her, / very slowly, a'X waters &c,—back to Glory Arch.* As the song ends, the *Chorus / of Spirits / In the flies /* repeats the last four lines and the prompter directs his men to # *Take up Glory Arch, and Raise Border Lights*—and *Light all the White fires R & L.*

CURTAIN

To the Miltonist the ending of Macready's version will seem an almost criminal sacrifice of poetry to spectacle: of Milton's last 100 lines only 26 were sung or spoken. To the theatre-goer of 1843, on the other hand, who only the season before had luxuriated in the profusely magical effects of Madame Vestris' so-called *Comus*, it would have seemed either worthily "classical" or merely "tame." Compare, for instance, the simple stepping forward of Macready's Sabrina with the arrival of the Madame, who, playing Sabrina herself, "appeared at the head of the waterfall, immersed in the cup of a lily up to the shoulders, and in this fairy skiff floated over the fall and descended to the stage"![27] The popular appetite for spectacle is reflected (and dismissed) by Mrs. Samuel Carter Hall, who for her own part found Macready's *Comus* "charming." To Helen Faucit she wrote, "The

---

[26] According to *The Oxford Companion to the Theatre* the Slote as a device for conveying persons was invented by Charles Kean (in the 1850's) "so that the angels in *Faust* and *Henry VIII* should be without wires." Obviously it was in use at Drury Lane in 1843, and since there is no reason to believe it was invented for this *Comus* production, it is probably of much earlier origin.

[27] Vandenhoff, pp. 59–61.

people, I imagine, expected a fireworky finale; but Mr. Macready's pure taste is right. The elevated character of the sublime poet requires that it should end as it did."[28]

The reviewers paid relatively scant attention to this *Comus*— partly, I suppose, because it first appeared on the same bill with Macready's controversial Benedick in *Much Ado*.[29] Thus, the critic of *John Bull* was so infuriated by Benedick that he could not make himself stay to see *Comus;* and for the *Examiner* Charles Dickens wrote so long and excited a defense of Benedick that he could manage only a gasping sentence in praise of the afterpiece. The *Athenaeum* delivered a brief paragraph of generalized approval of it as a "classic spectacle," objecting only that the whoops of the bacchanalians during the dance "remind one too strongly of the Highland reel." The *Times* critic totally failed to recognize Macready's effort at restoration of the text, and put it down as "much the same as that which used to be performed some ten years ago." Beyond that he praised all the performers, giving especial attention to Macready's great directorial talent in creating the wild disorder, drunken dancing, and "sensual indolence" of the rabble rout; and he found the view of the river "a very beautiful scene, far superior to any which we have witnessed for a long time at this theatre."

By far the most interesting account that I have seen appeared in the *Spectator*, written, I would guess, not by a regular staff critic, but by an old and experienced theatre-goer who was also a devotee of Milton. He reminds us that at no staging of *Comus* do we hear the masque that Milton wrote, and that Dr. Johnson's carping censure of it is beside the point, for it was never intended for the public theatre. He reviews the stage history of *Comus*, from Dalton to Colman to Madame Vestris' "most disgraceful of all the revivals," and makes the point that the composer Thomas Arne was himself a London bacchanalian, well suited to set Dalton's naughty songs but totally incompatible with the spirit of Milton. It is plain that he remembers well the Covent Garden *Comus* of 1815, in which the new music by Bishop and the vocalizing of the whole company "was trumps": it was "the most perfect exhibition of *Comus* as an *opera*

---

[28] Sir Theodore Martin, *Helena Faucit* (London, 1900), p. 107.

[29] See the *Times* (London), 25 February 1843; and *John Bull, Examiner, Athenaeum* and *Spectator*, all of 4 March 1843. For Dickens' authorship of the *Examiner* review see the *Catalogue* of the Forster Collection, p. 31.

that had ever been given. . . . But it was anything but the *Comus* of Milton." As for the present revival, "Macready's version indicates the taste and feeling of a scholar—of one who desires to retain as much of Milton's text as he dares, but who distrusts the power of his company to utter and that of his audience to enjoy it. He has cast out the greater portion of the added songs,—regarding them, probably, as unseemly excrescences; but he has also left but a fragment of the original poem." Although one of Henry Lawes' songs is said to have been retained, the writer failed to recognize it, though he claims to be "tolerably familiar" with Lawes' music. He speculates on the availability of Milton to contemporary audiences in view of the fact that he is read, in cheap editions, "by hundreds now where he was read by tens a century ago"; but he concludes nevertheless that Macready's reduction of the poem was discreet: "as much of recitation was given as it was prudent to give." The reason for the reduction is the fault of the actors, who have only "a very faint perception of the sweetness and majesty of Milton's verse." Milton's lyrical ear was perfect, but these actors ("our young ladies and gentlemen," he condescendingly calls them) can only "bandy" the verse "from mouth to mouth in pert and flippant dialogue." They "regard *Comus* as they regard any other play they have to enact, and deal with it accordingly. They look for 'points' and 'effects'—they seek out for lines and phrases which shall produce thunders of applause: and failing to find, they strive to make them. They are mistaken." He singles out Miss Faucit, alas, as "the chief offender," and asserts that she has "neither the tongue, demeanour, nor address of *a* Lady, much less of *the* Lady of *Comus*." He praises the scenery and the disposition and grouping of the performers: "The classic eye and feeling of the manager pervade all that is concerned with display. The spectator has nothing to desire—the auditor much." There has been no perfect exhibition of *Comus* yet, and probably there never will be.

By now, more than a century later, there have been many more stagings of *Comus*, and I suppose more of them have followed Macready's way with the text than John Dalton's. But it is not likely that this crotchety *Spectator* essayist would yet have had to eat his words. For the special beauty of Milton's poem comes to us better in the study than in the theatre. Yet Macready in his time did what a scholar and gentleman, who was also an actor, might be expected to do to "restore" it to the stage.

THE TEXT OF MACREADY'S COMUS

The lines deleted, the words altered, the transpositions, and the insertions are here listed. Numbers standing alone are lines to be deleted. Half-line deletions are indicated by words in parentheses.

Delete the opening stage direction; insert at head of text stanza xiii of "On the Morning of Christ's Nativity," with these three alterations: our human ears > our raptured ears—to touch our senses so > to gladden Spirits so—And let your > Now let your; 4; 6 (and with)–30; insert "But here my errand is"; 33 An > This; 34 Where > And; 36 delete "And new intrusted sceptre"; 37 Lies > Lying; 38–41; 42 Was > am; 43–62; insert here 520–22; 63 Excels > Who 'bove; 64 Offering > Offers; 67; 71–75; 76 And all > And they; 77 To > And; 85 this > their; 86–91; insert "But hark! the tread"; after 110 insert song beginning "Now Phoebus sinketh in the west, Welcome song and welcome jest" and repeating lines 103–106, with choral repetition of 105–106; 119–26 is a song, of which the fourth and eighth lines are repeated in chorus; transpose 127 and 128; 129–33; insert "Dark-veiled Cotytto, mystic Dame"; after 144 insert song which is lines 33–34 of "L'Allegro"; 151 (I shall)–153 (Circe); 156 (lest)–164; insert "When her eye"; 167; 168 (I fairly)–169; 173–77 (amiss); 179 such late > boisterous; 183–84; 188–90, 192 ('Tis)–200.

211–16; 217 That He > For He; 223 (there)–224; 225 And > It; 228 venter > venture; 238–41; 246–48; 249 they > it; 254–55; 257 (Scylla)–261; 266; 267 Unless > Or else; 271 (ill)–273 (skill); insert "naught"; 281–82; 285–86; 293–96; 307–10; 314; 315 attendance > attendants; 326 (In a)–328; after 330 insert song which is lines 93–96 of "L'Allegro"; 336–49; 350 But, Oh, that > Oh, me, that; 352–56; 357 Or > E'en; 361–65; 368; 370; 372; 375 (And Wisdom's)–380; 386–405; insert "Yet ah! I fear"; 407 (I do)–413; 414 My > Our; 422–52; 462 (But)–480 (reigns); 482 delete "For certain"; 497 (Hath)–500; 502 such a > any; 503–506; 513 ('Tis)–539; insert "night by night within this wood Comus's monstrous rout are heard to howl"; 543–48; 550–54; 557 (that)–560 (displaced); 565–67; 569; 573; 575–78; insert "I durst not stay, but swift away I sprung"; 580 delete "But furder know I not"; 585–88; 593–99 (But).

602 (let)–609; insert "Oh! good youth"; 610 yet > well; 611–48; after 658 insert Song II from *Arcades* with these four alterations: delete second "Follow me,"—Clad in splendour > in beauty's splendour—Her deity > A deity—hath not > ne'er hath; after stage direction insert Song I, stanza 2, from *Arcades* with this alteration: This, this is she alone > This, this is she, is she alone; after 669 insert song which is lines 25–26, 31–32 of "L'Allegro," the whole quatrain being repeated in chorus; 670–71; 672 first > now; 675–78; 680 (which)–687; 694 (What)–695; 697–700; 702 (None)–705; 707–708; 709 Praising the > To praise of; 712–13; 715–20 (with); 725–36; 740–61; 773; 776 (for)–779 (Feeder); 784–89.

802–805 (crew); 806 delete "And try her yet more strongly"; 807–808; 812 in > with; 817; 821–23; 827–28; 831 Commended > Commending; 832–40; 841 And > Straight; 842 (Still)–852 (said); 855–57 (need); 869–76;

879–82; in stage direction delete "and sings"; 890–901; in stage direction after 921 delete "and the lady rises out of her seat"; 922–38 (Come); 939 Let us fly > Fly from—cursed > accursed; 940 us > you; 942–45; 946 And > See—thence > hence; 948–53; 956 Come, let us > Thither; delete stage direction; 958–69; 970–71 their > your; 972 them > you; transpose 970–75 to follow 979; delete stage direction; 980–1017; 1018–23 is a song of which 1020–23 is repeated in chorus.

MILTON'S IDLE RIGHT HAND

Ernest Sirluck, The University of Chicago

In 1642 Milton found that his participation in the ecclesiastical controversy was being "imputed" to a "self-pleasing humor of vainglory . . . to contest with men of high estimation." He denies that it is so. He does not, of course, deny that he hopes one day to earn an honest fame by his writings, but he gives reasons to show that if he "were wise only to [his] own ends" he would not be writing pamphlets against episcopacy. Of these reasons the most important is that "if I hunted after praise" "I should not chuse this manner of writing [i.e., "the cool element of prose"] wherin knowing my self inferior to my self, led by the genial power of nature to another task, I have the use, as I may account it, but of my left hand." He then gives the famous account of his preparation to write poetry "doctrinal and exemplary to a Nation," asserts that "none hath by more studious ways endeavor'd [the accomplishment of such intentions], and with more unwearied spirit that none shall," covenants with the "knowing reader, that for some few yeers yet I may go on trust with him toward the payment of what I am now indebted," and trusts that he has hereby made it "manifest with what small willingnesse I endure to interrupt the pursuit of no lesse hopes then these . . . to imbark in a troubl'd sea of noises and hoars disputes."[1]

We accept all this (within the limits which we instinctively associate with polemical self-portraiture) because much of it is demonstrably true, and the rest is in the highest degree characteristic and probable. We know that Milton had at an early age committed himself with high ambition to the calling of poet, that he had for many years trained and disciplined himself for it, and that in the period immediately before the anti-episcopal pamphlets he had at last been closing in upon his subject: he had been systematically surveying both the Bible and early British history for suitable material, had compiled a list of possible topics, and worked up enough notes on some of them to make it clear that he was thinking about them seriously. One topic in particular received a good deal of attention: we have four separate drafts for a tragedy to be called *Paradise Lost* or *Adam Unparadised*,

---

[1] *Reason of Church-Government;* Columbia *Milton*, III, 234–41. When not otherwise indicated, references to the text of Milton are to this edition.

and Milton had actually begun to write verses for it (although beginning the drama with what is now Satan's soliloquy in Book IV does not fit any of the drafts we possess). So immersed was he in his poetic plans that they broke into the foreground of four of the five anti-episcopal pamphlets.[2] Perhaps we may suspect that Milton may not have been wholly unwilling a little to intermit the strain of creative "labour and intent study"[3] with the exhilaration of banging the bishops about, but we can hardly doubt his proclaimed reluctance to endure a serious interruption to his poetic enterprises. Hence we accept, in good faith, the image of a dedicated poet longing to get on with his great enterprise but impelled by his conscience to set it aside for a while because the church needs his instant service—a service in which he cannot work at full strength, has, as it were, the use of only his left hand, but thinks that in some respects that left is more effective than the collective right hand of Smectymnuus; and I think we are right to accept this image.

But then, and not without a great deal of help from Milton's other writings, we vastly extend the image's scope. The interruption would not after all be a brief one; the "few years" for which Milton had covenanted with the knowing reader stretched to a quarter-century before that worthy's patience would be rewarded with *Paradise Lost*. In understanding how the interruption grew so protracted, we have taken our cue from the *Second Defence* of 1654. There, looking back over his pamphleteering career, Milton sees no gaps, no intermissions of battle when the poet might have returned to his poetry; just one campaign after another in the wars of liberty. After the bishops had been defeated and the church delivered from "the yoke of slavery and superstition," Milton perceived that there were two further species of essential liberty, the domestic and the civil. The "magistrates" were looking after the latter, so he turned to the former, and since it involved "three material questions" he wrote, in turn, the divorce tracts, *Of Education*, and *Areopagitica*. Then it became necessary to turn to "civil" (i.e., political) liberty, and he wrote the *Tenure*. Thereafter, when he thought that he was to enjoy "an interval of uninterrupted ease," he was "surprised by an invitation" to become Secretary for Foreign Tongues, and, as Secretary, was ordered, among other things, to write *Eikonoklastes* and the *Defences of the English People*.[4]

---

[2] In addition to the passage in *Church-Government* already discussed, see *Of Reformation* (III, 78), *Animadversions* (III, 148), and *Apology for Smectymnuus* (III, 302–304).

[3] *Church-Government;* III, 236.

[4] Tr. Robert Fellowes; Bohn *Prose Works*, I, 258–61.

Guided so far by Milton's account, we easily extend its theme to cover the remaining years of the Puritan Revolution, and get the standard image of the dedicated poet at first postponing his poetic enterprise a little in the service of the church, but then, when reformation became revolution and crisis deepened into war, stoically foregoing the use of his poetic right hand for as long as necessity required him to ply his left in the Revolution's defense—which was until blindness earned him some respite, and finally defeat made the old warrior tragically impotent, but fortunately released the long-suffering poet to resume his creative labors. These labors, of course, have been profoundly affected by the experience of the intervening years: an Arthuriad has become impossible for the man so disillusioned about England, *Paradise Lost* is written as an epic rather than a dramatic poem, and there are a multitude of other changes; but the potential continuity was always there, the sense of a special calling and special equipment was uninterrupted, only the exigent needs of the great religious and political revolution to which he was committed kept the poet from his poetry.

And the facts of the left hand's productivity would at first sight seem to support this image. Between 1641 and 1660 Milton wrote some twenty-nine books and pamphlets, several in Latin; besides this, he had many official duties in the Council of State and for the Protectors; and during this time he suffered acutely from ill health, went blind, buried two wives and three children, and underwent a number of other pressures which interfered with his work. It would indeed seem that the left hand was fully and urgently occupied.

But it was not. If we apply a simple arithmetic and chronological test we find that while there is no reason to question the original image created by Milton, the extended image, encouraged by Milton but made by ourselves, does not correspond with the facts. The twenty-nine prose works are by no means evenly distributed through the twenty years. Not counting new editions which are substantially unchanged or only somewhat enlarged, but including the two radical revisions,[5] and using dates of publication except for the three works not published immediately upon completion,[6] we find that from May 1641 to April 1642 there were five pamphlets, from August 1643 to March 1645 there were seven, at some time during the next four years there was part of the *History of Britain*, during 1649 there were three

---

[5] *Doctrine and Discipline of Divorce* and *Readie and Easie Way.*

[6] *History of Britain, State Letters, Christian Doctrine.* I have not included the *Grammar* (1669), although it is possible that some work was done on this in the 1640's.

books or pamphlets and more of the *History of Britain,* as well as the first state papers and the beginning of other official duties, in 1651 there was one considerable book, a smaller one in 1654, a pamphlet in 1655; now or a little later the *Christian Doctrine* was begun; from February 1659 to April 1660 there are eight pamphlets.

What we have here is not unremitting, urgent labor of the left hand for twenty years but an initial controversial undertaking lasting a year; then a silence[7] of fifteen months; then a new burst of activity lasting about twenty months; then near silence for four years; then renewed activity for something over two years; then for about three years nothing except a greatly reduced official load; then increased activity for about two years, followed by three years in which there is some reduction of prose work but, when the distribution of the State Letters and the composition of the *Christian Doctrine* are taken into account, not as much as at first appears; and then a final burst of activity lasting just over a year.

What about the periods when the left hand was unengaged?

The question becomes even more urgent if we look more carefully at the passage in the *Second Defence* which has been so instrumental in causing us to extend the image of the reluctantly-interrupted poet created by Milton in the *Reason of Church-Government.* After he has completed his account of "the fruits of my private studies, which I gratuitously presented to the church and to the state" down to and including the *Tenure,* he says: "When I was released from these engagements, and thought that I was about to enjoy an interval of uninterrupted ease, I turned my thoughts to. . . . " We recall his pledge of seven years earlier that when "life and free leisure" will permit, and when the land is "once infranchis'd . . . from this impertinent yoke of prelaty, under whose inquisitorious and tyrannical duncery no free and splendid wit can flourish," none shall "with more unwearied spirit" than himself endeavor to accomplish the great poem "doctrinal and exemplary to a Nation";[8] and then we read on in the *Second Defence:* "I turned my thoughts to a continued history of my country, from the earliest times to the present period."[9] He turned to the *History of Britain,* with its apologetic explanation of why he has de-

---

[7] We are speaking of prose works. Of course during the two decades under consideration Milton wrote sixteen sonnets and a little occasional verse in other forms, and translated two groups of psalms; *Poems 1645,* except for three sonnets of this period, had been written before the anti-episcopal pamphlets.

[8] *Church-Government;* III, 240.

[9] Bohn, I, 260–61.

cided "to bestow the telling over ev'n of these reputed Tales,"[10] the history which in fact he never brought beyond the Norman Conquest, and which he did not trouble to publish until 1670! And what about the earlier periods of leisure after the two bursts of activity? He does not mention them.

Milton does not mean, really, to mislead us; he is accounting here for what he wrote, not for what he did not write; but we have been misled all the same, with our image of the dedicated poet sacrificing his poetic plans to the relentless and unremitting exigencies of the twenty-year-long Revolution. Milton's left hand was by no means in constant demand; when it was unengaged, why did he not use his right?

Let us start by narrowing the enquiry. The absence of new publications between mid-1655 and early 1659 does not really pose our problem. It is not merely that this is the period of Milton's most numerous and some of his most important state papers, but more, it is the time when he was working on the *Christian Doctrine*—a task probably amounting for him to a precondition for his poem—and when he did in fact at last return to his projected *Paradise Lost*.

Nor does it seem helpful to ask why Milton was silent[11] for the three years from the spring of 1651 to the spring of 1654. It was during this period that he fell into prolonged and severe ill-health, went totally blind, lost his wife and a child, had to be relieved of most of his official duties, went into a rather deep depression, and finally roused himself and wrote the *Second Defence*. This period will, I think, have something to tell us later on, but it hardly seems necessary to ask why he did not at this time take up the work of his right hand.

It is the silences[12] of the first decade which pose our problem most acutely. He was doing nothing urgent during them, nothing, so far as we know, of any immediate importance. This inactivity has drawn attention to itself, and has given rise to suggestions that it may have been at these times, rather than after the Restoration, that *Samson Agonistes* was written; but the argument will not bear examination.[13] The sole strength of these suggestions is the obvious and disturbing

---

[10] Columbia, x, 3.

[11] Except for two, perhaps three, sonnets and Psalms I–VII.

[12] During the first Milton wrote Sonnet VIII, during the second Sonnets XI–XIV (IX–X probably precede the publication of the final divorce tracts), "New Forcers," and "Ad Rousium"—all occasional or complimentary pieces—and translated Psalms LXXX–LXXXVIII.

[13] See Appendix, Section I, following.

emptiness of these years, but the emptiness cannot be filled with *Samson Agonistes*. It is during these two silent periods that it is most surprising that Milton's well-trained and -prepared right hand did not resume its labors, and it is here that we must look for our clue.

Let us recall the sequence of events. Back from his continental tour, Milton settled in London and prepared to come to grips with his poetic ambitions. He made a list of possible topics, worked some of them up a little, and seems to have got one in particular, *Paradise Lost*, actually under way. Then, either asked by the Smectymnuans to contribute the "Postscript" to their *Answer to the Humble Remonstrance* or otherwise brought into the controversy about episcopacy, he feels impelled by conscience to interrupt for a time the work for which he has been preparing all his adult life in order to do his duty to the church. One pamphlet leads to another and Milton cannot easily get back to his poetry; this troubles him, and he talks about it a good deal, especially in the fourth and fifth pamphlets. At last, after a year, the duty is discharged and he is free. It is now April 1642. Does he return to his poetry?

No. Instead, he gets married.

I believe that Milton's marriage and its failure hold the solution to our problem. What I am going to suggest is that Milton's concept of his role as a poet developed in such a way as to make the failure of his marriage a direct blow to his poetic inspiration (or, what amounts to the same thing, to his faith in it).

Let us review this development, not from the beginning (for that would take too long, and anyway the earliest stages are not especially pertinent here), but from the crucial Christmas season of 1629. Since Hanford's indispensable pioneering discussion[14] of the poems of this period as Milton's coming-of-age stock-taking of himself and dedication to the calling of poet, together with the superb firstfruit of that dedication, much has been added to our understanding of what took place in Milton's mind. We see him in Prolusion II, probably written not long before his twenty-first birthday,[15] securely possessing himself of the Pythagorean and Platonic doctrine that the celestial spheres make a heavenly music audible only to the pure. We may also, I think, see him working this notion into usable form by annexing to it such

---

[14] "The Youth of Milton," *Studies in Shakespeare, Milton and Donne* (New York, 1925), pp. 89–163.
[15] E. M. W. and Phyllis B. Tillyard, *Milton's Private Correspondence and Academic Exercises* (Cambridge, Eng., 1932), pp. xxv-xxix.

interpretations of the Promethean disobedience and of the golden age as almost inevitably become metaphors for the fall of man and the millennium:

Moreover, the boldness of the thieving Prometheus seems to be the reason why we hear so little this harmony, a deed which brought upon humanity so many ills and likewise took away this happiness from us, which we shall never be permitted to enjoy so long as we remain brutish and overwhelmed by wicked animal desires; for how can those be susceptible of that heavenly sound whose souls, as Persius says, are bent toward the earth and absolutely devoid of celestial matters? But if we possessed hearts so pure, so spotless, so snowy, as once upon a time Pythagoras had, then indeed would our ears be made to resound and to be completely filled with that most delicious music of the revolving stars; and then all things would return immediately as it were to that golden age; then, at length, freed from miseries we should spend our time in peace, blessed and envied even by the gods.[16]

Just after Christmas Milton writes Elegy VI, which reads almost like a manifesto. Diodati had sent him some verses and had purported to deprecate their quality on the ground of the seasonal festivities. Milton, of course, meets politeness with politeness: "Why do you complain that poetry absents itself from wine and feasting? Song loves Bacchus and Bacchus loves song." For the makers of "light Elegy," "bountiful feasts are permitted, and frequent draughts of old wine." But there are other, nobler kinds of poetry, and from those who would write them something different is required.

But the poet who sings of wars and of heaven subject now to mature Jove, and of pious heroes and leaders half divine, who sings now of the sacred conferences of the high gods, now of the abysmal realms where barks a savage dog, that poet should live sparingly as did the Samian teacher and should find in herbs his simple food. Let the crystal water stand beside him in a beechen cup, and let him drink only sober draughts from a pure spring. Let him have, in addition, a youth chaste and free from evil, uncompromising standards, and stainless hands.[17]

This, clearly, is the moment to which Milton was referring when he wrote, in *An Apology*,

And long it was not after, when I was confirm'd in this opinion, that he who would not be frustrate of his hope to write well hereafter in laudable things, ought him selfe to bee a true Poem, that is, a composition, and patterne of the best and honourablest things; not presuming to sing high praises of heroick men, or famous Cities, unlesse he have in himselfe the experience and the practice of all that which is praiseworthy.[18]

[16] Tr. Bromley Smith; Columbia, XII, 157.
[17] Tr. Nelson G. McCrea; *Student's Milton*, ed. F. A. Patterson (1939), pp. 91–92.
[18] Columbia, III, 303–304.

But Elegy VI does not leave the matter at the ethical level. It continues, "Such is your character, augur, when, bright with sacred vestments and lustral waters, you rise to approach the angry gods. . . . For the poet is sacred to the gods and is their priest."

Then, abruptly, Milton declares, in effect, that he is talking about himself:

But if you shall desire to know what I am doing . . . I am hymning the king of heavenly lineage, prince of peace, and the happy days promised by the sacred books; the wailing of the Christ child and the stabling under a poor roof of Him who rules, together with his Father, the realms on high; and the starry heavens and the hosts that sang in the upper air and the gods suddenly shattered in their own shrines. This is my gift to the birthday of Christ, the first rays of its dawn brought the theme to me.[19]

The "Nativity Ode" is the inspired rendition of these themes. The heavenly choir which promulgates the Nativity makes such music as was never made before except by that other heavenly choir which sang the creation; and in telescoping the familiar pair of Biblical phrases describing that earlier occasion "When the morning stars sang together, and all the sons of God shouted for joy"[20] into the single phrase in the line "When of old the sons of morning sung" (evoking the Hebraic tradition that the stars were angels), Milton forges a link with the music of the spheres, which are invited to join their music to that of the stars:

> Ring out ye Crystall sphears,
> Once bless our human ears,
>   (If ye have power to touch our senses so)
> And let your silver chime
> Move in melodious time;
>   And let the Base of Heav'ns deep Organ blow,
>   And with your ninefold harmony
> Make up full consort to th'Angelike symphony. (ll. 125–32)

The mathematical preconditions for harmony are satisfied by the correspondence between the nine ranks in the angelic hierarchy and the nine spheres. But the tradition[21] (invoked explicitly in *Arcades*, ll. 62

---

[19] *Student's Milton*, p. 92.
[20] Job 38:7.
[21] In Plutarch's *Symposiacs*, IX, 14 ("Some Observations about the Number of the Muses, not commonly known"), one of the disputants points out that Plato "committed the Revolutions of the eight Spheres to so many *Sirens*, and not Muses." Another replies that "*Plato* is absurd" in this because Daemons are not benevolent to mankind. A third says that the Sirens in Homer are not hurtful but delightful, and, confused by this, Plato "strangely and unaccountably . . . named the Muses *Sirens*." Eight of them

ff., and implicitly here) that each sphere was presided over by one of the nine muses prepares a path for the poet's participation in the music of the Nativity, as he invokes the "Heav'nly Muse" for aid in providing some verse, or hymn, or solemn strain "To welcome him to this his new abode." Another path lies not by way of the muses and the spheres but directly through the angelic choir. In that covenant with the knowing reader with which we began, Milton used the experience of Isaiah to explain what must be the source of inspired utterance: "that eternall Spirit who can enrich with all utterance and knowledge, and sends out his Seraphim with the hallow'd fire of his Altar to touch and purify the lips of whom he pleases."[22] Thus, if the Nativity poet can join his voice

> unto the Angel Quire,
> From out his secret Altar toucht with hallow'd fire (ll. 27–28)

it is because his lips, like Isaiah's, have been purged by God, and thus consecrated in His service.

I will not argue (although I think it not unlikely) that in thus dedicating himself, as he comes of age, God's poet, and (in the metaphorical sense) priest, he has already decided not to become a priest in the literal sense. But the elements of that decision are all present in this dedication of his poetic talent to God's service.

Milton's next poem, "The Passion," probably written during the following Lent, is, as the opening lines make clear, conceived as a companion-piece to the "Nativity Ode," celebrating another event in the life of Christ; that is, Milton is attempting to discharge the duties of a dedicated poet of God. But the thing is no good. Milton saw that it was no good, left it unfinished, and cultivated other veins, producing some wonderful successes, such as "On Shakespeare," "L'Allegro," and "Il Penseroso." But it is most interesting that when, fifteen years later, he published his first collection of poems, he included the unsuccessful fragment on "The Passion," complete with the apologetic and deprecatory note about being "nothing satisfi'd with what was begun." Why, if he was dissatisfied, should he have published it? I think it is because from the outset he had something of a con-

---

take care of the spheres, and the ninth "looks after the Place betwixt the Earth and Moon." But from this Plutarch dissents, suggesting a different disposition of the ninth muse: "let us place in Heaven, and over heavenly things, one of the Muses *viz. Urania*" (*Plutarch's Morals:* Translated from the Greek by Several Hands, 5th ed., 5 vols. [London, 1718], III, 474–80).

[22] Columbia, III, 241. Cf. Isaiah 6:5–7.

science about his decision not to take orders, and was unwilling to dispense with any bit of the meager evidence that he had been God's servant in another guise. Surely there is some uneasiness in the document from which we first learn explicitly of this decision, the "Letter to a Friend" written soon after Milton's twenty-third birthday.[23] That the decision has now been taken seems to me the inescapable inference from the additions in the second draft of the letter. What the friend admonished Milton about must have been his failure to take orders, for when Milton interrupts the flow of his self-justification with a jest, it is to say that unless he stops he will "doe that which I excuse my selfe for not doing preach & not preach." And what is involved is not merely a postponement of ordination but a decision against it, for after Milton has written out for his friend the twenty-third birthday sonnet, composed "some while since," he makes another deprecatory jest. If he has not won his friend to his point, he has at least wearied him to it; "this therfore alone may be a sufficient reason for me to keepe me as I am least having thus tired you singly, I should deale worse with a whole congregation, & spoyle all the patience of a Parish."[24] The decision to "keep me as I am"—i.e., unordained—has been taken.[25] The friend's warning, based on the parable of the hidden talent, is answered with the help of another parable, that of the laborers in the vineyard of whom "those that were latest lost nothing." And there are also answers for the friend's detailed arguments. Against his suspicion that excessive love of learning is drawing him into a dream-life of retirement, Milton cites the many motives there are, and which he feels, for plunging into the world of action. And to the suggestion that his retirement may be due to a "naturall pronenesse," Milton replies: "there is against that a much more potent inclination & inbred which about this tyme of a mans life

[23] See Appendix, Section II, following.

[24] Columbia, XII, 325.

[25] Failure to recognize the earnest beneath the jest leads to the conclusion that Milton was undecided, or partly disingenuous, or both. Thus Hanford ("Youth of Milton," p. 130): "the plain implication of the language [is] that he intends, when he is ready, to labor in the vineyard as a minister. It is possible, of course, that in the suggestion about a congregation and preaching Milton was maintaining a mental reservation, having already determined to interpret his ministry in terms of the poetic enunciation of divine truth. More probably he had not yet altogether abandoned the plan of entering the church. In any case, there is a misleading suppression of a part of his full mind, which we may regard as a characteristic manifestation of Miltonic strategy." Tillyard (*Milton* [London, 1930], p. 57) is uncertain "if indeed he had already decided to be a poet."

sollicits most, the desire of house & family of his owne." In short, Milton argues that the sole reason he is not yet visibly launched on his life's work is that he has not yet completed his preparations for so high an enterprise. "Yet," he writes, "that you may see that I am something suspicious of my selfe . . . I . . . send you some of my nightward thoughts some while since"; and here he transcribes the sonnet "How soon hath Time," in which he pledges to use his talent "As ever in my great task Masters eye."[26]

And in fact the three poems which follow show that he was attempting to direct his talent in accordance with his original dedication and its recent reiteration. "On Time" presents the contrast of the "meerly mortal dross" which exists in time with the perfect joy of the eternity which will succeed the Second Coming. "Upon the Circumcision," which, like "The Passion," begins with a reference to the "Nativity Ode," celebrates another event in the life of Christ. "At a Solemn Musick" moves from religious song to the imaginative contemplation of the angelic choir which eternally sings before the throne of heaven, accompanied by "those just Spirits that wear victorious Palms," in the hope that this contemplation will enable the poet rightly to answer to that "Song of pure concent," as men once did, before sin broke "natures chime."

This poem is, I believe, now being very widely misinterpreted to antedate by about five years a very important development in Milton's thought and art.

It was Tillyard who, in 1930, introduced the interpretation I have to challenge, which is, in brief, that the poem gives us "a hint of the doctrine that chastity is the means of hearing the celestial music."[27] Beginning with the declaration that the "Song of pure concent" is the singing of Plato's celestial sirens, Tillyard goes on to say that "the Platonic music of the spheres is identified with the song sung before the throne in the *Book of Revelation* . . . [which] is not only referred to several times in Milton's poems, but is cited in the *Apology for Smectymnuus* as one of the passages which particularly affected him in his practice of chastity."[28] He then quotes Revelation 14: 1–5, which had better be transcribed here as well:

And I looked, and, lo, a Lamb stood on the mount Sion, and with him an hundred forty and four thousand, having his Father's name written in their

[26] Columbia, XII, 323–25.
[27] *Milton*, p. 376.
[28] *Milton*, p. 377.

foreheads. And I heard a voice from heaven, as the voice of many waters, and as the voice of a great thunder: and I heard the voice of harpers harping with their harps: And they sung as it were a new song before the throne, and before the four beasts, and the elders: and no man could learn that song but the hundred and forty and four thousand, which were redeemed from the earth. These are they which were not defiled with women; for they are virgins. These are they which follow the Lamb whithersoever he goeth. These were redeemed from among men, being the firstfruits unto God and to the Lamb. And in their mouth was found no guile: for they are without fault before the throne of God.

Tillyard then continues:

The 'just spirits' in line thirteen of *At a Solemn Music* are these 'men [*sic*] without fault before the throne of God.' It is this making of chastity the condition of hearing and learning the song before the throne that gives a new turn to the ideas we are discussing. Milton had supposed that a heart of snowy purity could hear the music of the Spheres, but the music is no other than the song sung by the one hundred and forty-four thousand men in heaven, and chastity was the condition of their learning it. It follows then that chastity is the magic means of hearing the planetary music likewise, the means of supernatural powers in this life.[29]

Tillyard explains the consequence for the interpretation of *Comus* of this "uncommon theory of virginity . . . *deduced from a previous poem,*"[30] and then turns to Milton's statement, in *An Apology*, repudiating the charge that he was a haunter of bordellos and setting forth the means by which the idea of chastity grew upon him.

This that I have hitherto related, hath bin to shew, that though Christianity had bin but slightly taught me, yet a certain reserv'dnesse of naturall disposition, and morall discipline learnt out of the noblest Philosophy was anough to keep me in disdain of farre lesse incontinences then this of the Burdello. But having had the doctrine of holy Scripture unfolding those chaste and high mysteries with timeliest care infus'd, that *the body is for the Lord and the Lord for the body,* thus also I argu'd to my selfe; that if unchastity in a woman whom Saint Paul termes the glory of man, be such a scandall and dishonour, then certainly in a man who is both the image and glory of God, it must, though commonly not so thought, be much more deflouring and dishonourable. . . . Nor did I slumber over that place expressing such high rewards of ever accompanying the Lambe, with those celestiall songs to others inapprehensible, but not to those who were not defil'd with women, which doubtlesse meanes fornication: For mariage must not be call'd a defilement.[31]

---

[29] *Milton*, pp. 377–78.
[30] *Milton*, p. 378; my italics.
[31] Columbia, III, 305–306.

Of this Tillyard writes:

The end refers of course to the song sung in *Revelation* by the one hundred and forty-four thousand men who were not defiled with women, the song already identified in Milton's poetry with the music of the planets. The last sentence would seem to prove that Milton did not arrogate special powers to lifelong chastity. Certainly he did not in 1642 when he wrote the *Apology for Smectymnuus*, but eight years separate this work from *Comus*, during which his opinions may have changed. . . . I believe that at that time . . . Milton intended his celibacy to last his life.[32]

In 1937 Merritt Y. Hughes, in his widely used edition of the minor poems, adopted this identification of the "undisturbed Song of pure concent" with the "new song" of Revelation 14 which could be learned only by those "which were not defiled with women," although he rather confusingly referred the "just Spirits" to another place;[33] in his 1957 edition of the poems he refers everything to Revelation 14.[34] In 1941 Arthur Barker, in his very influential study of "The Pattern of Milton's *Nativity Ode*," also accepted this identification,[35] and it has since become commonplace.

Now this identification seems to me to rise from an anticipation of something unquestionably present in "Lycidas" and in *Epitaphium Damonis*—an anticipation helped, and indeed probably caused, by a peculiarity of the latter poem which will be noticed below. I can find nothing in the text of "A Solemn Musick" to link the "undisturbed Song of pure concent"[36] with the particular song of Revelation 14:1–5, or the "just Spirits that wear victorious Palms" with the hundred and forty and four thousand virgins. Indeed, if we turn to the seventh chapter of Revelation, where we are first introduced to the 144,000, we

---

[32] P. 380.

[33] *Paradise Regained, the Minor Poems, and Samson Agonistes* (New York, 1937), p. 207.

[34] *Complete Poems and Major Prose* (New York, 1957), p. 81.

[35] UTQ, x (1941), 179.

[36] Which, despite Tillyard's confident assertion, is not the song of Plato's celestial sirens. The syntax, while involved, is unambiguous: "That undisturbed Song of pure concent, Ay sung . . . With Saintly shout, . . . Where the bright Seraphim . . . Their . . . Angel trumpets blow, And the Cherubick host . . . Touch their . . . Harps, With those just Spirits . . . , Hymns devout and holy Psalms Singing everlastingly" (ll. 7–16). "Natures chime," unheard since the Fall, is not mentioned until lines 19–20. The "Blest pair of *Sirens*" with which the poem opens are not Plato's celestial sirens (which, as *Arcades*, ll. 62–67, informs us, numbered not two but nine, the original eight of *Republic*, 616–17 having been increased to nine and identified with the muses by Plutarch; see n. 21, above) but the "Sphear-born harmonious Sisters, Voice, and Vers," of the poem's second line.

find that the "victorious Palms" which are the principal individuating feature of Milton's "just Spirits" serve to mark them off from the 144,000. The Biblical writer here learns of two distinct groups. He does not see the first group, but hears of it, the angel who ascends from the east warning the four angels holding the four winds (Rev. 7:3–4),

Hurt not the earth, neither the sea, nor the trees, till we have sealed the servants of our God in their foreheads. And I heard the number of them which were sealed: and there were sealed an hundred and forty and four thousand of all the tribes of the children of Israel.

The angel goes on to give a precise census of the 144,000 (Rev. 7:5–8):

Of the tribe of Juda were sealed twelve thousand. Of the tribe of Reuben were sealed twelve thousand. Of the tribe of Gad were sealed twelve thousand. Of the tribe of Aser were sealed twelve thousand. Of the tribe of Nepthalim were sealed twelve thousand. Of the tribe of Manasses were sealed twelve thousand. Of the tribe of Simeon were sealed twelve thousand. Of the tribe of Levi were sealed twelve thousand. Of the tribe of Issachar were sealed twelve thousand. Of the tribe of Zabulon were sealed twelve thousand. Of the tribe of Joseph were sealed twelve thousand. Of the tribe of Benjamin were sealed twelve thousand.

The rubric for these first eight verses reads, "1. The four angels holding the four winds, and the angel who sealed the servants of God. 4. The number of the sealed." For the rest of the chapter it reads. "9. The multitude before the throne: their song. 13. Who they are." The text itself goes on (Rev. 7:9–15):

After this I beheld, and, lo, a great multitude, which no man could number, of all nations, and kindreds, and people, and tongues, stood before the throne, and before the Lamb, clothed with white robes and palms in their hands; And cried with a loud voice, saying, Salvation to our God which sitteth upon the throne, and unto the Lamb. And all the angels stood round about the throne, and about the elders and the four beasts, and fell before the throne on their faces, and worshipped God, Saying, Amen: Blessing, and glory, and wisdom, and thanksgiving, and honour, and power, and might, be unto our God for ever and ever. Amen. And one of the elders answered, saying unto me, What are these which are arrayed in white robes? and whence came they? And I said unto him, Sir, thou knowest. And he said to me, These are they which came out of great tribulation, and have washed their robes, and made them white in the blood of the Lamb. Therefore are they before the throne of God, and serve him day and night in his temple: and he that sitteth on the throne shall dwell among them.

The differentiation of the precisely enumerated twelve times twelve thousand children of Israel of the angel's speech who are to bear the special seal in their foreheads, but who are not yet seen, from the visible multitude of all nations, and kindreds, and people, and tongues, which no man could number, who carry palms in their hands, sing with a loud voice day and night (accompanied by the angels) before him that sitteth on the throne, and have been justified by the blood of the Lamb, seems to me strongly enforced. Then the biblical author, who has seen the great multitude but not the 144,000, is, after several chapters devoted to the account of the opening of the seventh seal and the events that follow, shown the 144,000. The rubric of chapter 14 begins, "The Lamb and his company: who they are." The text we have already seen (above), with its specification of the precise number of children of Israel having the Father's name written in their foreheads, singing a new song which no man could learn but the 144,000 virgins who were the firstfruits unto God and to the Lamb. This is obviously enough the passage echoed in Milton's *Apology*, but I can find nothing in "A Solemn Musick" to suggest it. On the contrary, it seems to me clear that the "just Spirits that wear victorious Palms" and everlastingly sing "Hymns devout and holy Psalms" are the "great multitude, which no man could number, of all nations," "clothed with white robes, and palms in their hands," who have come out of "great tribulation" and have been justified by the blood of the Lamb, and who, with the angels, sing before the throne day and night of salvation and blessing. (The Greek *textus receptus*, which Milton may well have used, has "palms" in the accusative—i.e., as the object, along with "white robes," of "clothed with" or, more precisely, "wearing"; "that wear victorious Palms" is therefore a straight translation with the white robes left out.) "At a Solemn Musick" is certainly a religious poem in which the poet aspires rightly to answer the melodious noise made by the angels and the just spirits in heaven, but I cannot see that sacrificial celibacy has anything to do with hearing or answering this song.

Nor can I really see that Milton was embracing a life of celibacy in the original version of the poem which we do so ill to call *Comus* (it is as if Milton had left *Paradise Lost* unnamed and we were to call it "Satan's Revenge"). The 1634 version of *A Mask at Ludlow Castle* has chastity for its theme, and it certainly treats of the powers of virginity; but these are almost wholly defensive powers, powers that clothe the virgin in "compleat steel" (l. 420), remove all hurtful power from "goblin, or swart Faëry of the mine" (l. 435). There is one thing beyond this: Milton's treatment of Plato's doctrine that "the soul which is pure at departing and draws after her no bodily taint, having never voluntarily had connection with the body, which she is ever avoiding, . . . departs to the invisible world—to the divine and immortal and rational, . . . But the soul which has been polluted . . . and is the companion and servant of the body always . . . is held fast by the corporeal . . . [and] is depressed and dragged down again into the visible world."[37] This Milton adapts in the famous lines (452–68)

> So dear to Heav'n is Saintly chastity,
> That when a soul is found sincerely so,
> A thousand liveried Angels lacky her,
> Driving far off each thing of sin and guilt,
> And in cleer dream, and solemn vision
> Tell her of things that no gross ear can hear,
> Till oft convers with heav'nly habitants
> Begin to cast a beam on th'outward shape
> The unpolluted temple of the mind,
> And turns it by degrees to the souls essence,
> Till all be made immortal: but when lust
> By unchaste looks, loose gestures, and foul talk,
> But most by leud and lavish act of sin,
> Lets in defilement to the inward parts,
> The soul grows clotted by contagion,
> Imbodies, and imbrutes, till she quite loose
> The divine property of her first being.

But these lines, by themselves, come nowhere near a personal pledge of celibacy (although once that pledge has been taken, they may be seen to foreshadow it). The passages which do suggest such a pledge, and which unmistakably resound in Milton's account of himself in *An Apology*, were added in 1637. It is then that Milton feels that the argument from the "holy dictate of spare Temperance" (l. 766) with which the Lady had replied to Comus' temptation is not enough, and interpolates (ll. 778–86):

> Shall I go on?
> Or have I said anough? To him that dares
> Arm his profane tongue with contemptuous words
> Against the Sun-clad power of Chastity,
> Fain would I somthing say, yet to what end?
> Thou hast nor Eare, nor Soul to apprehend
> The sublime notion, and high mystery
> That must be utter'd to unfold the sage
> And serious doctrine of Virginity. . . .

[37] *Phaedo*, 80–81; tr. Benjamin Jowett, *The Dialogues of Plato*, 2 ed., 5 vols. (Oxford, 1875), I, 457–58.

And Comus, who in 1634 had contemptuously brushed her original argument aside as "meer moral babble," in 1637 feels that he fears "Her words set off by som superior power," and is only dissembling his fear ("a cold shuddring dew Dips me all o're") when he characterizes the Lady's new "sacred vehemence" as "meer moral babble" (ll. 799–805).[38] It is in 1637 that Milton, again calling attention to the new matter—"(List mortals, if your ears be true)"—interpolates the passage in the epilogue (ll. 996, 998–1010) which begins with Venus and Adonis and continues:

> But farr above in spangled sheen
> Celestial *Cupid* her fam'd Son advanc't,
> Holds his dear *Psyche* sweet intranc't
> After her wandring labours long,
> Till free consent the gods among
> Make her his eternal Bride,
> And from her fair unspotted side
> Two blissful twins are to be born,
> Youth and Joy; so *Jove* hath sworn.[39]

The year 1637 is also the date of "Lycidas," the poem which brings priest and poet closer together than they have found themselves since the "Nativity Ode," and in which the apotheosized Lycidas finds his "large recompense" for dying unfulfilled (we recall that "the rathe primrose that forsaken dies" was originally written "that unwedded dies") in hearing "the unexpressive nuptial Song, In the blest Kingdoms meek of joy and love."

All this inevitably suggests the autobiographical passage of *An Apology*, setting forth what Milton learnt from poets and philosophers (especially Plato) "of chastity and love, I meane that which is truly so, whose charming cup is only vertue which she bears in her hand to those who are worthy. The rest are cheated with a thick intoxicating potion which a certaine Sorceresse the abuser of loves name carries

---

[38] Harris F. Fletcher, *John Milton's Complete Poetical Works Reproduced in Photographic Facsimile*, 4 vols. (Urbana, 1943–48), gives both manuscript versions of the mask, as well as the three editions printed during Milton's lifetime. See I, 331–32, 424–25, for the relevant passages in the Bridgewater and Trinity MSS respectively, neither of which have ll. 778–805. They are in the printed editions of 1637, 1645, and 1673.

[39] In the Bridgewater manuscript, which does not contain these lines, the portion of the epilogue to which the passage was subsequently attached is used as a prologue; see Fletcher, I, 303. The Trinity MS has two final pages for the mask. The original, which does not contain these lines, has been canceled. The revised page has the passage, with the monitory line 996 written into the right margin. See Fletcher, I, 430–33.

about; and how the first and chiefest office of love, begins and ends in the soule, producing those happy twins of her divine generation knowledge and vertue, with such abstracted sublimities as these,"[40] and the further impact of "those chaste and high mysteries" of Christianity which taught that "the body is for the Lord and the Lord for the body," particularly as these mysteries are seen in the light of "that place expressing such high rewards of ever accompanying the Lambe, with those celestiall songs to others inapprehensible, but not to those who were not defil'd with women." And "it is not without significance," as Hanford long ago pointed out, "that the first prose letters to . . . Diodati, which Milton cared to preserve and publish, should date from the year 1637."[41] Hanford argued most convincingly that the early intimacy had faded, and that Milton took the initiative to revive it and put it on a very different basis: "a fully developed Platonic relationship" which he "substituted consciously and deliberately" for "the earthly Aphrodite."

In 1637, then, we clearly are in the presence of some personal relation to celibacy. Now 1637 or early 1638 is also, I believe, the date of *Ad Patrem*,[42] and I think that piece can throw some light on what took place. Behind the elaborate compliment of the poem, and providing its occasion, is clearly some remonstrance by the father, some warning that it was time for Milton to do something with his life—some repetition, that is, this time by the father rather than by a friend, and perhaps not for the first time, of the admonition of five years earlier which called forth the "Letter" we have already noticed. The poem replies that what the son intends to do with his life is to be a poet; but it also reveals that the father betrayed some uneasiness about this ambition. In the discussion (or the several discussions) which gave the occasion for the poem, the son may well have said, as he was to say in *The Reason of Church-Government*, that poetry was "of power beside the office of a pulpit,"[43] to serve God and one's country; he may have said, as he had done in his manifesto on coming of age and repeated in

[40] Columbia, III, 305.

[41] "Youth of Milton," pp. 143–47. The significance of the date for Hanford lies in its contemporaneity with "Lycidas." It seems to me that only his failure to notice that lines 998–1010 of *Comus* were added for the 1637 edition (he discussed them as written three years before "Lycidas"; see p. 152) prevented him from seeing, in this wonderfully perceptive study, how all the indications of a personal relation to celibacy for Milton really date from 1637.

[42] See Appendix, Section III, following.

[43] Columbia, III, 238.

"Lycidas," that the poet is God's priest. But at this point either the father or the poet's own conscience—which five years earlier was already "something suspicious of my selfe," as he told the friend who confronted him with the parable of the talents, and five years later, as he told the world in explanation of his entering into the ecclesiastical controversy because of "the enforcement of conscience only,"[44] was still "suspitious of my self and mine own doings,"[45] "remembring also that God even to a strictnesse requires the improvment of these his entrusted gifts"[46]—must have said something like the following: "It was on this ground that you refused to take orders; it was with this argument that you met the suspicion that you were surrendering to the allurements of a life of retirement and books; but many years have gone by, and the work 'doctrinal and exemplary to a Nation' is nowhere to be seen. How can you know that you are not deceiving yourself: avoiding a duty which you find distasteful, not performing the duty which you proclaim its surrogate, taking all—a life of ease and scholarly pleasure—and giving nothing?"

All his life Milton made covenants and gave pledges: with the knowing reader, with his friends, with his father, with the "Heav'nly Muse," with the covenant-takers and protestation-makers of the Puritan Revolution, presumably with himself. (The word "covenant" requires more than five columns of the *Columbia Index*.) It seems to me that, confronted by the kind of challenge I have here imagined (and, whether by his father or by his own conscience, I am sure that he was so challenged), he would have made a covenant with himself and given a pledge. I think that the 1637 additions to *A Mask*, and "Lycidas," *Epitaphium Damonis*, and *An Apology* tell us what the covenant and pledge were. The covenant was the renewal yet again of his self-dedication as God's poet, and the pledge which made this self-dedication more convincing than its predecessors was sacrificial celibacy.

The celibacy which had until recently been imposed upon the priesthood was wrong, of course. But it had nevertheless been for many ages the sacrifice demanded of those who would be God's priests. Had he taken orders as intended, he would not have been called upon to make this sacrifice. But what if he now made it voluntarily, as the symbol of his poet-priesthood? Such a sacrifice would be pledge enough

---

[44] *Church-Government;* III, 234.
[45] Columbia, III, 232.
[46] Columbia, III, 229.

of his sincerity, proof that in refusing orders he was so far from unwilling to submit to a strict discipline that, like Isabella in *Measure for
Measure*, he desired "a more strict restraint Upon the . . . votarists"
whom, in another vesture, he was joining. And the pledge would have
a further propriety. Chastity in the sense of the eschewing of fornication he had always practised merely as a moral duty. Chastity in the
Platonic sense he had long brooded on, and practised, so far as that
could be said of a Christian. To rise from this to permanent, sacrificial
celibacy in the sense of Paul and John the Divine ought to enable him
to claim the reward promised by them; and the poet-priest who heard
the "unexpressive nuptial song" of the Lamb would surely have his
lips touched and purified "with the hallow'd fire of his Altar"—and, at
last, unlocked; so that the prayer of Milton's first pamphlet would be
met, and "amidst the *Hymns*, and *Halleluiahs* of *Saints* some one"
would "bee heard offering at high *strains* in new and lofty *Measures* to
sing and celebrate thy *divine Mercies*, and *marvelous Judgements* in
this *Land* throughout all *Ages*."[47]

Some such covenant and pledge, rising out of the challenge of conscience and friends, were, I am arguing, made about 1637, and hence
the additions to *A Mask* and "Lycidas." Two years later the theme is
even more explicit in *Epitaphium Damonis*, that more emphatic re-
working of the "Lycidas" material. "You, too, have a place among
the gods . . . Damon. . . . Tears fit not you: so I will weep no more. . . .
Now that you have received your due rights in heaven, stand by me,
at my right hand, graciously give me your favor. . . . Because the
crimson flush of modesty, and youth without stain were your pleasure,
because you ne'er tasted the joys of the marriage couch, see! virginal
honors are reserved for you. With your bright head encircled by a
radiant crown, and carrying the gladsome shade of the broadleaved
palm, you will consummate, eternally, immortal nuptials, where there
is singing, where the lyre revels madly, mingled with choirs beatific,
and festal orgies run riot, in bacchante fashion, with the thyrsus of
Zion."[48]

Here is the peculiarity I mentioned as being instrumental in the
reading into "A Solemn Musick" of a meaning not there. *Epitaphium
Damonis* indisputably provides one of the 144,000 virgins with palms.
This is surely why the "just Spirits who wear victorious palms" of "A
Solemn Musick" were assumed to be the 144,000 virgins. But it is now
seven years later; Milton has, for some two or three years, been con-

[47] *Of Reformation;* III, 78.
[48] Tr. Charles Knapp; Columbia, I, 316–17.

centrating his aspirations on the 144,000 virgins, rather than on the countless multitude; his vision is of Damon participating in "festal orgies"; and, whether deliberately or instinctively, he fits him out suitably for such revels with joyous palms, either not now remembering or not caring that John the Divine provided the virgins who sang and harped before the throne with no such equipment, but reserved it for the multitude. (The joyous palms were, of course, familiar enough from the annual Feast of the Tabernacles [Lev. 23:40] and from Christ's entry into Jerusalem [John 12:13].) For the sake of his earlier poem Milton ought not to have confused matters, but he did.

We do not know when Milton underwent the inner change represented by that incongruous afterthought, "which doubtlesse meanes fornication: For mariage must not be call'd a defilement," except that it must have been after *Epitaphium Damonis*. Probably the change was completed not long before he wrote the sentence and went off to get married, which he did in a haste emphasized by his nephew. Presumably he had decided that he did not have what Paul called the "gift" of celibacy. Perhaps the glamor of the sacrifice had begun to wear off, aided by the fact that Diodati, that unmarried friend of his heart, had been dead for almost four years, and that Milton was now living in the busy world of London, not in the virtual cloister of Horton. Most influential of all, it may be thought, was the fact of his participation in the fight against episcopacy. Here at last, visible and undeniable, was meaningful action—and in the service of God's church. It seems to me just the kind of thing needed before Milton would release himself from the pledge which was both symbol and counterpart of the service yet to be performed in God's church with the other hand. The left hand had earned the commutation of the sacrifice pledged in the name of the right hand.

The marriage was a disaster of strangely mixed effects, some liberating and enlarging, others permanently embittering. I want to concentrate, however, on the effect it had on his faith in his poetic inspiration. From the beginning, almost, certainly from his coming-of-age, and more insistently since the decision not to take orders, he had conceived this inspiration almost sacramentally. He had made something like a sacramental vow on its behalf; and then he had released himself from it and allowed himself the contrary alternative. He would but change the circumstances of his dedication, would add the strength of a loving help-mate, and two would serve God instead of one. But at once he was met with a blank; abandoned; made a mock.

Fierce as was his resentment against his wife, could he, brooding in his house for a year, have avoided questioning himself? Had he done anything to deserve this blow? That he had made a mistake in judgment was obvious, but was there not something worse? He had offered God a sacrifice and then withdrawn it; he had pledged celibacy and then substituted marriage; had God rejected the substitute in anger? And if he had, was he also rejecting the service whose pledge had been withdrawn?

Such inner questionings may have been fugitive, but it will be many, many years before we again hear of the poem which is to be "doctrinal and exemplary to a Nation." It has not been enough noticed that for the next decade Milton wrote almost nothing, aside from the *History of Britain*, that did not rise from an immediate personal occasion. The first divorce tract rose out of the failure of his marriage. It earned him a reputation as a libertine and heretic, which affected the revision. This in turn was "lavishly traduc't" and "odious inferences"[49] drawn therefrom, and apparently there was an effort to get it suppressed and the author punished.[50] This leads to the "Postscript" in *Martin Bucer* which so clearly anticipates *Areopagitica*; and the continuing controversy brings on that great pamphlet and the two final divorce tracts. Meanwhile, the personal solicitation of Hartlib has occasioned *Of Education*, and various personal incidents or relations have occasioned or will occasion (with one exception) the few poems of this period: the sonnet on his door when the city expected an assault, those to the lady in the prime of youth, to Lady Margaret Ley, to Henry Lawes, on the death of Mrs. Thomason, on the reception given his pamphlets, the ode to Rouse. I am assuming that the *Tenure* and the sonnet to Fairfax rose out of some decision to cast his lot in with the Army, perhaps precipitated by some discussions (for the invitation to become Secretary for Foreign Tongues cannot have been made wholly without preparatory discussions). The *Observations*, *Eikonoklastes*, and first *Defence* are, of course, written to order.

The exception is most interesting. In the spring of 1648 he translated nine psalms. He had paraphrased or translated two psalms when he was fifteen, and had done one into Greek in 1637; otherwise he had shown no interest in such work. Now he translates nine psalms, and in 1653 eight more. Why would he have taken up this work at this juncture? Is it not because, after the long intermission, the long

---

[49] *Bucer;* IV, 12.
[50] See my introduction, Yale *Complete Prose Works*, II, 140–41. See pp. 137–45 for a discussion of the immediate occasions of the pamphlets of 1643–45.

silences, he was trying to renew his dedication as God's poet, trying to rekindle his sense of inspiration?

But when at length he does regain his sense of inspiration its symbol will not be celibacy. Every reader must be struck by the energy with which he repudiates, in *Paradise Lost*, what had once been for him a "chaste and high mystery." Adam and Eve (IV, 741-49)

> Strait side by side were laid, nor turnd I weene
> *Adam* from his fair Spouse, nor *Eve* the Rites
> Mysterious of connubial Love refus'd:
> Whatever Hypocrites austerely talk
> Of puritie and place and innocence,
> Defaming as impure what God declares
> Pure, and commands to som, leaves free to all.
> Our Maker bids increase, who bids abstain
> But our Destroyer, foe to God and Man?

The new symbol of poetic inspiration will be his blindness. He can be seen working his way out of the depression that acccompanied his blindness and toward its appropriation as symbol and, if not source, at least avenue of inspiration. In 1652,[51] when he considers how his light is spent, "And that one Talent which is death to hide, Lodg'd with [him] useless," the best he can manage is resignation: "They also serve who only stand and waite." By 1654, however, answering the charge that his blindness is God's punishment for his part in the regicide, he goes far beyond a denial of guilt, to the assertion that

There is a way, and the Apostle is my authority, through weakness to the greatest strength. May I be one of the weakest, provided only in my weakness that immortal and better vigour be put forth with greater effect; provided only in my darkness the light of the divine countenance does but the more brightly shine: for then I shall at once be the weakest and the most mighty; shall be at once blind, and of the most piercing sight. Thus, through this infirmity should I be consummated, perfected; thus, through this darkness should I be enrobed in light.[52]

[51] Smart's date (*Sonnets* [1921], p. 108), "when the calamity was fresh" and before Milton "had become accustomed to a life in darkness." Hanford, "The Arrangement and Dates of Milton's Sonnets," *MP*, XVIII (1921), 475-83, argued from what he thought the predominantly chronological order of the 1673 edition and from the presumed arrangement of the Trinity MS (from which the leaf containing this poem is missing) that the date was 1655. Although a number of scholars have accepted Hanford's view, many have thought that it ran counter to the evidence of the poem itself, and Fitzroy Pyle, "Milton's First Sonnet on His Blindness," *RES*, new ser., IX (1958), 376-87, has recently shown that the ordering cannot be chronological, and has strongly reinforced Smart's date.

[52] *Second Defence*, tr. G. Burnett, rev. M. Hadas; Columbia, VIII, 73.

We remember this when, the following year, in marking the third anniversary of his complete blindness, he answers the question of what it is that supports him in his affliction:

> The conscience, Friend, to have lost them overply'd
> In liberty's defence, my noble task,
> Of which all Europe talks from side to side.
> This thought might lead me through the world's vain mask
> Content though blind, had I no better guide.[53]

And we know not only who is the better guide, but Milton's sense of how and why he gives his guidance.

The invocation of *Paradise Lost* would seem to be another step in developing the blindness into the symbol of poetic inspiration, if we adopt the very persuasive suggestion, proposed independently in two recent discussions,[54] that when Milton at the outset of his "great Argument" prays that the Spirit instruct him ("What in me is dark Illumine"), the reason he adds to the names of the three famous mountains, Oreb, Sinai, and Sion, the relatively unknown brook of Siloam is that he is alluding to John 9:1–3: "And as Jesus passed by, he saw a man which was blind from his birth. And his disciples asked him, saying, Master, who did sin, this man, or his parents, that he was born blind? Jesus answered, Neither hath this man sinned, nor his parents: but that the works of God should be made manifest in him." Thereupon Jesus cures the blind man with the water of the pool of Siloam, and uses him as a symbol: "For judgment I am come into this world, that they which see not might see; and that they which see might be made blind" (v. 39).

No one, of course, has ever failed to see the relation between Milton's physical blindness and his sense of spiritual illumination in the invocation to "holy light" at the beginning of Book III. Milton's eyes "rowle in vain" to find the light, "So thick a drop serene hath quencht thir Orbs";

> But cloud in stead, and ever-during dark
> Surrounds me, from the chearful waies of men
> Cut off, and for the Book of knowledg fair
> Presented with a Universal blanc
> Of Natures works to mee expung'd and ras'd,
> And wisdome at one entrance quite shut out.

---

[53] Sonnet XXII.

[54] Jackson I. Cope, "Milton's Muse in *Paradise Lost*," *MP*, LV (1957–58), 6–10, and Paul Lauter, "Milton's 'Siloa's Brook,' " *N&Q*, CCIII (1958), 204–205. For a contrary view see George W. Whiting and Ann Gossman, "Siloa's Brook, the Pool of Siloam, and Milton's Muse," *SP*, LVIII (1961), 193–205.

So much the rather thou Celestial light
Shine inward, and the mind through all her powers
Irradiate, there plant eyes, all mist from thence
Purge and disperse, that I may see and tell
Of things invisible to mortal sight.   (ll. 45–55)

APPENDIX

Some Recent Suggested Changes in the Chronology of Milton's Poems

I. *SAMSON AGONISTES*

There are two main arguments for dating the composition of *S.A.* in the period from the early 1640's to the early 1650's, both advanced in a special Milton number of *Philological Quarterly* (xxvIII, 1949). One, by William R. Parker, is entitled "The Date of *Samson Agonistes*"; the other, by Allan H. Gilbert, is called "Is *Samson Agonistes* Unfinished?" Mr. Parker subsequently published "The Date of *Samson Agonistes:* A Postscript," *Notes and Queries,* ccIII (1958), 201–202. Mr. Parker's argument, which is the more serious and has had considerable influence, may be considered first.

It begins with the contention (*a*) that there is no solid basis for the traditional late date for the poem. We have nothing from Milton about the date; neither Aubrey nor Wood mentioned the poem at all; "the Anonymous Biographer merely lumped it with seven other works 'finished after the Restoration'—an unhelpful comment. Toland . . . said nothing about the time of its composition. When Bishop Newton stated, in 1749, 'This I conceive to be the last of his poetical pieces,' he expressed an uncritical assumption. . . . *Samson Agonistes* was printed last; *ergo* it was written last. No one, of course, would dream of applying such dubious logic to Milton's *Grammar* or *History of Britain*" (*PQ*, p. 145). Next, Parker argues (*b*) that the traditional date is doubtful. For one thing, Edward Phillips, who said that *P.R.* was "begun and finished and printed after the other [*P.L.*] was published, and that in a wonderful short space considering the sublimeness of it," also said that "It cannot certainly be concluded when he wrote his excellent Tragedy entitled *Samson Agonistes*, but sure enough it is that it came forth after his publication of *Paradise Lost*, together with his other poem called *Paradise Regained*." Since it would be a much greater wonder if Milton had written both poems in so short a time, Parker concludes that the two statements together "make it quite clear that he, for one, does not believe the *Samson* to have been written after *Paradise Lost*" (*PQ*, pp. 146–47). Again, (*c*) "the years *immediately preceding or immediately following*" the publication of *P.L.* are highly unlikely ones for the composition of *S.A.* because 154 lines (about one-eleventh of the poem) contain rhyme, and when he wrote them Milton "could not have felt about riming as he did while composing the paragraph on 'The Verse' for *Paradise Lost*," with its attack on rhyme (pp. 147–49). Next, under the heading "The Autobiographical Fallacy," Parker (*d*) dismisses all critical and biographical inferences from the poem which point to the traditional date, arguing that the method is fallacious and the particulars unreliable. But, since "it is a game at which anyone can play blindfold, and . . .

the scales of subjective criticism need balancing," Parker proposes his own
biographical inferences from internal evidence. One dominant idea in the
poem, Parker thinks, so heavily emphasized as to make it seem "a passion,
a deep personal conviction of the author," is that God chooses a few in-
dividuals "for the fulfilment of His mysterious purposes." This, he says,
points to the period 1648–54, when Milton's "belief in chosen ones amounted
to an emotional necessity. . . . Cromwell was elected to power, not by the will
of the majority, but 'by the special direction of God.' Milton wanted to
believe that the great Protector was 'almost instructed by divine inspiration,'
just as Samson acted 'from intimate impulse,' from 'divine impulsion.' The
justification of success is, of course, a dangerous doctrine, and Milton found it
increasingly difficult to hold as the Restoration grew imminent; and after the
Restoration he could not, in logic, believe it. . . . Neither *Paradise Lost* nor
Paradise Regained contains such an emphasis . . . " (pp. 149–53). Again,
(*e*) *S.A.* is, in Parker's view, not didactic in mood and tone (like the epics)
but prophetic; and this would fit the Milton of the 1640's and early 1650's,
but not the later Milton (pp. 153–55). Next, Parker gives other "Reasons for
an Early Date." (*f*) Although most stylistic tests are "inconclusive," "the
audacious metrical experiments" in *S.A.* link it with similar experiments in
the ode to Rouse, and hence point to a period "as early as 1647" (pp. 155–56).
Again, (*g*) "the *only evidence* of Milton's interest in dramatic composition
dates from the period 1641–1645. Both . . . *The Reason of Church Government*
. . . and . . . the Trinity Manuscript indicate clearly that Milton was con-
templating writing a tragedy in 1641." When the pamphlets of 1643–45 were
finished "and the poet enjoyed almost four years of freedom from pamphleteering (1645–1648), he almost certainly returned to his idea of writing a
tragedy." If Aubrey and Edward Phillips can be taken at face value, Milton
had in 1642–43 composed some ten lines for a drama on the subject of *P.L.*,
having "evidently decided then that a drama could be brought to completion
with less difficulty than a longer poem. Is there the slightest reason to suppose
that he changed his mind in 1645?" (pp. 156–57). Further, (*h*) since Edward
Phillips did not know when *S.A.* was written, Parker infers that it was
"chiefly done" during some period when the nephew was not seeing much of
the uncle. He believes that Phillips would have left Milton's care about 1646,
"making it at least possible that *Samson Agonistes* was begun in the year 1647,
when Phillips might have known nothing about it" (pp. 157–58). Now (*i*)
Parker gives it as his "guess" that *S.A.* was "begun in 1646 or 1647, . . . discontinued in April of 1648, . . . taken up again for its possible *katharsis* in
1652 or 1653, . . . again discontinued in August of 1653. Whatever the exact
facts, both the style and the characterization . . . persuade me that its composition was several times interrupted" (pp. 158–59). Parker anticipates (*j*)
that "The reader may wonder at my inclination to link conjectured interruptions with experiments in translation. It seems to me that Milton's mood in
April of 1648 was obviously unable to sustain original composition, and that
it is clearly reflected in his translations of nine psalms into English riming
verse. . . . The spirit of *Samson Agonistes* is everywhere in these psalms. . . .
Milton's translations were exercises in morale as well as in linguistics; they
compensated for unaccountable stoppages in direct personal expression." As

for the psalm translations of 1653, they contain "a great variety of rime and metrical patterns, and strangely anarchic rhythms which may remind one somewhat of *Samson Agonistes*" (pp. 159–61). Finally, (*k*) "it is a simple matter to reconcile a conjectured early date with other facts of Milton's thought and art." Parker emphasizes that "Samson had 'quit himself like Samson' *before* he pulled down destruction upon the Philistines. The psychological development is the thing that makes the play. And this psychological development, the regeneration of the fallen leader, is Milton's invention; it is not even hinted at in the Old Testament story. It provides, therefore, a potential clue to Milton's choice of Samson as a subject for tragedy." The Trinity Manuscript and the published works show that Milton had been interested in the Samson story before 1646–48, but not very immediately; it was in these years, "when he realized that blindness threatened him, when the clergy were still damning his views on marriage and divorce, when he felt lonely and miserable and frustrated in his life's work, he may have wondered how Samson managed to rise above his troubles and fulfil, at last, his great purpose. The moment at which the poet first considered the mental process that led to Samson's regeneration was the moment at which the drama was conceived; for then, and only then, did the Old Testament story cease to be a possible plot, listed with a hundred others in a notebook, and become instead a compelling theme for tragedy." This is unlikely to have happened before Milton realized his own approaching blindness (i.e., about 1647). On the other side, "we can believe" that the passages on blindness "have about them the eloquence and conviction of newly-met reality," and it is unlikely that Milton would have risked writing them after he had achieved tranquility under the affliction (pp. 162–64).

Parker's arguments are best discussed seriatim. (*a*) He has not fully stated the external, objective basis for the traditional date, nor has he stated fairly that part which is reported. How is it that he passes from Toland (1698) to Newton (1749) without mentioning Richardson, whose *Life* of 1734 is so important an authority, who eagerly questioned so many persons who had been acquainted with Milton during his latter life (or who had known such acquaintances), and who was therefore able to give so many "fresh details that have the stamp of personal knowledge"? (Helen Darbishire, *The Early Lives of Milton* [London, 1932], pp. xxix-xxx). Richardson declares without any trace of uncertainty that *S.A.* was written after *P.L.* and *P.R.*: "His Time was Now Employ'd in Writing and Publishing, particularly *Paradise Lost.* and after That, *Paradise Regain'd*, and *Samson Agonistes*" (Darbishire, p. 275). As for Newton, why should he be presumed guilty of "an uncritical assumption"? He tells us that in order to present a reliable account he "not only read and compared" all written accounts of Milton's life and work but "also collected some other particulars . . . from credible tradition" (9th ed., 2 vols. [1790], I, sig. a3ᵛ); among others to whom he talked was Milton's grand-daughter Elizabeth. Nor is it clear that the element of opinion apparent in the phrase "I conceive" is concerned with uncertainty about whether *S.A.* was written after *P.L.* and *P.R.* Newton is discussing Milton's work in chronological order, and after having dealt with *P.R.* he says (I, lxiii-iv): "His Samson

Agonistes is the only tragedy that he has finished, tho' he has sketched out the plans of several, . . . and we may suppose that he was determined to the choice of this particular subject by the similitude of his own circumstances to those of Samson blind among the Philistines. This I conceive to be the last of his poetical pieces. . . . There are also some other pieces of Milton, for he continued publishing to the last. . . . [In 1673] his poems, which had been printed in 1645, were reprinted with the addition of several others. . . . [In 1694] his excellent sonnets to Fairfax, Cromwell, Sir Henry Vane, and Cyriack Skinner, on his blindness, were first printed." Newton seems to me to be expressing no lack of confidence about when Milton wrote *S.A.*, but rather giving his opinion that although certain other poems were published for the first time at a later date, they had been written earlier. We may note in passing that in the articles of 1935 and 1952 which are discussed below, Parker takes as prime evidence of chronological order the sequence in which Milton arranged the poems of the 1645 and 1673 editions, but the present article (which comes between the other two) scorns the "dubious logic" which would assume that Milton placed *S.A.* after *P.R.* in the 1671 volume because it was composed later.

(*b*) If Edward Phillips thought *S.A.* written before *P.L.*, why did he not say so? What he says is that the date of composition is not known but that the date of publication is; if he thought that there was a great disparity between them—that is, that the latter gave a misleading impression about the former—would he not have said so? Incidentally, it is not very wonderful that he should be unsure of the date of *S.A.*; Miss Darbishire points out that dates are his weak suit: "he gets wrong both the year of Milton's birth . . . and the year of his death" (*Early Lives*, p. xiii).

(*c*) Some indication of the blatancy of the question-begging here may be obtained by observing that when Milton revised *P.L.* for the second edition and added four lines to introduce the newly separated eighth book, what he wrote was a quatrain with the first and third lines rhyming and the second and fourth assonantal. Actually, there is a considerable amount of rhyme in *P.L.*, as John S. Diekhoff has partly shown ("Rhyme in *Paradise Lost*," *PMLA*, XLIX [1934], 539–43). Parker knew this article, but instead of being warned by it against his *petitio principii* he dismissed it in a footnote: "There are even rimes in *Paradise Lost*, but they are so inconspicuous and infrequent that a scholarly article was published to call attention to them" (p. 148). In fact, Diekhoff reported seventeen actual couplets, forty-five instances of rhymes separated by a single line, fifty-two instances of rhyming lines enclosing two not rhyming ("in several cases the enclosed lines themselves contribute to other rhymes"), twenty-seven instances of rhyming lines enclosing three not rhyming (some of the enclosed lines being themselves interlaced with rhymes), "many other rhymes . . . more widely separated," and a large number ("nearly two score . . . in the first two books alone") of rhymes at medial caesurae. To Diekhoff's count may be added two more couplets (II, 893–94; X, 544–45), seven more rhymes with a single intervening line (IV, 482–84; V, 349–51, 857–59; VIII, 171–73; IX, 228–30, 361–63; XI, 637–39), and ten more rhymes with two intervening lines (I, 553–56; IV, 729–32; 825–28; VI, 530–33, 601–604, 658–61; VII, 251–54; IX, 720–23, 1101–04; X,

712-15). Since Diekhoff does not list his twenty-seven rhymes with three intervening lines, nor the many which are more widely separated, nor any of the medial rhymes, it is not easy to know whether his count could be further enlarged. There are, however, well over four hundred line-end rhymes close enough together to be picked up by ear, and a very large number of caesural rhymes. It is not clear how we are to reconcile all this rhyme in *P.L.* with Milton's note explaining why he did not rhyme his poem (perhaps the answer is that as he used rhyme here it neither produced a "jingling sound" nor was it a "bondage"); but it is obvious that the presence of rhyme in *S.A.* cannot be used to prove that it belongs to an earlier period than *P.L.* We may add S. E. Sprott's remark (*Milton's Art of Prosody* [Oxford, 1953], p. 37) that the rhyme in *S.A.* "occurs in lyrical choruses along with shortened lines, and the preface to *Paradise Lost* may not wholly apply."

(*d*) It may be thought a pity that Parker chose to "play blindfold" his "game" of autobiographical inference; without the blindfold he might have seen that "the deep personal conviction" which he found in *S.A.* was not as absent from the works written just before, during, and after the Restoration as he thought. In August 1659, Milton opened *Hirelings* with the declaration that the Rump, "after a short but scandalous night of interruption, is now again by a new dawning of Gods miraculous providence among us," restored (Columbia, vi, 43). The first edition of *Readie and Easie Way* (Feb. 1660) declares that while the majority of the nation who insist upon running "thir necks again into the yoke" may be worthy to be slaves, the minority must resist them by force, for they are "reservd, I trust, by Divine providence to a better end; since God hath yet his remnant" (ed. E. M. Clark [New Haven, 1915], pp. 18-19). "The justification of success" was never used more explicitly by Milton than in the second edition of *Readie and Easie Way* (see Columbia, vi, 140-41). The blindfold's harmful effects are most obvious in the reference to *P.L.* and *P.R.* All the heroes of Michael's preview of history in Books XI and XII of the former poem—Enoch, Noah, Abraham, Moses, Joshua, David, Jesus—were, like Samson, chosen by God, not elected by the will of the majority; and this is *a fortiori* so of the hero of *P.R.* The emphasis is heavy in *S.A.* (but not heavier than in *P.R.*) because the fallen hero's inner torment rises chiefly from the guilt of having betrayed God's trust.

(*e*) Not Moses and all the prophets could have understood this distinction, for were they not sent to "teach the good way" as well as to foretell the future? (Incidentally, does *P.L.* foretell the future less than *S.A.*?)

(*f*) What, precisely, can a comparison of the metrics of poems in different languages prove? But this general question aside, since Parker does not particularize his comparison, let us look at the conclusions of two prosodic studies which do. After examining all the relevant prosodic data, Sprott says (pp. 129-31): "Milton's most advanced prosodic theory is employed in *Samson Agonistes*. . . . [It] is metrically the pinnacle of its author's achievement . . . gathers up all his experience in previous works." Similarly, Ants Oras ("Milton's Blank Verse and the Chronology of His Major Poems," *SAMLA Studies in Milton*, ed. J. Max Patrick [Gainesville, Fla., 1953], pp. 128-97), says (p. 191): "The continuity of the statistical sequences is too striking, and the emerging patterns occur too persistently and seem too natural to be accidental. Certain features in particular, such as the treatment of feminine endings, of syllabized *-ed* endings, and of terminal pyrrhics, show a compelling logic in their development with which no order of composition very different from the traditionally accepted one seems at all compatible. . . . The second half of *PL* is linked in so many ways with *PR*, and *PR*, in its turn, with *SA*, that the chronological sequence *PL* vii-xii: *PR: SA* seems inescapable."

(*g*) What Milton contemplated writing at the time of *Reason of Church-Government* was a poem "so written to aftertimes, as they should not willingly let it die," but he was undecided "whether that Epick form whereof the two poems of *Homer*, and those other two of *Virgil* and *Tasso* are a diffuse, and the book of *Job* a brief model. . . . Or whether those Dramatick constitutions, wherein *Sophocles* and *Euripides* raigne shall be found more doctrinal and exemplary to a Nation" (Columbia, iii, 236–37). As was long ago pointed out (see Hanford, *Milton Handbook*, pp. 181–82, and further reference there given), the fact that the only worked-up plans that happen to have been preserved in the Trinity Manuscript are for dramas does not mean that there were no plans for other kinds of poems. The subjects which were worked up in the Trinity Manuscript were not the Samson story but the stories of Adam and Eve, Noah, Abraham, Lot, Phineas, John the Baptist, and Jesus. If Milton did begin a drama in 1642, one can think of at least two reasons, neither particularly "slight," which might have made him turn to some other form if he attempted to return to poetic composition in 1645 or 1646: the closing of the theatres in 1642 and the increasing hostility of his own party toward plays. But these are all secondary matters; the main point here is that it is another *petitio principii* to say that Milton returned in any significant way to the writing of poetry at this time. There is no positive evidence for it; the negative evidence is against it, for there is nothing about it in the account of his writings in the *Second Defence*. (It must not be thought that this statement reported only published or completed works, for it includes the *History of Britain*, which was neither.)

(*h*) There is in fact nothing to show that Milton and his nephew were not seeing each other as much as usual during 1647, but there are quite other times when it is most unlikely that they did; for example, Edward Phillips was living away from London in 1664–65 (also in 1650–51, and he may well have been away at other times). And of course Milton was in hiding in 1660, and in Chalfont in 1665.

(*i*) Since the stylistic characteristics which persuade Parker of discontinuous composition are not given, it is impossible to examine them. We may however put against this impression of discontinuity of style Oras' numerical analysis of the style of *S.A.*, which concludes (p. 197): "Steady progression or regression is the most striking characteristic of the majority of these ratios. . . . This steadiness of direction suggests a subconscious unity of impulse and inspiration that could hardly have survived such prolonged interruptions of the process of composition as Professor W. R. Parker thinks probable." (See also the opinion of Sprott, quoted above.) There is no need to discuss the professed "guesses" about just when the work was taken up and laid down until it is established that there were such interruptions.

(*j*) With respect to the "anarchic" rhythms Parker thinks he sees in

S.A., we may add to the views of Oras and Sprott already quoted the opinion of F. T. Prince (*The Italian Element in Milton's Verse* [Oxford, 1954]), who says (p. 153) that because of the "severely logical . . . metrical construction" the affinities of *S.A.* are seen to be "only with the more disciplined of the Italian poetic dramas," and explains (pp. 164–65) that "the apparent freedom of the choruses" is a "legal, or even legalistic, freedom" whose governing law lies in the rules of Italian prosody. We have already dealt with the "conjectured interruptions" of composition. I agree that Milton's mood in April 1648 —and, I would add, for several years before and some time after—was unable to sustain original composition, and that the psalm translations were exercises in morale as well as in linguistics.

(*k*) All the speculation and inference here is built upon a demonstrable error of fact. Milton did not invent the regeneration of the fallen Samson. Writing before the appearance of F. M. Krouse's *Milton's Samson and the Christian Tradition* (Princeton, 1949), Parker was unaware of the seventeenth-century view of Samson. Even so, he was somewhat categorical in ascribing the "invention" to Milton; it may be true that there is no hint of Samson's spiritual regeneration in the Old Testament, but there is in the New: the Epistle to the Hebrews, under the rubric "On faith: what it is; its powers; its heroes," includes Samson (11:32–34). Krouse gives many examples, from earliest Christian times down to the seventeenth century, of exegetes who declared that Samson repented of his sin after his captivity, was thereupon restored to grace, and as a regenerate saint brought down the temple under God's immediate impulsion; he also makes it quite clear that all this was a part of the popular seventeenth-century conception of Samson (see especially pp. 31, 37–38, 43, 45, 48–49, 77, and 78–79).

In his note of 1958 Parker returns to the Anonymous Biographer, whose comment he had in 1949 termed "unhelpful." He briefly recapitulates his 1949 statement about the absence of specific dating in the early biographers, and again says nothing of Richardson. Nor does he say anything of the effect upon his argument of the various studies published since and cited above. He only quotes the comment which he had previously "misread" and explains what he "now understands" it to mean: "It was now that hee began that laborious work of amassing . . . a *Latin Thesaurus* . . . ; Also the composing *Paradise Lost* And the framing a *Body of Divinity* out of the Bible: All which, notwithstanding the several Calamities befalling him in his fortunes, hee finish'd after the Restoration: As also the *Brittish history* down to the Conquest, *Paradise regaind, Samson Agonistes*, a Tragedy, *Logica* & *Accedence commenc'd Grammar* & had begun a Greek Thesaurus. . . . " This, says Parker, distinguishes between two groups of works: the first three, begun after blindness and completed after the Restoration, and the remaining six, begun at some unspecified time and (except for the Greek Thesaurus) also completed after the Restoration. If there is such a distinction in the passage (so skillfully concealed that it has taken three centuries to become discernible) it would involve an early date for *P.R.*, but this does not deter Parker; instead, he cheerfully promises to make this consequence good in a subsequent article! He recognizes that the Anonymous Biographer contradicts Edward Phillips, who said that all three of the first group were begun before Milton's blindness; this he attributes to what he thinks the Anonymous Biographer's inferior knowledge of matters pertaining to 1640–43. He does not say why, if the Anonymous Biographer is wrong in respect of all three of the works about which he is explicit and confident, we should take his word (if one grants for the moment that Parker has correctly inferred what this word is) for the six works about which he is so vague and uncertain. It will be most interesting to see Parker's argument for redating *P.R.*, since so much of his argument (see [*b*] and [*h*] above) for redating *S.A.* derived from the contrast between Edward Phillips' uncertainty about when the latter was written and his confidence that the former was "begun and finisht and Printed after . . . [*P.L.*] was publisht."

As for the Anonymous Biographer's meaning, it seems to me that in this very summary, very incomplete, and, if Edward Phillips is right, very erroneous paragraph the author has taken as his basic framework the order of publication of the works he remembers. This he supplements by reporting three unpublished works, the two thesauri and the body of divinity, disposed among the published works in what he thinks to have been the order in which they were undertaken. The two great events to which this list of works is related are Milton's blindness and the Restoration. But the biographer got his original framework wrong in one respect: the *Grammar* should have come at the beginning of his list of works published after *P.L.*, instead of at the end. Otherwise the publication dates are in sequence: 1667, 1670, 1671, 1672. If the biographer at first omitted the *Grammar* (1669), and then bethought himself of it and tacked it on, it would not be very surprising: he omitted altogether the tracts of 1659–60 and 1773 and the letters and prolusions of 1674 (to speak only of published works).

Gilbert begins with what he believes to be discrepancies between *S.A.* and its "Argument." Almost a third of the poem is occupied by the Dalila and Harapha incidents, but the Argument says only that Samson "in the mean while is visited by other persons"; the Argument speaks of the Chorus and Manoa seeking "to comfort [Samson] what they can," but Gilbert does not think they "make much effort at comfort"; the Argument does not mention the offstage shout when the temple falls; it seems to suggest a more protracted inner debate before Samson's decision to accompany the Philistine officer; and so forth. From all this Gilbert concludes that the Argument was probably not written after the poem was finished, but rather "was an outline for a proposed play, which the poet modified as he worked" (p. 99). Next, he asserts that Dalila and Harapha are comic characters who do not fit Milton's preliminary critical note, in which he condemns "intermixing Comic stuff with Tragic sadness and gravity." Hence he concludes that "the development of these visits appears to have been an afterthought" (p. 101). The poem itself has things which Gilbert thinks abrupt and others which he thinks unintegrated. He also thinks there is inartistic repetition of words and figures, and of ideas. All these things seem to him indications of lack of care and failure to revise. His explanation for the discrepancies and crudities which he believes he sees is the following: "My own impression, for many reasons that cannot be here presented, is that the tragedy is essentially an early work, following soon after the making of the notes in the Cambridge Manuscript. . . . The manuscript perhaps lay with him until he had *Paradise Regained* ready for printing. The publisher of that short epic [may have asked for something to eke it out]. . . . The poet thought of his old tragedy, had it found, and turned it over to the bookseller. I incline to think that he did no further work on it . . . " (p. 106).

It is difficult to know how to take such an argument seriously. One may urge that the alleged discrepancies are not discrepancies, that the alleged crudities are not crudities, that Dalila and Harapha are not comic characters. One may ask how the alleged carelessness and failure to revise squares with such printed *errata* as "Page 16, verse 127. for Irresistable, r. *Irresistible*" (1671, sig. [P4ʳ]; see Fletcher, facsimile ed., IV, 298–99). One may ask why Milton, who in 1645 published every scrap of verse which would help make good his poetic claims, failed to publish (and in 1654 to mention) a *S.A.* which he judged sufficiently good and sufficiently finished to publish without change in 1671, when his poetic achievement was no longer in question. But there is no need to answer "impressions" based on "reasons which cannot be presented," open guesswork, and almost equally open question-begging.

In summary, it may be said that of those who have argued for a date in the 1640's and early 1650's, one has not acknowledged any need to disprove the traditional date, and the other has failed to state fully the external, objective basis for the traditional late date, and has not stated fairly that part which he does report; that the objections which they have brought against the traditional date are sometimes meaningless, sometimes groundless, sometimes trivial, sometimes inapplicable; and that the grounds on which they have suggested early dates are either admitted conjecture, impressionistic speculation, or demonstrable fallacy.

II. SONNET VII

If the dating proposed by W. R. Parker ("Some Problems in the Chronology of Milton's Early Poems," *RES*, XI [1935], 276–83) is correct, the time referred to in the text of my essay above would be after Milton's twenty-fourth birthday, or early 1663. Such a change would not affect the present argument, for Parker retains the usual sequence for Sonnet VII and the three poems which follow. Nevertheless, in view of the strange influence Parker's article has exerted, it is more than time to examine its method and findings—indeed, it may well be too late, so widely have its conclusions been accepted; see, for example, Diekhoff, *Milton on Himself* (New York, 1939), p. 112; A. S. P. Woodhouse, "Notes on Milton's Early Development," *UTQ*, XIII (1943), 67, 99–100; Hanford, *Poems of Milton*, 2nd ed. (New York, 1953), p. 93; W. A. and Alberta T. Turner, Yale *Complete Prose Works*, I (1953), 318; M. Y. Hughes, *Milton's Complete Poems and Major Prose* (New York, 1957), p. 76.

The main contention of Parker's article is that when Milton says that Time has stolen on his wing his three-and-twentieth year he means his four-and-twentieth. After showing, without difficulty, that the title "On his being arrived at the age of 23" is without Miltonic authority (Milton gave the sonnet no title, only a number), Parker (p. 277) lays down the basic proposition

of his argument, which I here transcribe *in its entirety:* "When Milton wrote 'Anno aetatis 17,' he meant, not 'in his seventeenth year of age,' but always 'at the age of seventeen'. With this phrase he dated eight of his Latin and two of his English poems, and *in most instances* we are able to prove his memory accurate. It is clear that, in Latin at least, he meant 'at the age of' when he wrote 'in the year of age' " (my italics). This now becomes the major premise of all that follows. The second proposition is that "Milton made this particular error in English as well as in Latin." Again I transcribe the argument in its entirety (*ibid.*): "In the *History of Britain* he cites Asser as his authority for his facts about the death of Alfred; and according to Milton, Alfred 'ended his daies in the year 900. the 51. of his age.' Asser writes: 'anno vero aetatis suae 51.' Remembering Milton's usual interpretation of 'anno aetatis 51.' we can see that '51st year of age' likewise meant to him 'aged 51.' A less confusing illustration, however, is to be found a few pages later in the *History*. 'This year,' he writes, 'dy'd *Swarling* a Monk of *Croyland*, the 142. year of his Age, and another soon after him in the 115th.' His authority for this statement is given in the margin as '*Ingulf.*,' and in the latter's *Historia* we read: 'Anno proxime sequente obiit dominus *Swarlingus* completis annis vitae suae 142 . . . Tandem anno proximo vltimus omnium obiit Dominus *Turgarus* venerabilis senex completis annis vitae suae 115.' "
The third proposition is that the circumstances of December 1632 better fit the mood of Sonnet VII than do those of December 1631; the argument is the usual fitting of inference to inference, including the suggestion (p. 278) that "twenty-four, unlike twenty-three, suggests the completion of a cycle. There are twenty-four hours in a day. . . . " Without further ado Parker writes (*ibid.*), "Faced with this much evidence, we cannot, I think avoid the conclusion that the sonnet was written in December, 1632." Then he uses this date as a fixed point from which to argue the redating of a number of other works.

Now how valid is this argument? Let us begin with the major premise. Is the evidence for it correctly stated? To see that it is not we need go no farther than the same author's restatement of his case in 1952 ("Notes on the Chronology of Milton's Latin Poems," *A Tribute to George Coffin Taylor*, p. 114): "When Milton wrote 'Anno aetatis 17' he seems to have meant, not literally 'in the seventeenth year of age,' but 'at the age of seventeen' or, literally, in his eighteenth year. He used this Latin phrase for dating eight of his Latin and two of his English poems; and from *three of these ten* (Elegies II and III and the verses on the Bishop of Ely, all concerned with deaths for which there are verifiable dates) *scholars have inferred* that he meant 'at the age of' whenever he wrote 'in the year of age.' . . . The evidence, I repeat, consists of only three of ten poems. Two others of the ten (the Fair Infant elegy and the verses on Gostlin) are dated wrongly whichever way we interpret Milton's Latin, and, as we shall see, several of the remaining five are perhaps dated wrongly" (my italics).

It is not now "in most instances" but in three of ten cases that the hypothesized error will bring Milton's dating into conformity with the facts. But this revised assessment of the evidence does not mean that Parker intends to modify his major premise; on the contrary, while he wishes to shift the groundwork on which he erected it (the dates of the other poems), he wishes also to retain the premise as an accepted and unquestionable *datum*. Is this the reason for the strikingly modest "scholars have inferred"?

Not only does the postulated error fail to account for 70 per cent of the relevant data, but it is, by Parker's own showing, far from the only way to account for the 30 per cent to which it conforms. Parker not only emphasizes (p. 113) Milton's demonstrably faulty memory in dating his early compositions, but also argues (p. 115), with good evidence, that "it pleased Milton to emphasize his own precocity when he published his minor verse." He applies these inferences very freely in redating many of the poems which Milton dated; he need only extend them to the three poems on which what is left of his major premise is founded, and they will account perfectly for Milton's having given a date one year too early, without asking us to suppose that Milton, the son of a scrivener and himself much occupied with legal affairs, and whose Latinity was so much admired in his own day and since, did not understand the inescapable documentary phrase.

With the major premise gone, what is left of Parker's second proposition? Since there is now no "usual interpretation" to "remember," the obvious thing to say about the first piece of "evidence," the use of Asser, is that Milton simply gave a correct English translation of what he found. As for the second, "less confusing," piece of evidence, which now stands alone, it is surely fair comment to say that if Milton, in poring over the vast and weary deserts of the medieval chroniclers, never made a worse error of transcription and translation than, on a single occasion, in paraphrasing in one English sentence the content of two Latin ones, to neglect in each the word "completis," then his standard of accuracy is beyond all praise. Thus, the removal of the first proposition (that Milton did not understand the Latin phrase "Anno aetatis 17") leaves totally unsupported the second—and breath-taking—proposition, that Milton did not understand the English phrase "three and twentieth year."

The third proposition need not be examined. There would be no difficulty in drawing up a similar argument for 1631 (see, for example, D. C. Dorian, *The English Diodatis* [1950], pp. 122–23). What counts is that there is now no reason to hypothesize that when Milton contemplates

> How soon hath time the suttle theef of youth,
> Stoln on his wing my three and twentieth yeer,

he had just turned twenty-five; and we may return to the poem's perfectly plain meaning. This, in turn, means, I think, that discussion of the chronology of Milton's early poems should return to the *status quo ante* 1935.

While this appendix cannot be made the occasion for examining all of the ways in which Parker has changed the meaning of Milton's testimony concerning dates of composition, it seems worthwhile to analyze the most important of his proposals of 1952 before it becomes as widely accepted as that concerning Sonnet VII. Both the 1645 and the 1673 editions of the *Poems* date *Elegia Septima* "Anno aetatis undevigesimo." But Parker, who is concerned to establish that the sequence in which the poems are printed is an important guide to the order of their composition, wishes to show that Elegy VII was written later than Elegy VI, which we know to have been composed

shortly after 25 December 1629—i.e., just after Milton had turned twenty-
one. His ordinary interpretation would advance "nineteenth" to "twentieth,"
but what is required here is "twenty-second." Accordingly, Parker writes
(p. 120): "Why 'Anno aetatis undevigesimo' instead of the usual 'Anno
aetatis 19'? . . . I conjecture that he used the ordinal in this solitary instance
in order to make the record—what it certainly is—conspicuous, but that he
actually wrote 'Anno aetatis uno et vigesimo' or 'uno&vigesimo.' This age is
ever an occasion of importance and deserves more notice. . . . A careless
compositor . . . may have misread Milton's date as 'undevigesimo' . . . ."

Now, at the beginning of his chronological speculations, in the well-
known 1935 article, Parker rested a good deal of his case for the chronological
ordering of most of *1645* and *1673* on the fact that one item in the *1673
Errata* shows care for the arrangement (he assumed it must be a chronological
arrangement). But some dozen and a half other items in the same *Errata*
show care for other things, like turned or dropped letters, misplaced or missing commas, etc. Parker's argument would have Milton using the ordinal *for
the sole purpose of making the date conspicuous*, and then not noticing that this
conspicuous dating—*in the title line*—was two years off in *1645* and again in
1673, while carefully providing corrections for matters of merely typographic
significance!

III. *AD PATREM*

Masson (*Life*, I, 324) summarily assigned *Ad Patrem* to 1632 because he associated it with the "Letter to a Friend." In 1925 ("Youth of Milton," pp.
130–31) Hanford was willing to accept this view, although he pointed out
that the contrast between the two pieces was striking. In the same year
Grierson (*Poems*, 2 vols. [1925], I, xxii), enforcing the contrast more strongly,
argued for 1637 (or possibly 1638). Milton's father, he pointed out, had been
prepared to allow his son ample time for study, and had no objection to poetry
occupying some of this time, as with other learned men and divines. "But
when it became clear that poetry was to be, not an occasional bypath, but the
main highway of his son's career, he seems to have been taken aback and to
have demurred. Milton's poem would seem to be his reply. This crisis can, I
think, hardly have arisen till the performance and publication of 'Comus'
revealed clearly both to Milton and his father whither the long-waited-for
prompting of the spirit was preparing to carry him." Grierson also noted
some verbal echoes in "Lycidas" and "Mansus." Tillyard, in 1930 (*Milton*,
p. 384), accepted this argument, reinforcing it with another echo in "Mansus"
and with an argument from style. Woodhouse ("Notes on Milton's Early
Development," pp. 89–91), although repudiating Masson's reason, argues for
his date, while J. M. French (*Life Records*, 5 vols. [1949–58], I, 274) continues
to find Masson's reason persuasive; but the arguments of Grierson and Tillyard have been increasingly accepted. Hanford is now persuaded (*Poems*, 2nd
ed. [1953], p. 151), putting *Ad Patrem* in 1637 after "Lycidas" and saying that
it is "more mature in feeling and expression than anything Milton had written
hitherto." Hughes (*Minor Poems* [1937], p. 282) dated it 1636–37; Diekhoff
(*Milton on Himself* [1939], p. 117) gives 1637 as the probable date; and Barker
(*Milton and the Puritan Dilemma* [1942], p. 347, n. 2) gives "c. 1636." Harris

Fletcher has argued for dates as late as 1645 (*Poetical Works* [1941], p. 524), but now appears willing to accept the bracket 1635–45 (*Intellectual Development of John Milton* [1956], p. 283). Parker ("Notes on the Chronology of Milton's Latin Poems," pp. 125–28) accepts Grierson's general argument, but opts for 1634 (after the production of *Comus*) rather than 1637 (after its publication), on the ground that the earlier date would preserve the partial chronological order he sees in the printed *Poems;* Tillyard's argument he finds "subjective" and unconvincing. Hughes, in his new edition (*Complete Poetry and Major Prose* [1957], p. 85), adopts Parker's intermediate date. As the preceding discussion of "Sonnet VII" and *Elegia Septima* shows, I think Parker's argument that, apart from what he thinks a relatively few "obvious" exceptions for "artistic reasons," the order of the poems in the printed editions, "within their respective groups," corresponds to the order of their composition, is without validity, and the fact that *Ad Patrem* is printed before the Greek version of Psalm 114 is no evidence that it was composed first (and indeed what reason is there to share Masson's odd assumption that the "ode" Milton sent Gill in December 1634 is the Greek psalm?). But even if one were to allow that Milton had intended a chronological ordering within the groups ("occasionally" disturbed "for artistic reasons"), this would not be decisive for *Ad Patrem*. J. T. Shawcross ("The Date of *Ad Patrem*," *N & Q*, ccIV [1959], 358–59), beginning with Parker's suggested dates for the neighboring poems and his postulated chronological sequence, shows most convincingly how "the apparent chronological order could have been disturbed by exigencies of printing," and returns to the "more meaningful and convincing" dating of Grierson and Tillyard.

MILTON'S HARAPHA AND GOLIATH

John M. Steadman, Atlanta, Georgia

I

The literary parentage of Milton's "Giant *Harapha* of *Gath*" has been a controversial subject for contemporary scholars. In Parker's opinion, "Harapha had some Euripidean blood in his veins";[1] "the introduction of an insolent giant, the frank depiction of a noisy quarrel; the tendency to mix laconic insult with formal debate—these are all things which we expect from Euripides."[2] Gilbert, on the other hand, suggested the influence of the romances of chivalry. "Harapha," he maintained, "is a boastful knight, own brother to Spenser's Braggadocchio."[3] Boughner believed that "the giant of Gath is . . . a figure conceived in the comic spirit and woven out of the same comic stuff that Milton so sweepingly disparages in the preface." The cowardly braggart of Renaissance Italian comedy contributed the salient characteristics of this figure—

Harapha's emphasis on his "honour," which he has won by "mortal duel"; his knightly disdain for Samson's feats of strength and unchivalric equipment, and a preference for the "glorious arms" worn in battle by heroes and for a combat "in camp or listed field"; his pretended lament that "fortune" in the past has prevented the two from meeting and now makes it impossible for a "noble warriour" to stoop to such an unworthy "match"; and his taking refuge, when directly challenged by Samson, in the pretext that "no man of arms" would fight with a condemned man.

This behavior, Boughner argued, reflected the influence of the Renaissance dramatists, who had "ordinarily made the soldier the victim of a situation in which he must either accept a challenge and by fighting run the risk of wounds or blows, or decline the challenge on some pretext by which the code of arms permitted him to retain his honor. . . ."[4]

Actually, there is no need to look so far afield. For a prototype

---

[1] William R. Parker, "Milton's Harapha," *TLS*, 2 January 1937, p. 12.

[2] William R. Parker, *Milton's Debt to Greek Tragedy in Samson Agonistes* (Baltimore, 1937), p. 123.

[3] Allan Gilbert, "*Samson Agonistes* 1096," *MLN*, XXIX (1914), 161 n.

[4] Daniel C. Boughner, "Milton's Harapha and Renaissance Comedy," *ELH*, XI (1944), 297–306. For criticism of Boughner's view, see F. Michael Krouse, *Milton's Samson and the Christian Tradition* (Princeton, 1949), p. 129.

for the Philistine giant Milton could have turned simply to the account of Goliath in I Samuel 17. Many of Harapha's attributes could have been derived from the Biblical portrait of his son.

In describing this figure as a "Giant . . . of *Gath*" and the "Father of five Sons All of Gigantic size, *Goliah* chief," Milton was exploiting the Hebrew word for giant (*raphah*)[5] and the Biblical references to "the sonnes of Haraphah," who had been "borne unto Haraphah at Gath, and fel by the hand of David, and by the hands of his servants" (II Samuel 21:16–22; I Chronicles 20:4–8). Of these four "children of Haraphah," one (Lahmi) had been identified as "the brother of Goliath the Gittite, whose spearestaffe was like a weavers beame." In investing the father with many of the characteristics of his more famous son, Milton was following one of the cardinal principles of the poetic art—decorum, "the grand masterpiece to observe."[6]

Goliath and Harapha share several affinities besides their father-son relationship: Both are giants of Gath. Both are champions of the Philistines. Both hurl insults at the Israelites. Both boast of exploits they never fulfill. Both invoke Philistine gods.[7] Both scoff at the "trivial" weapons of their adversaries, and mock the latters' disregard for the conventional armaments of warfare. Both are finally humiliated[8] by the Hebrew opponents they have scorned.

Conversely, David and Samson resemble each other in their roles as God's champions against Philistine champions, their obvious physical handicaps, and their disregard for armor and arms.

Samson's catalogue of the giant's "gorgeous arms" includes many items listed among Goliath's paraphernalia—helmet, coat of mail, greaves, spear, and shield.[9] Though Milton amplifies this list, to underline still further the giant's reliance on arms ("Brigandine," "Vant-brass," "Gauntlet"), he adds two further details strongly

---

[5] Parker, "Milton's Harapha"; E. N. Adler, "Milton's Harapha," *TLS*, 16 January 1937, p. 44; Jacob Leveen, "Milton's Harapha," *TLS*, 23 January 1937, p. 60; H. Loewe, "Milton's Harapha," *TLS*, 23 January 1937, p. 60; Merritt Y. Hughes, ed., *Samson Agonistes* (New York, 1937), pp. 588 n., 596 n.; James Hastings, ed., *A Dictionary of the Bible* (Edinburgh, 1902), *s.v. Rapha.*

[6] John Milton, *Of Education;* see Bohn edition, III (London, 1883), 474.

[7] I Sam. 17:43 ("And the Philistine cursed David by his gods"); Milton's Harapha invokes Baal-zebub (l. 1231) and swears by Astaroth (l. 1242).

[8] It is interesting to note that the Vulgate uses the word *humiliavit* in describing the victory of David and his warriors over four Philistine giants (I Chron. 20:4): "percussit Sobochai Husaithites, Saphai de genere Raphaim, et humiliavit eos."

[9] I Sam. 17:5–7. The Biblical account of the victory of David and his men over the four giant "sonnes of Haraphah" (see Geneva version) likewise stresses the giants' arms and armor (II Sam. 21:16, 19; I Chron. 20:5).

reminiscent of Goliath. Like his son, Harapha wears helmet and body-armor of brass. Like Goliath's, his spear-shaft resembles "A Weavers beam."[10]

Conversely, Samson, like David, bears only the most trivial weapons. Though the "Oak'n staff" with which he threatens his opponent has no parallel in Judges, there is a suggestive analogue in the staff David carries in I Samuel 17:40—a weapon Goliath despises ("Am I a dog, that thou comest to me with staves?"). Harapha's "knightly disdain for Samson's . . . unchivalric equipment, and a preference for the 'glorious arms' worn in battle by heroes"[11] are paralleled by Goliath's contempt for David's rustic arms and the Biblical emphasis on his own massive weapons and armor.

Analogous too are the giants' emphasis on "mortal duel" and "preference for . . . a combat 'in camp or listed field' " and their disdain for their Hebrew antagonists as "an unworthy 'match.' "[12] In the Biblical account, Goliath ("a champion out of the camp of the Philistines") had challenged the Israelites to "choose you a man for you" for single combat to the death, in full view of the two armies in "battle . . . array." This "mortal duel" became a favorite theme for Renaissance Biblical epic, and Milton could have encountered the theme of the *Monomachia* of David and Goliath in several heroic poems.[13] Unlike the Renaissance playwrights cited by Boughner, these poets treated the single combat as a heroic theme, rather than as a subject "for farce."[14]

Like Harapha, who despises Samson as "no worthy match For valour to assail," Goliath feels contempt for his adversary:

And when the Philistine looked about, and saw David, he disdained him: for he was but a youth, and ruddy, and of a fair countenance.

In DuBartas' *La Seconde Sepmaine*, Goliath warns David that this is no shepherds' contest; like Harapha, he initially refuses to fight with so unworthy an antagonist:

> Mais non, je ne veux point, ô pucelle affetee,
> Souiller dedans ton sang ma dextre redoutee,

---

[10] See Hughes, p. 1120 n.
[11] Boughner, p. 298.
[12] Boughner, p. 298.
[13] For DuBellay's *Monomachie de David et de Goliath* and other epic treatments of this subject, see R. A. Sayce, *The French Biblical Epic in the Seventeenth Century* (Oxford, 1955), *passim*. See also Rudolph Walther, *Monomachia Davidis et Goliae* (Tiguri, n.d.).
[14] Boughner, p. 298.

Cerche [*sic*] quelque autre main, trouve un autre Atropos,
Et ne fonde, insolent, sur ma honte ton los.[15]

Harapha declares that a combat with Samson would "stain his honour"; DuBartas' Goliath regards a duel with David as shameful to himself and disdains to soil his hand in such a fight.

In both encounters the giant's boasts prove substanceless. Goliath threatens to "give thy flesh unto the fowls of the air, and to the beasts of the field." Harapha vaunts that

I should have forc'd thee soon wish other arms,
Or left thy carcase where the Ass lay thrown. . . .

Both engagements culminate in the giant's humiliation. Goliath is ignominiously slain by a boy with the shepherd's weapons he had despised. Harapha departs "somewhat crestfall'n"—compelled to "Hear these dishonours, and not render death"—a "vain boaster" and "baffl'd coward."

Though there are several obvious differences between the two situations[16] (Samson's victory over the giant is essentially moral, for his adversary refuses to fight), most of the salient features of the encounter between Samson and Harapha appear in the Biblical account of the duel between David and Goliath. The giant's character derives, on the whole, less from Renaissance comedy than from I Samuel 17.

II

In the encounter with Harapha, Krouse has recognized the third and last of "three trials of faith." The giant serves as "the instrument of temptation by violence and fear," but Samson is "ready to engage in mortal combat with Harapha because his 'trust . . . in the living God' is still strong."[17] The Biblical account of David's *monomachia* with Goliath places a similar emphasis on the Hebrew champion's reliance on God for victory. Like Samson, David is zealous for Jehovah's honor. Like Samson, he depends on divine aid rather than on arms and armor. In both encounters the essential elements are the

[15] *The Works of Guillaume de Salluste Sieur Du Bartas*, ed. U. T. Holmes, Jr., J. C. Lyons, R. W. Linker (Chapel Hill, 1940), III, 341–42. For DuBartas' influence on *Paradise Lost*, see George C. Taylor, *Milton's Use of Du Bartas* (Cambridge, Mass., 1934).

[16] The most obvious differences are that Samson and Harapha never come to blows, that Goliath never reveals himself a coward, and that (though Harapha first brings up the subject of the duel) it is Samson, rather than the Philistine giant, who issues the formal challenge.

[17] Krouse, pp. 129–30.

same—on the one hand, the giant's boasts and reliance on arms; on the other, the Hebrew's disdain of fleshly weapons and an unshaken confidence in God.

Although Milton gives this antithesis its clearest dramatic expression in the Harapha episode, it recurs throughout the drama. The opening speech of the Chorus describes the hero as one "whom unarm'd No strength of man, or fiercest wild beast could withstand" and relates how, before his downfall, he

> Ran on embattelld Armies clad in Iron,
> And weaponless himself
> Made Arms ridiculous, useless the forgery
> Of brazen shield and spear, the hammer'd Cuirass,
> *Chalybean* temper'd steel, and frock of mail
> Adamantean Proof.

Scorning "thir proud arms and warlike tools," he had compelled seasoned warriors to turn "Thir plated backs under his heel" or soil "thir crested helmets in the dust." Fighting with "what trivial weapon came to hand, The Jaw of a dead Ass," he had slain a thousand Philistines at Ramath-lechi. Samson himself reiterates this contrast:

> . . . on thir whole Host I flew
> Unarm'd, and with a trivial weapon fell'd
> Thir choicest youth. . . .

Thus the essential features of Samson's challenge to Harapha had been clearly stated at the very beginning of the drama, and, significantly, the Chorus reaffirms them immediately after the Harapha episode:

> He all thir Ammunition
> And feats of War defeats
> With plain Heroic magnitude of mind
> And celestial vigour arm'd,
> Thir Armories and Magazins contemns,
> Renders them useless, while. . .
> Swift as the lightning glance he executes
> His errand on the wicked, who surpris'd
> Lose thir defence distracted and amaz'd.

In I Samuel 17 the contrast between the virtually unarmed Israelite and the heavily armed Philistine giant had been emphasized by the detailed catalogue of Goliath's massive armaments (verses 5–7), David's explicit rejection of Saul's armor for the trivial weapons of the shepherd (38–40), and his reply to the giant's taunts (45–47):

Thou comest to me with a sword, and with a spear, and with a shield: but I come to thee in the name of the LORD of hosts, the God of the armies of

Israel, whom thou hast defied. And all this assembly shall know that the LORD saveth not with sword and spear: for the battle is the LORD's, and he will give you into our hands.

Could we ask for a more explicit statement of the basic antithesis underlying Samson's challenge to Harapha—the ethical opposition of *fiducia in Deo* (trust in God) and *fiducia carnalis* (carnal reliance)?[18] Like David, Samson chooses to fight in God's name, for God's honor, against the blaspheming infidel. Like David, he confesses that "the battle is the LORD'S":

> . . . all the contest is now
> 'Twixt God and *Dagon*. . . .
> . . . these Magic spells,
> Which I to be the power of *Israel's* God
> Avow, and challenge *Dagon* to the test. . . .

Like David, he rejects the conventional paraphernalia of warfare and relies instead on divine aid. The parallel between the two Hebrew champions is still further enhanced by their physical handicaps— Samson's fetters and blindness, and David's youth:

And Saul said to David, Thou art not able to go against this Philistine to fight with him: for thou art but a youth, and he a man of war from his youth.

The moral values Milton emphasizes in the Harapha episode had, moreover, been traditionally recognized by commentators on I Samuel 17. Procopius of Gaza observed that God did not permit David to bear Saul's weapons, lest the victory be attributed in part to arms:

Saul arma sua dedit, at David gestare non potuit. Etenim Deus hoc non concedit, sed necdum vult reportare victoriam, ne armis victoriae virtute partae pars attribuatur.[19]

Theodoretus stressed David's trust in divine aid and the contrast between the unarmed shepherd youth and the seasoned man of war:

Erat adolescens quindecim aut sedecim annorum. . . . Nihil, inquit, differt a bestia qui vivit in impietate, et qui est nudatus divino auxilio. Ego autem confido in illius [Dei] auxilio. . . . Cum hac fide profectus spe non fuit frustratus: sed cum esset nudus, vicit armatum, et qui pascebat oves, eum qui erat exercitatus in bellis et tropaeis; et qui erat parvus et juvenis, eum qui de tanta se jactabat magnitudine.[20]

---

[18] See Milton's *De Doctrina Christiana*, Bk. II, ch. 3; cf. my article, " 'Faithful Champion': The Theological Basis of Milton's Hero of Faith," *Anglia*, LXXVII (1959), 12–28.

[19] *PG*, LXXXVII, col. 1102.

[20] *PG*, LXXX, cols. 566–67.

Theodorus Prodromus likewise emphasized the gulf between the two champions in arms, size, and military experience:

David upilio, per aetatem pusillus corpore, Goliae procero giganti mortem infert, inermis armato. . . .

Ante Philistaeorum cuneos prosiliens barbarus, provocabat ad singulare certamen virum bello instructissimum, qui visu quidem horribilis erat, sed ab exili David prostratus est. . . .[21]

Calvin's *Homiliae in Primum Librum Samuelis*[22] laid considerable stress on many of the principal concepts of the Harapha episode— the giant's vaunts and blasphemies, the apparent inequality of the conflict, and—above all—the Hebrew's confidence in God. Unterrified by the giant's threats, David treats them as an occasion for magnifying God:

Quam blasphemus iste gigas, Davidi maledicens in idolis quae a Philistaeis colebantur? quasi adversus Deum possit aliquid idola gentium. Atque istis minis Davidem ille gigas terrere voluit: sed ille contra maiorem inde occasionem Dei magnificiendi capit: et blasphemi hominis in Dei maiestatem contumeliis excitatur.[23]

The most striking feature of the duel, however, is the antithesis between the unarmed shepherd and the fully equipped warrior:

Sed quam impari certamine! Nae veluti si musca elephantum, vel formica taurum vel aliquam similem feram lacesseret . . . . Sed quum certamen illud impar aggressum, et velut in immensam abyssum immersum, Deus facit emergere, et victoriam insignem ipsi de hoste concedit: quum, inquam, gigas, et quidem sic omnibus armis instructus, et in re militari exercitatus, ut rupes quaedam aut propugnaculum videretur, a Davide superatur, et eo iuvene, et inermi, nisi quod aliquot lapillis in pera pastorali sumptis, funda turrem illam et propugnaculum evertere conatus est. Nam ipsius gigantis staturam et armaturam attendite, *erat altitudinis sex cubitorum et palmi: Et cassis aerea super caput eius: et lorica squamata induebatur. Et ocreas aereas habebat in cruribus: et clypeus aereus tegebat humeros eius.* Quibus vero contra munitus armis erat David? Nae, nudus et inermis adversum tam bene armatum gigantem progreditur. . . .[24]

[21] *PG*, cxxxiii, col. 1152.

[22] *Corpus Reformatorum*, ed. G. Baum, E. Cunitz, and E. Reuss (Brunsvigae, 1886), lviii, cols. 184–253.

[23] *Corpus Reformatorum*, col. 227.

[24] *Corpus Reformatorum*, col. 190. Cf. col. 215, "Ecquis enim adolescentem, et inexercitatum, ferat cum gigante exercitato in armis congredi? quis inermem cum cataphracto milite, et quidem non pari cum aliis statura, sed qui erat turris instar, ut vidimus: cuius lancea tanti ponderis et tantae longitudinis erat ut a nullo alio portari posset? Denique qui clypeum, galeam, thoracem, ocreas immensi ponderis habebat? et qui unus erat instar propugnaculi?" See also col. 224, "Quid enim effecturus videtur

Nevertheless, trusting not in his own strength, but in God, the Hebrew champion remained unshaken by the giant's threats and superior weapons:

Nihil enim de suis viribus sibi pollicitus est, adversus gigantem Goliathum singulari certamine congredi paratus: . . . sed in Deum spem omnem collocavit, et coelitus auxilium exspectavit, de se ipso nihil sperans . . . . Talis est fiducia illa Davidis in Dei potentia:[25]

Nunquam ergo David, mente titubavit nunquam immutatus est: quam mentem habuit rusticus et opilio, et quam in Deo fiduciam. . . .[26]

Hoc sane David auxilium divinum sensit, exprobrans giganti gladium et lanceam, qua Davidem se confossurum gloriabatur, sed vana gloriatione.[27]

In the *Homilies*, as in *Samson Agonistes*, the giant's vaunting proves vain ("vana gloriatio"). Calvin, like Milton, compares the giant to a tower ("his pile high-built and proud," "lay thy structure low").[28] Finally, in Calvin's account, as in Milton's, the giant arrogantly mocks his Hebrew antagonist as below his own "quality":

Itaque Goliathus arroganter et fastuose adversus illum progressus despexit, quod non esset eiusdem cum ipso qualitatis . . . Davidem ludibrio habuit quod cum baculo pastorali seu pedo progrederetur, tanquam adversus canem. . . .[29]

The marginal glosses on I Samuel 17 in the Geneva Bible[30] emphasize many of the same points. The note on verse 33 stresses the trial of faith:

Here Satan proveth Davids faith by the infidelitie of Saul.

The observations on verses 34, 46, and 48 call attention to David's trust in God, assurance of his cause and calling, and zeal for God's honor:

David by the experience that he hath had in time past of Gods helpe, nothing doubteth to overcome this danger, seeing he was zealous for Gods honor.

---

rusticus homo et ovium pastor, qui praelio nunquam interfuerat, qui cum hoste manum nunquam conserverat? qui vel a stabulis vel a domo paterna nunquam recesserat? qui denique innermis [*sic*], sine galea, sine lorica, sine clypeo, solo baculo armatus adversus hostem progrediebatur?"

[25] *Corpus Reformatorum*, cols. 213–14
[26] *Corpus Reformatorum*, col. 228.
[27] *Corpus Reformatorum*, col. 229.
[28] Hughes, pp. 588 n., 596 n.
[29] Calvin, col. 226
[30] *The Bible . . . Imprinted at London by Robert Barker* (1607). For close parallels between *Samson Agonistes* and the Geneva version's glosses on Judges, see George W. Whiting, *"Samson Agonistes* and the Geneva Bible," *Rice Institute Pamphlet*, xxxviii, no. 1 (1951), 18–35.

David being assured both of his cause and of his calling, prophesieth of the destruction of the Philistims.

Being moved with a fervent zeale to be revenged upon the blasphemer of Gods Name.

The commentary on verses 37 and 40 declares that David's victory was due not to his own might, but to the "power of God":

For by these examples he [Saul] saw that the power of God was with him [David].

To the intent that by these weake meanes, God might onely be knowen to be the author of this victorie.

The headnote at the beginning of the chapter reiterates the essential point of verse 47, *"The Lord saveth not by sword nor speare."*

Though David and Samson had long been associated (Hebrews 11:32–34) as "heroes of faith"[31] who "out of weakness were made strong," Keckermann's *Systema SS. Theologicae* stressed an additional point of resemblance. The exploits of both champions were "mixed" miracles—miracles in which God controls the "second causes" and both directs and increases their forces beyond nature:[32]

Talia mixta miracula multa occurrunt in sacris: quale est miraculosum illud robur Simsonis, qui naturae & temperamenti fuit robustissimi, sed ita, ut Deus vires illas naturales in eo auxerit, ut ea efficeret Simson, quae impossibile fuit efficere solis naturae viribus, ut videre est, Iud. 14.15 & 16. Sic 1. Sam. 17. David adolescens vastissimi corporis, & roboris Goliatum lapillo è funda eiecto, prosternit, adhibens naturae vires brachium & fundam; sed quae minime suffecissent ad hoc opus emoliendum, nisi naturam auxisset vis quaedam superior. Nimirum quotiescunque potest per naturae vires fieri, solet Deus adhibere naturam ad miraculosos effectus, tum ne ociosa sit natura, quando potest agere; tum ut testetur causas, secundas non pugnare, sed subordinari suae potentiae; tum denique, ut ostendit se esse autorem naturae, eamque amare, & eius vires posse prout licet vel intendere, vel remittere.[33]

III

The primary source of Milton's giant is thus Biblical rather than secular. Though classical tragedy and Renaissance comedy may have been contributing influences, his character and significance

---

[31] See Krouse, pp. 130–31; Parker, *Milton's Debt*, p. 236.

[32] *Systema SS. Theologiae . . . per Bartholomaeum Keckermannum* (Hanoviae, 1602), p. 467: "Mixta sunt, cum Deus assumit causas secundas, earumque vires supra naturam intendit & auget." In line 364 of Milton's drama, Samson is called "the miracle of men."

[33] Keckermann, pp. 466–67.

derive largely from I Samuel 17, and his name from II Samuel 21. Milton introduced him into the story of Samson on the analogy of Goliath in the story of David, in order to convey the same moral opposition which had been manifested in David's duel—the antithesis between the Hebrew's trust in God and disdain of fleshly weapons and the Philistine's pride and carnal reliance. Both Goliath and Harapha trust in "glorious arms" for "safety," but this is a false security, a *vana salus*.[34] "The LORD saveth not with sword and spear," and both giants, for all their strength, are ignominiously defeated by their unarmed opponents. The true prototype of the spiritual duel between Samson and Harapha is the *monomachia* between David and Goliath. In the encounter between a physically handicapped "hero of faith" and a Philistine giant in full armor, Milton found an ideal vehicle for the ethical opposition between *fiducia in Deo* and *fiducia carnalis*.

[34] Cf. Rabanus' comment on the Israelites' battles with four Philistine giants in II Sam. 21 (*Patrologia Latina*, CIX, col. 114): "Quid autem quatuor bella ista David et servorum ejus contra Palaestinos significant, nisi bellum Christi, quod omni tempore istius vitae in membris suis contra perfidos quosque istius saeculi, et contra spiritales nequitias incessanter agit? . . . Unde Psalmista ex persona Ecclesiae confidenter dicit: 'In Deo faciemus virtutem, et ipse ad nihilum deducet tribulantes nos (*Psal.* LIX).'" In the Authorized Version this text is Psalm 60:11; in the Vulgate, Psalm 59:13.

MILTON AND ALEXANDER MORE: NEW DOCUMENTS

Kester Svendsen, University of Oregon

The Middelburg, Amsterdam, and Charenton phases of Alexander More's turbulent career, as reported by Bayle and Haags, have to some extent been documented in recent times by Masson, Stern, and French.[1] But the equally well advertised tempests and turmoil at Geneva, though fortified with an extract or two in Stern, have remained pretty much a matter of Milton's charges in *Defensio Secunda* (1652) and *Pro Se Defensio* (1655) and More's denials in *Fides Publica* (1654–55). Unquestionably the poet obtained firsthand information through Ezekiel Spanheim, the Turretins, and the Calandrinis to supplement the gossip forwarded by Thurloe's agents; but the true state of More's affairs in Geneva for the period 1639–49 has not been verified. Now through the courtesy of Dr. Peter Wegelin, of Berne, and M. Louis Binz, associate archivist of Geneva, the entries about More in the *Registres des Conseils* and the *Registres de la Vénérable Compagnie des Pasteurs et Professeurs* have been supplied me in microfilm. They tell an involved and somewhat pathetic story of More's difficulties, not least of which was being the stubborn focus of a struggle for power between civil and ecclesiastical authorities.[2]

The present article concerns the 125 entries about More in the *Registres des Conseils*, Nos. 138–150, which extend from 3 August 1639, when the Council approved his appointment as Professor of Greek, to 22 July 1651, when it authorized an official copy of its attestations about him sent to Montauban, where the luckless pastor

[1] See my "Milton's *Pro Se Defensio* and Alexander More," University of Texas *Studies in Language and Literature*, I (1959), 12, n. 2, for the bibliography of More's life and his conflict with Milton. Alfred Stern, *Milton und sein Zeit*, 2 vols. (Leipzig, 1877–79), II, 297–303, quotes briefly from Salmasius' letter (*Archives de Genève* No. 3194) and from *Registres de la Vénérable Compagnie*, 25 July 1648, 24 November 1648, and 16 February 1649. The rest of Stern's appendix documents synod proceedings at ter Goude, April 1659; the relation of his findings to Milton's charges is discussed in the article referred to above. Other relevant information, including a great deal in Thurloe and Burmann missed by Masson, has been assembled by J. Milton French, *The Life Records of John Milton*, 5 vols. (New Brunswick, N. J., 1949–58).

[2] I am indebted to the University of Oregon Office of Scientific and Scholarly Research for a grant which enabled the microfilming and Xeroxing of these entries. The study has been advanced at various stages by grants from the University of Oklahoma, the Folger Shakespeare Library, and the Huntington Library and Art Gallery for an edition of *Pro Se Defensio* for the Yale *Complete Prose Works of Milton*.

was once more seeking a post.[3] In the critical years 1648–49, the Council devoted nearly a hundred discussions to More's manners and morals, his testimonials, his invitations to Middelburg and Lyons, and to the evasions and resistance of the Company to the Council's plans for him. The minutes of these meetings substantiate nearly every accusation Milton made about More's troubles at Geneva, and they identify most of the Genevans named in *Defensio Secunda, Fides Publica,* and *Pro Se Defensio.*[4] A summary of Milton's principal charges will simplify reference and comparison.

Once Milton committed himself in *Defensio Secunda* to the subsequently embarrassing attribution of *Regii Sanguinis Clamor* (1652) to Alexander More, he went after his antagonist with a fury exceeded only by the ferocity of his return to the same victim in *Pro Se Defensio.* The endless iterations about More's adultery and heterodoxy in the former are particularized and expanded in the latter, together with a systematic devaluation of the twenty-three testimonials printed in More's *Fides Publica* and its *Supplementum.*[5] In *Defensio Secunda*

---

[3] The extracts from *Registres de la Vénérable Compagnie* date from No. 8, 19 July 1639, to No. 9, 23 May 1651. In addition to these two sets of entries, M. Binz has kindly provided microfilm of *Archives de Genève* No. 3111, three letters of 1642 from the French Church of London asking More's assignment as pastor; No. 3191, two letters (one of them also in translation) of 1648 from the burgomasters of Middelburg concerning More's appointment there and one from Elizabeth of Bohemia urging approval; No. 3194, Salmasius' letter of 8 June 1648 about the charges against More (Stern, II, 297, quotes a sentence from this). Donald A. Roberts informs me of several other documents in a Geneva *Manuscript Français* 468 entitled "Affaire Alexandre Morus." Since one of these relates the story of More's adultery with Claudia Pelletta, it is doubtless part of the "hundred articles" referred to by both Milton and *Registres des Conseils.* Roberts has made these available to me in advance of his edition of *Defensio Secunda* for the Yale *Complete Prose Works of John Milton.* Correlation of the Registers of Council and Company and of the other archival material may be expected as a sequel to the present study.

[4] In this period, the effective civil power was the Petit Conseil, though the Genevan structure included a Sénat du Syndics, a Grand Conseil de Deux Cents, and a Conseil Général of all citizens. Several times the Company of Ministers upset the Petty Council by suggesting an appeal to the Grand Council or to the General Council (see particularly *Registres des Conseils,* No. 148, 12 February 1649, pp. 77–79; 18 April 1649, pp. 203–206—hereafter cited as *R.C.*). The Petty Council met two or three times a week and at call of one of the Syndics for special emergencies. A brief relation of its conflict with the Company over More and other matters appears in Charles Borgeaud, *Histoire de l'Université de Genève: L'Académie de Calvin* (Geneva, 1900), pp. 353–57.

[5] I use *Defensio Secunda* and *Pro Se Defensio* in *The Works of John Milton,* 18 vols. (New York, 1933–38), VII–IX (hereafter cited as *Works*), and the Huntington Library copy of *Alexandri Mori Ecclesiastae & Sacrarum Litterarum Professoris Fides Publica, Contra Calumnias Ioannis Miltoni* (Hagae-Comitum, MDCLIV), which includes the separately bound but continuously paged *Supplementum* of 1655.

Milton described More as a professor of Greek dismissed with ignominy or ejected from Geneva because of flagrant immorality and heresy. He noted a preliminary censure by the ministry of More's doctrinal aberrations, his recantation upon oath, and his escape from further prosecution by contriving an invitation to Middelburg through the influence of Salmasius. In order to get rid of him, the Genevans issued him perfunctory testimonial letters; but even these cold declarations were offensive to Frederick Spanheim, who had known him at Geneva and who had warned Salmasius against sponsoring so impious a man. They let him go, said Milton, but they kept on file in the Geneva library the written evidence of his subversive opinions and of his summer house affair with a serving woman.[6]

After the publication of *Fides Publica* with More's defense of his reputation at Geneva and with copies of various testimonials, Milton enlarged his attack. In the interim he had accumulated much precise information, including what presumably he had not known earlier, that More's departure for Middelburg was delayed on account of difficulty about the certification of his character and doctrine. He repeated charges about the adultery in the garden, now naming the paramour as Claudia Pelletta; he reasserted the cacheting of these and other indictments to the number of nearly a hundred in the public library; and he traced the stages by which the ministers discredited More but permitted his transfer with testimonials to avert public scandal.[7] His inspection of More's activities is so circumstantial as almost to indicate access through an intermediary to the official records. One shrewd stroke was his suggestion that More received invitations with the understanding that he would not accept.[8]

Now he adds that More had indeed been accorded testimonials prior to the threatened trial over the Pelletta affair; but this was long before his actual departure. Even these were suspect as having been passed in less than a full assembly and not on a regular meeting day. Furthermore, some in the assembly objected to their issue and others repented having authorized them; they were simply an expedient to avoid disgracing Geneva. When later More was about to be tried, he suddenly requested permission to accept the invitation to Middelburg. This was granted as another uneasy expedient, but More was deprived of his office and denied the additional letter of recommendation he had

[6] *Works*, VIII, 31–35, 149.
[7] *Works*, IX, 135–37, 193, 233, 271, 281 *et passim*.
[8] *Works*, IX, 157–59.

the effrontery to ask for. So he remained in Geneva some eight or ten months, unwilling to transfer to Middelburg empty-handed and unable to obtain the new clearance paper necessary to his reputation.[9] Then for a second time his trial was prepared; but the authorities decided instead to give him a new letter, which was, however, so little to his liking that More omitted it from *Fides Publica*.[10] Milton hammers at More's failure to produce this last letter and names Mermilliod, Theodore Tronchin, and Pictet as Genevan ministers violently opposed to him.[11] He disparages letters More did obtain as partial, partisan, and unsatisfactory. It is clear from the evidence supplied by the Registers that Milton knew more about the murky circumstances lying back of the testimonials than do any of his biographers, including Masson, who took them at face value as the most splendid set ever provided a migrating divine.[12] Milton speaks of More's "[standing] by while they were written"; and he reads between the lines something of the extortion and imposition which will now be apparent from the Council minutes.[13]

The first note of discord in More's career, according to the Council Registers, was struck in June 1641, nearly two years after his election as professor of Greek. In that month he appealed to the Council to direct the Company of Ministers to re-examine him for admission to their number.[14] From then until long after his flight to Middelburg, Church and State clashed over his case. The Venerable Company of Pastors and Professors, jealous of their privilege and mainly conservative in their outlook, fought within against the "new" Protestantism of Amyrault and Saumur and without against a civil authority less concerned for refinements of doctrine but prudent about the reputation of Geneva as a center of religion and of learning. The brilliant and wayward young Alexander More, now in his middle twenties, capti-

---

[9] *Works*, IX, 137, 209.

[10] *Works*, IX, 193–211.

[11] *Works*, IX, 233. The names are misspelled Mermillio, Troncini, and Pittet in this edition, which is based on George Burnet's translation of 1809. So with Otto for Hotton, Duraer for Dury, Vlaccus for Vlacq.

[12] *The Life of John Milton*, 7 vols. (London, 1859–94), IV, 460.

[13] It should be noted here that in addition to documenting the facts already known, the Council and Company Registers supplement, amplify, and correct the accounts of More in Bayle, Masson, Borgeaud, and that curious panegyric by Archibald Bruce, *Critical Account of the Life, Character and Discourses of Mr. Alexander Morus* (Edinburgh, 1813).

[14] *R.C.*, No. 140, fol. 76[r–v]. Approval of More's professorship is recorded in No. 138, pp. 506–507, under date of 3 August 1639.

vated the Council, as he was all his life to ingratiate himself with governors, public officials, and even princes. Poet, preacher, and scholar, gifted as Hermes, yet he was Ares to these men of the world, and into the bargain a catastrophic philanderer. The Council supported him even when his very existence was a liability. Utterly without diplomacy himself, he was the center of infinitely patient maneuvering by both Company and Council, each for its own reasons avoiding open warfare. Eventually the Council won, but as by Pyrrhus and not until its competitors had exhausted every delaying tactic.

In July 1641 the Company was still wrangling with the Council over a list of dubious points in More's theology: he was unsound on grace, original sin, predestination, and the divinity of the Holy Spirit. It was not until 5 October 1641 that More signed a satisfactory confession of faith and was approved by the Company and the Council.[15] In December he still had not been ordained, and as late as 22 January 1642 arrangements for allowing him to preach were unsettled.

Monsieur le premier Syndic ayant representé que plusieurs personnes s'éstonnent de ce que Spect. Alexandre Morus ayant fait diuers Exercises en Theologie et trois Sermons par lesquels on a suffisament recogneu son scauoir et doctrine orthodoxe, neantmoins on a differe iusqua ici de luy donner l'imposition des mains. Arreste que ledit Seigr premier Syndic fasse appeler le Spect. ministre qui preside ceste semaine et luy dit que Messieurs voulent et entendent que ladit imposition de mains se fasse dimanche prochain.[16]

Soon he was back, asking for testimonial letters to offset rumors stirred up by conflicts over his sermons, which (as Borgeaud points out) were more liberal than conservative Calvinists would endure.[17] Administrative procedure referred such solicitations to the Company for its recommendations; civil endorsement without concurrence from the ecclesiastical body was useless to a cleric of that time and place. The Councils of Geneva had the last word, but the Company's voice was loud and clear; and though it could not fight *hôtel de ville*, it could hamper and hinder by the kind of testimonial it would allow. Yet the two organizations worked closely together. At this stage in More's history, for example, Company and Council tactfully agreed to decline the request for More's services which had been made by the French

---

[15] *R.C.*, No. 140, fols. 81r–v, 87r, 139r–v.

[16] *R.C.*, No. 140, fol. 165r; No. 141, pp. 20–24, 35–36. I have transcribed the Registers literally, expanding contracted forms of *ledit, lesdites, pour,* and *-ment,* but not attempting to normalize inconsistencies in spelling and punctuation.

[17] *R.C.*, No. 141, p. 239. Borgeaud, pp. 355–56.

Church in London, though final decision was not passed until 7 December 1642.[18]

In 1646 More had risen to the office of Rector, only to encounter a new challenge to his theology by the Company; and there were rumors outside Geneva about his addiction to the liberal protestantism of Saumur and to sins of the flesh.[19] By this time too he had resumed his contest with Frederick Spanheim, who had left for Leyden in 1642; and so More had to contend with that distinguished scholar's relatives and friends. Once again he was grudgingly cleared after signing a second attestation of faith, but on 21 April 1646 he found it necessary to solicit confirmation of the clearance which he could send to the Low Countries.

Monsieur le premier Syndique rapporte que le Sieur Morus l'estant venu voir le jour d'hier luy tesmoigne d'estre grandement afflige des bruits qu'on faisoit courir contre luy dehors, et dont son pere luy a escript luy faisant entendre qu'yl desire venir par deca pour faire leurs des sinistres impressions qu on tasche de donner contre luy—prie Messrs de luy voulent donner pour le contentement de son espere et le sien propre une attestation en bonne forme de ce que s'est passe ceans entre Messrs les Ministres et luy. Arreste qu'on luy ottroye ladit attestation laquelle sera veue ceans deuant qu'estre expediée.[20]

These new letters met prompt counter-action in Holland, partly because Spanheim opposed him on doctrinal grounds. The fight continued into 1648, with Spanheim repeatedly urging the Council not to authorize anything that reflected on him in their support of More.[21]

On 25 January 1648, after fearful combat behind the scenes, More was given additional testimonials, but four days later the Company refused to recommend him to Lyons despite his plea that he could thereby counteract slanders in both Switzerland and in the Low Countries.

Spectable Paul Bacuet a presenté la lettre escripte par les Spectables Pasteurs & anciens de l'Eglise de Lyon aux Spectables Pasteurs & Professeurs de ceste

[18] *R.C.*, No. 141, pp. 406–407.
[19] *R.C.*, No. 145, pp. 17–18. Eugène and Émile Haag, *La France Protestante*, 8 vols. (Paris, 1857), VII, 544, remark that when attack on More's dogma failed, his enemies "se mirent à épier sa conduite, et bientôt de sourdes rumeurs circulerent sur la dépravation de ses moeurs, non seulement à Genève, mais à l'estranger."
[20] *R.C.*, No. 145, pp. 143–44.
[21] *R.C.*, No. 147, pp. 149–51, 154–55, 181–82. This was one battle More helped Salmasius win. Spanheim died in May 1649, shortly before More's departure from Geneva. The *Dictionary Historical and Critical of Mr. Peter Bayle*, ed. Des Maizeaux, 2nd ed. (London, 1734–38), IV, 272, repeats the epigram that went the rounds in Europe: "Salmasius killed him, and More was the dagger."

Eglise en date du 26 de ce mois par lesquelles ils les prient derechef de leur ottroyer en prest le Ministere de Spect. Alexandre Morus: Et rapporte que leur Compagnie en ayant deliberé a resolu unanimement de leur faire refus de la personne dudit Sieur Morus. Sur quoy arresté que les dites Spect. Pasteurs & Professeurs faient response aux dites Sieurs Pasteurs & anciens de Lyon que l'estat & necessité de nostre Eglise & Academic ne peuuent permettre qu'on leur accorde ledit Spect. Morus en prest ni autrement.

The Council's dictation of the pretext for refusal indicates their effort to prevent leakage of the real reason, the Company's disinclination to send abroad one who could not or would not conform to the testimonials just subscribed. More argued his case at length before the Council on 5 February without success: "arresté qu'il soit dict audict Spect. Morus que le Conseil ne peut en fason que ce soit luy ottroyer le congé par luy demandé." On 29 March, however, he managed to extract a confirmation of his January testimonials from the Council itself. He quoted Salmasius and the Council of Paris to the effect that gossip in the Low Countries described them as "extorques par surprise, & à ces fins mendie les suffrages des Ministres des champs." The Company objected after the fact so strenuously that the Council tried to retrieve the certificate from More, who had cannily dispatched it; and so to satisfy the Company a second confirmation was drawn and signed 12 April.[22]

On 24 May 1648 Salmasius' efforts succeeded at least in Holland: the burgomasters and elders of Middelburg invited More as pastor and professor.[23] On 28 July, while the Company was debating whether to grant him a three-month leave, the Council suddenly authorized it; and "La Compagnie ne peut qu'y souscrire." But when he asked for a new letter to accompany the *congé*, the ministers declared themselves unwilling to issue one without reinvestigating More's doctrine and his

[22] *R.C.*, No. 147, pp. 39–43, 44–45, 49–50, 71, 148, 152–54, 162–63. Bayle, IV, 272, reports: "the greatest storm this minister met with at Geneva, was raised after his obtaining the testimonials of January 24, 1648." The only official Genevan documents printed in *Fides Publica* are these referred to in the meetings of 25 January and 12 April. They are five in number, some in both French and Latin: (1) "Testimonium Ecclesiae Genevensis" (25 January 1648), pp. 81–87; (2) "Tesmoinage du Senat de Geneve" (26 January 1648), pp. 88–92; (3) "Confirmatio praecedentis Testimonii Ecclesiae Genevensis" (12 April 1648), pp. 98–102; (4) "Approbation du Senat" (12 April 1648), pp. 102–103; (5) "Confirmation du te[s]moignage rendu par le Senat de Geneve" (29 March 1648), pp. 104–106. This last is the independent Council action against which the Company protested. The letter authorized 27 June 1649 (*R.C.*, No. 148, p. 393) is, as Milton pointed out, significantly omitted.

[23] *R.C.*, No. 147, pp. 229–30. On 21 June 1648, p. 259, the Council refused flatly. On 15 July 1648, pp. 288–89, the Council similarly rejected the suggestion by Salmasius in the letter of 8 June that More be allowed to come to Middelburg to clear himself.

deportment.[24] Here ensued the long delay Milton referred to. The Council then tried to divert More from the trip by offering to send Middelburg what it hoped to obtain as a special concession, a good letter about him. Even Diodati was enlisted to enforce the bribe. More turned it aside and demanded a supporting testimonial. Since he had already announced his visit and since a change of plans would betray the disorder in Geneva, the Council had no recourse, having authorized the three-month leave, except to order the Company to write the letter. From 2 August 1648 until 2 July 1649, however, the Company engaged in every available parliamentary device to avoid certifying More as a credit to the Church. They knew More's record could not survive official re-examination, and they declared that disclosing it would only bring disgrace to all concerned. Eventually they were overruled, but capitulation was protracted by still further Fabian removes. More would be required to sign yet another attestation of faith, article by article. When he added marginal reservations and qualifications, the Company refused to sanction the statement; and there followed much discussion between Company and Council over jurisdiction and over theological terms.[25] The Council, laboring to keep the investigation confined to More's theological suitability, could not push matters too far.

Middelburg repeated its invitation in September 1648; and the Council, perhaps in desperation, asked More (still at loose ends with his three-month leave in hand) if he wished to accept the permanent change.[26] Now obviously More as well as the Company had the Council at a disadvantage; and he declined unless the Company would provide a new and appropriate testimonial. At this conference he related his rough treatment in the Company assembly, mentioning for the first time in these records the hundred articles later sealed up in the library.

La Compagnie entrant en deliberation il fut ordonné à chascun de rapporter ce qu'il scauoit de la vie & moeurs dudit Sieur Morus. Chascun baille ce qu'il veut. On dresse cent ou six vingts articles des quels fut faict un triage. On l'oblige à y respondre, & fait on un Secretaire nouueau scauoir le Sieur Professeur Dupan. Les articles sont cacheter on preste serment de ne rien reueler. Ceux qui auoyent dit quelque chose contre luy sont retenus au iugement quoy que ce soyent ceux qui apportent toutes les nouuelles de Holande & d'ailleurs.

[24] *R.C.*, No. 147, 28 July 1648, pp. 297–300; 2 August 1648, pp. 306–307. Stern, ii, 298, gives the date of the *congé* incorrectly as 25 July.

[25] *R.C.*, No. 147, pp. 308, 313, 326–29.

[26] *R.C.*, No. 147, pp. 370, 376–80.

Le triage faict on l'appelle pour luy faire les questions & rediger les responses par escript.[27]

The articles were unmistakably compromising. More returned to them on 18 November 1648 when he asked the Council to force the Company to release the doctrinal part of those accusations for his reply. He complained that they were now deposited "dans l'aumoire de la Bibliotheque ou on tient entre autres choses les liures defendus & damnables de Seruet & Socin" and that the association with heretics was ruining his good name.[28] On the following Tuesday, Abraham Dupan and Daniel Chabrey appeared for the Company in defense of their right as ecclesiastics to judge More's conduct and religion. The papers concerning the affair had been filed as a protection to the Company.

... les cacheter a fin qu'ils ne fussent plus veus au cas que ledit Sieur Morus estant sorti de ceste ville ne remuast ni escriuist aucune chose, mais aussi que la Compagnie y peust recourir pour sa iustification en cas qu'il fist des plaintes ou escripts contra elle.

As to the contaminating bibliographical associations of the sealed articles, the ministers drily explained that in the same place were the official records of the Company and the works of Calvin.[29]

For a while the Company tried to argue that More's acceptance of the Middelburg post removed him from their jurisdiction. If he wanted to remain in Geneva he had to submit to their interrogation; if not, he was free to go with the same *congé* and the old letters. This did not work. When in a test of strength the Company was required to transmit their accusations, they offered once again an itemized confession of faith which More was to sign without addition or comment.[30] At this point, and in a manner since hallowed in legislative and academic senates, a committee was appointed from both groups to

---

[27] *R.C.*, No. 147, 27 September 1648, pp. 379–80.

[28] *R.C.*, No. 147, p. 438.

[29] *R.C.*, No. 147, 21 November 1648, pp. 445–49.

[30] *R.C.*, No. 148, 20 June 1649, pp. 325–27. At an earlier meeting, Etienne Girard and Paul Bacuet reported great disorder in the academy because of the lack for a long time of a Rector to replace More and requested permission to elect one, since David le Clerc could no longer serve as Prorector (16 March, pp. 127–29). Ten days later (pp. 147–48), the Council confirmed the election of Philippe Mestrezat. On 5 May 1649 (pp. 239–42) the Council concurred in the Company's refusal to let More march as a professor in the academic procession. These actions are of special interest because of Milton's claim that More was stripped of his office and because the interregnum presided over by le Clerc is not indicated in the lists of Rectors provided by Borgeaud and others.

study More's responses; for he had again refused to sign his name "simply and purely."[31] On this the Company's position was unassailable: if More was sincere ("march de bon pied") he would have no difficulty in signing the articles of faith held by everyone.[32] The Company, which all along had resisted Council intrusion into an ecclesiastical matter, resorted to still other delays and evasions to prevent an open contest. Sometimes it was impossible to get a quorum, sometimes contradictions were found in Council orders, and once Diodati (who seems to have blown hot and cold about More) excused himself from appearing before the Council because his horses were not available. Half a dozen exchanges were necessary for agreement on the membership of the review committee.[33]

In February 1649, after yet other disputes, the Council handed down a direct order that the matter was closed and that the Company should not even discuss it further.[34] But it was discussed, because the Council felt the pressure from the Low Countries for some explanation of the delay in More's announced departure. Minutes of the meeting of 18 April 1649 relate a long strategy session upon the rumor that the Company would appeal to the Council of the Two Hundred.[35] In all these transactions, Theodore Tronchin, Jean Francois Mermilliod, and Andre Pictet (Milton's Pittet) figure repeatedly.[36] Eventually More signed a negotiated attestation (his third in eight years) and then capitalized upon the tension, there being further awkward inquiries from Middelburg and Harlem to both Council and Company. David le Clerc was appointed by the Council to draft a testimonial

[31] *R.C.*, No. 148, 9 June 1649, pp. 295–303.

[32] *R.C.*, No. 148, pp. 307–308.

[33] *R.C.*, No. 148, 16 March 1649, pp. 127–29. A messenger was sent to subpoena Diodati after that report but "qu'ayant demandé de luy parler il n'auroit trouue que la chambriere qui luy auroit respondu qu'elle estoit toute seule dans la maison, & que ledit Spect. Deodati estoit allé aux champs auec la famille & pensionnaires."

[34] *Registres de la Vénérable Compagnie*, No. 9, p. 208; quoted by Stern, II, 297. But the Company recorded nonetheless its conviction "que le ministere du susdit sier Morus ne peut estre un edification en ceste église et académie." Both More and the Company were repeatedly warned by the Council not to write or publish anything about the controversy.

[35] *R.C.*, No. 148, pp. 203–206. It was perhaps symbolic that between this session and their joint meeting with the Company that afternoon, the Council received an application from one Joachim Andere of Caen to exhibit a lioness and a monkey for three days, devoting one day's receipts to the poor (p. 205). And shortly thereafter, Jeanne Courtet, convicted of fornication with a German servant of Diodati, was fined 50 florins and exiled (24 April 1649, pp. 215–16).

[36] E.g., *R.C.*, No. 148, pp. 217–20, 226–44, 295–303, and elsewhere. None of the testimonials in *Fides Publica* was signed by these three pastors.

reply. But the Company refused to approve that minister's white-washing of More and submitted other letters, drawn by Etienne Girard, which alluded to the Company's previous condemnation.[37] The Council, in alarm, disqualified Girard's version.[38] After nearly two weeks of haggling, in which More was allowed to see and to criticize Girard's letters, the two documents were conflated into something acceptable to both juries and to the plaintiff. In one of the concluding negotiations, 26 June 1649, may be observed both the extremes to which the Company was driven as well as the harried scholar's exasperation at paperwork. The Council had announced that le Clerc's letters would be sent unless the Company produced some of equal favor to More.

Spectables Philippe Mestrezat & Estienne Girard estants entres ont representé de la part de leur Compagnie que sabmedi dernier estants partis de deuant Messeigneurs ils croyoyent que toutes choses seroyent termineés & les difficultes concernant Spect. Alexandre Morus leueés & assoupies par le temperament trouue par le moyen des lettres en dernier lieu dressees. Mais qu'ayants appris par la bouche du Secretaire Colladon l'intention du Conseil que les lettres dresseés par Spect. Dauid le Clerc seroyent expedieés leur Compagnie leur a donné charge de venir ceans faire nouuelles remonstrances & declarer en premier lieu qu'ils souhaiteroyent tous grandement d'estre descharges de cest affaire & aimeroyent mieux estre dans leurs cabinets à estudier ou faire autres fonctions de leurs charges . . . . Quant aux lettres dresseés par le Sieur le Clerc que la plus grand voix de beaucoup a porté que dans le mouement de leurs consciences ils ne les peuuent signer non pas pour ce qu'elles n'ont pas este dresseés par ordre de la Compagnie ni pour les expressions comme de ces termes, *nous l'auons embrassé* &c mais pour le procedé d'autant que Messieurs du Synode de Harlem les ont tant obtesté & coniuré de leur escrire particulierement ce qui s'est passé au faict dudit Sieru Morus, à quoy n'est satisfaict par les lettres dudit Sieur le Clerc.

When this line of argument failed, the le Clerc letters were amended with the result just mentioned.[39]

The Company was thus finally beaten. Again More pressed his advantage, proposing that the Council sponsor his reconciliation with the ministers and a last appearance in the pulpit. Word was sent that the reconciliation was to be effected "par attouchment de mains sans

---

[37] *R.C.*, No. 148, 18 June 1649, pp. 318–19. Henri Heyer, *Catalogue des Thèses de Théologie soutenus a l'Académie de Genève* (Geneva, 1898), pp. lxxv–lxxxviii, quotes the "Thèses de 1649" on original sin, predestination, and grace as signed by J. Sartoris, E. Girard, Alexandre Morus.

[38] *R.C.*, No. 148, 19 June 1649, pp. 321–25. The Council met over this affair twenty-five times in May, June, and July 1649.

[39] *R.C.*, No. 148, pp. 335–38.

permettre que la Compagnie delibere la-dessus." On 2 July 1649 Dupan, Liffort, and Colladon escorted him to the Company chambers, exhorting him "de ne faire long discours & s'abstemir de tous termes qui pourroyent donner matiere d'offense." Some ministers balked, to no avail. More entered, spoke movingly about his regret at leaving, shook hands all around, and left.

One last flurry occurred that same night. The Council deferred until after the reconciliation episode the news that More was to preach a farewell sermon. When the Premier Syndic did notify the Moderator, "ledit Sr. Butiny a fait assembler la Compagnie laquelle auroit resolu que ledit Sieur Morus ne prescheroit point." Their reason was that Abraham Dupan was already scheduled. The Council in a final show of strength and for appearance's sake dissuaded Dupan and assigned More to his church, forbidding him "expressement de parler en fason que longue en son presche de ce qui s'est passé ni donner aucune matiere d'offense audits Spect. Pasteurs."[40]

In the light of these records, the Genevan testimonials printed in *Fides Publica* assume, more than Masson and others have supposed, the precise character given them by Milton. He knew, and not from inference only, that the very confirmations themselves bespoke trouble beneath the surface. The Registers confirm Milton's statements about the hundred articles, the trouble over More's misconduct, the stages of censure, and the extremely difficult situation of the Genevan authorities. They explain like a gloss on *Pro Se Defensio* why More printed outdated endorsements and omitted the one which actually accompanied him in July 1649. This is not the place to marshal the other details in *Pro Se Defensio* corroborated by the Registers of the Council; but their documentation of the charges about More's career and the difficulty with which he secured his testimonials reasserts Milton's veracity, even in polemic, and provides further source material for the illumination of his text and for the study of his style and method as a propagandist.

---

[40] *R.C.*, No. 148, pp. 334, 343–49. Jean Sénèbier, *Histoire Littéraire de Genève* (Geneva, 1786), II, 199, sums up one verdict of posterity on the testimonial: "Il partit au mois de Juillet 1649 avec un certificat d'orthodoxie, qu'il eut autant de tort de demander qu'on eut de lui donner." Some afterclaps indicate the truth of Milton's assertion that the signers of More's testimonials regretted their compliance. In May–June 1651, Tronchin and others rewrote, at Council insistence, the Company replies to searching inquiries from Montauban about the circumstances of More's endorsement at Geneva.

ON ANNOTATING *PARADISE LOST*, BOOKS IX AND X

E. M. W. Tillyard, Jesus College, Cambridge

To deal with this topic as I wish means being personal in a way unbefitting a learned journal. But, since for this issue the Journal has assumed the more personal guise of *Festschrift*, it may perhaps allow me the necessary latitude.

Rightly or wrongly, I have chosen to write books rather than to annotate texts, except when I anthologised the poems of Wyatt and felt obliged to try to explain such passages in them as seemed to me to need explanation. More recently I wrote introductions to school editions of some of Milton's shorter poems and of the first two books of *Paradise Lost*. And now, concerned with the neglect of the later books of *Paradise Lost* compared with the vogue of those first two, I have been moved to do something about it and have edited Books IX and X for use in schools. This time I could not escape with a bare introduction but had to write the notes also. My experience of annotating proved different from what I had expected and more interesting. It is this experience, with its lessons both critical and educational, that is the subject of this paper.

My first lesson was that more editors had dealt with the earlier than the later books of *Paradise Lost* and that they had concentrated most on the first two. Even so, with Todd's Variorum and the excellent editions of Verity and Merritt Hughes I expected to have little new to contribute myself. I had to allow that Todd and Hughes aimed their remarks at an older set of readers than I was to do; but Verity's edition, both in format and contents, was plainly intended for schools. So it was with some surprise, when I began on the first lines of the ninth book, to learn my second lesson: that I should have more work than I had bargained for; that in fact the schoolboy had been allowed a degree of intelligence and a capacity for understanding far greater than I should have thought possible, and even that there were things in these books that had been misinterpreted. Milton begins:

> No more of talk where god or angel guest
> With man, as with his friend, familiar used
> To sit indulgent and with him partake
> Rural repast, permitting him the while
> Venial discourse unblamed.

The difficulty here is of course in the first line. And Todd, through Pearce's retort to Bentley, duly records Bentley's annotation, in which, remembering that in the poem God when he visited Adam did not partake rural repast, he proposed the drastic remedy of emendation. Other annotators seemed to me to quibble in their efforts to justify Milton's text, the most plausible effort being that of Richardson, who tried to account for *god* by the episode in Genesis of Abraham being visited by angels. Even so, he has to admit that "God himself, indeed, is not properly a speaker in it" and to proceed to a pretty thin explanation of this absence. Verity has this note:

where God; understand from what follows some word like 'conversed', 'spoke.' The reference is to book viii, where Adam says that the Almighty gave him possession of the Garden of Eden, warned him not to touch the Tree of Knowledge, and then promised him a help-mate in Eve.

But he shirks the difficulty noted by Bentley: that God did not in fact take a meal. This clearly was not playing the game; and having read Verity's note I came to the depressing conclusion that I had taken on more than I had bargained for. On thinking about the passage afresh I decided desperately, that all the commentators were wrong; that, though *angel guest* referred (among others) to Raphael visiting Paradise, *god* did not refer to Book VIII at all; and that Milton's intention was roughly as follows. When he says *god* he is thinking not of a precise passage in his own epic but of the stories, sacred and pagan, of heavenly beings visiting men in disguise and eating with them. One such is indeed in Genesis, as noted by Richardson, and another is the tale, told by Ovid, of Philemon and Baucis, who entertained Jupiter and Mercury disguised as men. In short, Milton says, "I have finished with the type of literature in which heavenly beings pay genial visits to men and eat with them, to which type my account of Raphael visiting Adam and Eve belongs." This seems to me the obvious meaning but it leaves me apprehensive; for how could the commentators have missed it, if it is so obvious? surely there must be a snag? My hope is that annotators of whom I am unaware have had the same idea. And I hasten to add that I have not often had to accuse the commentators of being flat wrong; my usual criticism has concerned what they have seen good to pass over in silence: a remark which brings me back to the lines of Milton from which I began.

No recent commentator has thought fit to comment on the word *venial* in the passage before us. Experienced in Miltonic usage, knowing his proneness to use words in their basic Latin senses, they have no difficulty in perceiving its connotations. But they are sadly wrong if they think that schoolboys generally share these advantages with them. They might retort that all that needs to be known about *venial* in this passage is to be found in the Oxford Dictionary but do they really think that schoolboys make habitual use of it? Left alone with our passage the ordinary schoolboy would apply to it the notion he has of *venial* as currently used. He may have a notion of what a venial sin is and he may think the word *trivial* a pretty close alternative. *Venial discourse* might be about the weather or the pruning of the roses in Paradise: a conclusion hardly fair to the actual talk between Raphael and Adam. Or the schoolboy may approximate the sense to *pardonable*, which is very much nearer the truth and yet fails to hit it. There was nothing in the discourse that called for pardon; there was no initial hint of sin, however small. The word should convey to the reader that the discourse was permitted by God or even favoured by him; see the original sense of the Latin *venia*.

Through the commentators' failure to gloss *venial* I was confronted with the question: what kind of note really matters for the schoolboy? For instance, was it more important to point to a rather different meaning attached to a familiar word or to explain the meaning of *impreses, sewers,* and *seneschals,* occurring a little after *venial*? Verity by his acts is seen to think the latter; and I do not deny that the unfamiliar words should be explained: but if I had to say which was the more important for the schoolboy's education I should say the former without the least hesitation. Remember that this is a matter not confined to Milton; and here is a parallel from Shakespeare. Which of the following (both from *Troilus and Cressida*) are in the greater need of annotation for the good of the schoolboy's soul? Nestor speaks of the "ruffian Boreas enraging the gentle Thetis"; and it has been pointed out both that Thetis, as a sea-nymph, stands here for the sea, and that Shakespeare may have muddled her up with Tethys, who, as the wife of Oceanus himself, has a better right so to stand. Ulysses compared Time to "a fashionable host / That slightly shakes the parting guest by the hand"; and, as far as I know, it has not been pointed out that when Shakespeare wrote *fashionable* he did not mean by it quite what we mean today. Indeed I suspect that most readers or listeners, having the *cliché* "fashionable hostess" vaguely resounding in their ears, make the word mean *smart* and think of the host as serving a *de luxe* hotel or at least a four-star one.

Of course in the Shakespearean sense a host could be *fashionable* as well in a humble motel as in the Waldorf-Astoria; and the word means "adaptable to the changes in fashion." My point is that it would profit a schoolboy more to grasp the different sense of a word in a great speech of Shakespeare than to have to remember that Tethys was the wife of Oceanus.

Through such instances we arrive inevitably at the general question of how in fact it profits schoolboys to be put through a detailed study of a few classics of their own tongue. I shall not try to answer this terrifying question; but I shall plead that the education inherent in looking closely at the meanings of words is profitable. It would be foolish to expect that books of *Paradise Lost* or plays of Shakespeare will be read for pleasure in later years by most children made to study them at school. This happy issue will be exceptional. Anyhow, there is no compulsion in later life to read poetry. But no one, not even the man most able to conduct his life-work through mathematical and other symbols, can do without words; and competence in that traffic is one of the first conditions of happiness and success in life. To be aware of words not only enlarges a man's scope but protects him in a world which through the medium of words, seen in print or heard on the air, is, like Shakespeare's Ephesus,

> full of cozenage
> As, nimble jugglers that deceive the eye,
> Dark-working sorcerers that change the mind,
> Disguised cheaters, prating mountebanks,
> And many such-like liberties of sin.

Train a child to look for differences of meaning in the same word as used by Milton and ordinarily by himself, and you begin to make him critical of his own use of words and better aware of the power of words as used by others; more likely in later life to ask what the promises and pretentions of politicians and advertisers really amount to.

What I have just said about words began from Milton's use of *venial*. Here are other examples of words which call for similar annotation. When Satan first saw Eve among the flowers he was so charmed that for the time being he was bereft of the power of action and "remained stupidly good." Left to themselves most schoolboys and, I greatly fear, some of their teachers would think that Milton meant by *stupidly* what they mean by it in their ordinary talk. But Milton did not mean that Satan was foolish; he was using the word in one of its Latin senses and meant that Satan was dazed. As far as I know, no recent annotator has pointed this out.[1] More surprising still, when Satan tells Eve that if she eats the apple she will acquire glory by not having been prevented by "the pain of death denounced," his words have been passed over in silence. Any uninstructed schoolboy would take *pain* in its usual sense of *suffering*, would be hopelessly puzzled by the word *denounced*, which in its modern sense won't fit the passage, and could have no idea whether it is *pain* or *death* that is *denounced*. Warned by previous experience he might suspect a Latinism, but only a very gifted and well-instructed schoolboy would conclude that Satan's words mean "the proclamation of the penalty of death."

As with altered meaning, so with altered pronunciation. Schoolboys' ears can be trained; and that training will be impaired, if the versification of their texts is murdered by false accents. I still remember a boy in my class at school reading

'Tis sweet and comméndable in your nature, Hamlet,

and not being pulled up by his teacher. I also remember being vaguely puzzled by the way the line went; but no one ever told me that Elizabethan stresses did not always agree with ours. Todd marks many of the unusual stresses, and Merritt Hughes some. But an annotator for schools should note them all; and as much for the instruction of the teacher as of the pupil. Even at the best staffed universities, with the maximum of individual teaching, it is impossible, through lack of time, to train undergraduates in the reading of verse; and the spectacle of men getting degrees in English, learned in facts and incapable of reading verse aloud in a civilised manner, is distressingly frequent. If the teacher is constantly reminded by the notes in the edition he uses of archaic stresses he may be persuaded to take the matter of reading verse more seriously. There are many lines that need thus annotating, for instance: IX, 320, "less áttribúted to her faith sincere"; IX, 511, "At first, as one who sought accéss, but feared"; and probably (cf. Italian *rimédio*) IX, 919, "Submitting to what seemed remédiless." In the same way, if the annotator is at all puzzled by the rhythm of a line, he should say so and offer his

---

[1] Patrick Hume has a good note, but what schoolboy has access to Hume?

tentative suggestion in the hope of arousing discussion. I think that a schoolboy might find tricky the rhythm of X, 423, "far to the inland retired, about the walls"; and I guess that we should read it, "Far to th'inlánd," etc. Such prosodical matters are much more interesting and profitable to schoolchildren than the miscellaneous references to Bible or Classics which must indeed be explained for the sake of further profit but whose self-value is minimal.

Genuine alternative meanings are all to the good as providing material for dispute in class. These lines (X, 28–31), describing Gabriel and his guard making their report to God, give a good example:

> They towards the throne supreme
> Accountable made haste to make appear
> With righteous plea their utmost vigilance,
> And easily approved.

Verity thinks that *accountable* goes with *vigilance*, and the meaning would be: "They, approaching the throne, hastened to make their vigilance, which had been the best they were capable of, appear sufficient for the account they were expected to render; and they vindicated their conduct." But this interpretation demands the queer understanding of *going* before *towards* and a distortion of the natural word order violent even for Milton. It also demands a rhythm that strikes me as un-Miltonic. I prefer to make *accountable* agree with *they* and to interpret the lines thus: "Knowing that they were to be called to account, they hastened towards the throne in order to make evident that they had watched with the utmost care; and they vindicated their conduct." Todd does not annotate but through his pointing shows that the takes the sense in this way.

If an annotator is defeated by a passage he should own up; and most of all in a book meant for schools. Schoolboys easily imagine that the editors of their texts have some magic access to meaning that costs them no effort. If they can acquire even the dimmest realisation that annotators have to take trouble, to submit to tedium, and can be uncertain of themselves, they will have learnt a useful lesson, which might lead them on to think that some day they may have a right to their own differing opinions. It may even occur to them that the mysterious mortal who annotates from some remote academic citadel could be looked on as co-operator, not dictator. I now own up to a passage which has defeated me but which the annotators pass over as if it presented no difficulty. I am much embarrassed, for it is most likely that there is some quite obvious explanation to which I have been blind. This is the passage (X, 332–36):

> He, after Eve seduced, unminded slunk
> Into the wood fast by, and, changing shape
> To observe the sequel, saw his guileful act
> By Eve, though all unweeting, seconded
> Upon her husband.

Why *though*? I should have thought that Eve's unawareness was more rather than less likely to make her play on her husband the trick Satan had played on her. Nor can I find the *though* more apt if it is Adam and not Eve who was unweeting. The best explanation I can offer is lame indeed: that the *though* is retrospective, referring to Satan and Eve alone and implying that their two acts were not strictly parallel, for, while Satan knew what he was doing, Eve did not.

There is no harm in school editions being dated through following fashion, for they should not remain in use for long. Thus I did not feel at all apologetic when I yielded to the current proclivity to see double or multiple meanings. I found myself writing notes like these. In IX, 157, Satan, thinking of Gabriel's watch, speaks of ministers tending their earthy charge; and I could not restrain myself from commenting:

Milton probably wanted *earthy* to mean both *earthly* and *low*. Satan continues to rub in the indignity of angels having to do with their inferior, man. In Milton's day the word could bear both meanings.

And a few lines later when Satan expresses hatred of his animal disguise and contrasts his position of God's challenger to his present case of being "constrained into a beast," I found myself saying:

constrained: another instance of Milton making a word do more than one job of work. Satan says that he is *compressed* into a beast and is *compelled* to invest with flesh and to brutalise his airy and rarefied angelic substance.

Another modern fashion is to welcome, rather than to think trivial, a play on words. Verity, sparing of critical comments, cannot refrain from expressing his dislike of this passage (X, 92–97):

> Now was the sun in western cadence low
> From noon, and gentle airs due at their hour
> To fan the earth now waked and usher in
> The evening cool, when he, from wrath more cool,
> Came, the mild judge and intercessor both,
> To sentence man.

Verity was right from his point of view in admitting he disliked the yoking of the coolness of evening with the coolness of God; for he had the opinion of his age behind him, and his readers sharing his prejudice and ratifying his dislike would be the more inclined to trust him to do his job of editing well. In the same way I thought it legitimate to say of the passage:

Milton derived God's visiting Adam and Eve "in the cool of the day" from *Genesis*, but his making the coolness of evening correspond to the Son's "coolness" or freedom from anger is typical of his age. In Milton's day nature existed less as an independent set of phenomena than as a reflection of a set of human states of mind. The correspondence is much more than what Verity calls "not a very happy play on words."

Lastly, there is the difficult problem of how much aesthetic comment an annotator for schools should allow himself. I am sure he ought not to allow himself much, lest he should turn into a dictator whose opinions are *a priori* right and must be memorised and reproduced. On the other hand he ought to give enough critical remarks to show that he minds (for if he does not mind, he has no business to be editing for schools) and to catch the attention of the minority of children possessing a fine intuition for poetry. It does not matter if he is on the wild and provocative side, for the teacher can query his excesses, and children like grownups who commit themselves and risk ridicule, provided they are not their immediate relations. Thus I have not hesitated to say things that are likely to be contradicted. For instance, I have detected comic elements in Book IX, knowing that I am provoking opposition. I have also thought it worth while to make a reference or two to wider principles for the benefit of the few who may be interested and stimulated. When we know for certain that Satan is going to find and tempt Eve (IX, 494 ff.), there is a pause in the action and Milton inserts a gorgeous account of the serpent form Satan has assumed. I allowed myself this note:

Ornamentation, such as the comparisons that follow, comes best in the pauses of the action. We now know for certain that Satan is to make his culminating attack on Eve and in that certainty we are glad to pause and enjoy the digressive ornament that Milton gives us. The ornament also serves to emphasise what is to follow, hinting that it is too weighty and solemn to be entered on without ceremony. An example of similar technique is in Chaucer's *Knight's Tale*. We know at one point that the rival loves of Palamon and Arcite are to be settled by a tournament and because of that knowledge we welcome the elaborate account of the scenes depicted on the temples of Mars and Venus, where the two rivals go to offer their vows.

The last feeling set up by annotating great poetry is one of be-wilderment. What strange stuff it is; and the stranger and the more fascinating, the better you get to know it! And the richer; for if I re-did my annotation I should be amazed at the amount I had missed. What in the world, one asks, can schoolboys make of such richness and complexity? Actually, I think, a great deal. But the discrepancies between what this or that boy and girl will make of them are so wildly great that the topic is unmanageable and must be firmly dis-missed.

BAROQUE AND MANNERIST MILTON?

Rosemond Tuve, Connecticut College

It has become thoroughly conventional during the last ten years to speak of Milton as a baroque artist. When any label for a major figure is no longer simply a provocative term used by knowledgeable critics to suggest relations, or when a cliché in the easy-going journalism that likes to pick up such labels for the great becomes a cliché of the schools as well,[1] then it is valuable for as many serious students as possible to consider its usefulness, before the ticket begins to remake the poet. As is usual, terms beget terms, and the unfortunate tendency of every poem to differ from others has forced an extension into the Mannerist category to account for *Lycidas* (*Paradise Lost* being Baroque, and *Comus* being left to fill up "Renaissance"). Thus far, the equally awkward tendency of poets to differ from each other, so that a baroque Donne writing short *libertin* love poems is hard to square with the Milton of *Paradise Lost*, has been taken care of by careful choice of what to look at in the epic, or by devising verbal formulae which can somehow stretch to include differing things under a similarity. All comparisons and all classifications require some of these shifts. But if a category is to become fixed, the need is to make sure that terms which align—usually by differentiating from a third thing, in this case usually "the Renaissance"—can in truth align validly and differentiate surely.

One way to examine this is to look at the basis upon which each of the criteria used to delimit these categories is erected. The great desideratum in words which help us characterize and thence classify, is that they should point to the presence or absence of something sufficiently observable that men may agree about its being importantly in one thing and not in another. Despite wild variety on the fringes,

---

[1] Clichés about the greater poets are a more important matter than they seem. Milton has held a reading public better than most, but the last hundred years have seen changes; of the vast majority of those currently reading *Paradise Lost* in the English-speaking countries, the average age must be around 19, and the average age of those instructing the readers, around 29. Present "scholars" may be safe from clichés; the ones to come are at their mercy. They commonly penetrate rapidly down into the school handbooks; misconceptions created by the invalid ones (especially if they classify) are to be rooted out largely by the college instructor, and with difficulty, as everyone knows. Graduate-school clichés are thus endowed with an all but heel-less immortality.

the innumerable discussions[2] are enough alike to furnish a set of criteria or characteristics which recur faithfully. No violence is done by taking up singly these familiar differentiating traits, for discussions persistently fall into the pattern of putting this or that author into the category by finding them in him. This is perhaps a necessary feature of a classification borrowed from other arts, just as analogy is an inescapable method in the attempt to make the differentia applicable to literature.

The division made (p. 88) in Wellek's remarkably clear, inclusive, and temperate analysis still holds, and critics still adduce two sorts of criteria—touching stylistic elements or touching attitudes of mind. Somewhat to one's surprise, the first of these is not the staple of discussion in attempts to find Milton baroque. Actually, it is natural that great numbers of attempts to fasten the term on particular authors either slight the question of style, or else are highly impres-

---

[2] It would be idle to point to the users of each term or idea I take up; they overlap, and often differ chiefly in ingenuity of phrasing. Treatments are prodigiously numerous, and affect Milton study almost equally whether they mention him or not, in the latter case of course being all the less conscientiously applied by disciples; but I try to take locutions or paraphrases from those who bring Milton in directly. I am released from the necessity of space-taking citation by the chief bibliographical help, which is still René Wellek's "Concept of Baroque in Literary Scholarship," *JAAC*, v (1946), 77–109, if one adds the special number of the *Revue des sciences humaines* devoted to the subject (new ser., nos. 55–56, July-Dec. 1949), Helmut Hatzfeld's "Clarification of the Baroque Problem in the Romance Literatures," *CL*, I (1949), 113–39, and the notes in O. de Mourgues, *Metaphysical, Baroque and Précieux Poetry* (Oxford, 1953). For characterizations applicable and being applied to Milton, the most important forms of statement in recent years have been the numerous French treatments, by Lebègue, Raymond, Buffum, de Reynold, Rousset, and others, cited in the book which tries hardest to make the necessary distinctions of Baroque from neighboring categories (that by de Mourgues). Wölfflin's treatment is still fundamental, despite its virtual confinement to art history. But except for the form given to the problem by Curtius on Mannerism (ch. 15 of *European Literature and the Latin Middle Ages*, tr. Trask [New York, 1953]), German discussions are less important now than they were to the question of Baroque as a term applied to English writers (unless we except also for a very different reason—his notable caution—A. Esch, *Englische religiöse Lyrik des 17. Jahrhunderts* [Tübingen, 1955]). On the other hand, Croll's influence is pervasive; as with a few early or carefully delimited works like Austin Warren's on *Richard Crashaw* and Mario Praz's several essays, definitions are extended and traits widely applied by others, though the earlier writings were deliberately suggestive rather than dogmatic (and I suppose no one would deny Crashaw's baroque traits). Sometimes the application reaches Milton, as in Roy Daniells' "Baroque Form in English Literature," *UTQ*, XIV (1945), 393–408, or he takes a larger place as in M. Mahood, *Poetry and Humanism* (New Haven, 1950). But the book by far the most dogmatically and persistently concerned to fit Milton into these categories, is W. Sypher, *Four Stages of Renaissance Style* (New York, 1955), which I therefore use most for examples, or when a phrasing will delineate a criterion (without cluttering the text with references, since points are reiterated throughout the clusters of relevant material at pp. 1–5, 19–25, 104–19, 174–75, and Parts II and III of the section "Baroque").

sionistic, or rather elementary, or tied to a passage or two, in their treatment of it. For although the original use as a category in art criticism had the great merit of being based on definite stylistic elements provably in a monument or painting, these elements must all be translated before they can apply to form as literature shows it. Most remain only metaphorically intelligible (open and closed form); many stubbornly resist any but an impressionistic application (linear, painterly; absolute and relative clarity).

None depends on the presence of any isolatable verbal device such as the rhetorician can describe, and most tangle with difficulties raised by the inescapable conceptual dimension of words. From this attribute of the medium arises the fact that an author can control the relevance, more surely than the form, of the images we make: he does so especially through fairly precise indications of their relation to a poetic subject. Thus Sypher's statement, "If a Spenserian sonnet is 'linear,' Milton's vistas in *Il Penseroso* are 'painterly,' " turns out not to be a comment on style but an announcement of the fact that vistas are painterly, obscuring the further fact that Milton, whose poetic subject involved portraying, through concrete "circumstances," the nature of an abstraction governing a chosen kind of life, could do it with help from vistas, whereas Spenser's sonnets do not usually reflect about matters that can use any. Few sonnets do at this date and stage of the fashion, and neither adjective can be responsibly used about Milton's to Lady Margaret Ley, or either sonnet to Cyriack Skinner, or that on his blindness or on *Tetrachordon*, while if we become too ready to pause on what might be painterly in the Nightingale on the bloomy spray we are soon set right by the last two lines—as we are if we overstress what we "see" in "Methought I saw. . . ." This is not to say that "sonnets cannot paint"; many do, but in Keats and Wordsworth too, as in Donne, the nature of the poetic subject will be seen to be causally related, and the picture-evoking words will be seen to be too complicated as to connotations and conceptual significance for us to agree on any counting up of which is stressed, line or "paint."

Such problems about the presence of qualities and effects, even the simplest, thus turn into problems about decorum. Indeed, it was soon seen that Curtius' attempt to call literary pieces Mannerist if they *used* hyperbaton, *annominatio*, periphrasis (a thing we can indeed determine and agree on) provided no criterion; for all literature does so, and for a hundred reasons. This cannot even separate "Lycidas" from Drayton's *Mortimeriados*, to say nothing of severing a Mannerist

"Nativity Hymn" from a Renaissance *Comus*. Curtius himself moved toward one of the ways to make this observation of something ubiquitous into a criterion that can differentiate, by implying that it was the presence of very many or too many such devices which could bring a work under the rubric of Mannerism. But most critics have perceived that whenever we erect a criterion upon quantity, in any art, we run into the plain fact that quality makes much more difference to effects produced, and that one effective periphrasis will unaccountably seem like "more" use of periphrasis than five vapid ones.

Of course the moment "*too* many" comes in, our criterion is no longer based upon the presence of something determinably there, but upon a norm in the mind or sensibility of the judge. One's discomfort about this is not due to an unwillingness to admit evaluation as part of criticism (probably there is no criterion of any importance which does not draw in evaluations)—but an unwillingness to depend on evaluations referable chiefly to a reader's impressionistic report of his reactions. People can agree that there is "too much" of something, but usually they do so not because firm evidence can be brought to bear, but rather because their tastes click and their linguistic sensibilities are similar.

That one among Curtius' criteria which is most oblivious of this danger is the one which has lived longest in later discussions; he claims seemingly with no qualms that far-fetched metaphors ("manierierte," "studied") distinguish a Mannerist. This famous distance traversed by a mind fetching the second term of a comparison is not a measurable journey, as is obvious from constant disagreements, but critics continue to speak as if our quite different mental speedometers could be expected to agree, and put forward as criteria both "strain" and "incongruity" in the images, as well as "superabundance" of metaphors. The first is a very stubborn form of subjectivity, for readers seem unable to learn to experience connotations which are not their own by early unconscious habits of association, and the old remarks about Donne's "mechanical" or down-to-earth compass image roll on, no matter how much we learn about its seventeenth-century associations with symbols of perfection and of divine creation. In much the same way Crashaw's fires and perfumes are obstinately felt as primarily sensuous, though centuries of their history had shortened their "distance" from the spiritual states signified; it is as if we were to insist that "bread and wine" *must* seem as much closer to lunch than to heavenly love, to Herbert, as to Omar Khayyam.

No matter how adroitly it is phrased, or how persuasively it appears as a way of recognizing the "distorted vision" or "deformation" critics put forward as differentiating characteristics of Baroque, it is obligatory upon us to recall that unless we look at how close the link in a metaphor may have seemed to the man who "fetched" it, we merely point to what seems to us strained, distorted, or extravagant. This is one of the most famous wax noses in history. Almost anything can melt it—linguistic fad, small changes in environment, developments of any and every kind, from railroads to eschatology. Every change in mental furniture changes connotations and mental linkages; it is all but impossible to know any author's or any time's linguistic world this fastidiously. "Mannered metaphor," and other criteria having this environmentally regulated instrument hidden within them, could well be discouraged among those making the elementary decision of classifying, as requiring too much knowledge now impossible of discovery, a criterion largely suitable to those with absolute conceptions of "justness" in language or life.[3]

The superabundance of images, which Lebègue and others adduce (talking of richness not selectivity, of minuteness of description and details accumulated in a comparison), has the same difficulty of a subjective norm—that in the critic necessarily differing from that in the author, for, of course, no poet decides to put in too many or too much. This is less a difference in aesthetic than in simple judgment as to what will suffice. It is no accident that the criterion is generally employed as a whip, one of those chastising uses of the car-horn that someone has named "the pedagogical toot." But despite these difficulties it continues to be used as a differentiating characteristic; "baroque profusion" is a commonplace, usually illustrated by image-filled passages without special regard to whether a subject needs images; one critic speaks of profuse emblems, metaphors, conceits, another of jewelled richness.[4] But I do not find treatments of Milton

---

[3] As usual, a warning is necessary: this is not to say that there are no strained metaphors, or that linguistic wrenching does not characterize some authors and times, but that keeping in repair the proper equipment for recognizing them requires a scrutiny of such meticulousness as to be defeating. So far in literary history "common sense" has not proved enough, though it lasts during the time that our form of it is what is common. Supersemantics and detailed social history should not be asked of those trying merely to group authors in classes.

[4] De Mourgues can distinguish Metaphysical from Baroque, controlled equilibrium from an orgy of metaphors, by looking for those whose intelligence has put a check on sensuous visions and love of decorative imagery. Hatzfeld can divide multiplicity of figures in *secentismo, marinismo* from Baroque richness by assigning the first to "lack of discipline," thus by use of the same ground providing us with precisely opposed

which carry this point forward in two possible ways which could set a control on its subjectivity. One is to relate it strenuously to the author's conception of "decorum according with the subject" as we can detect that from his entire poem, and the other is to group metaphors more reliably according to their *formal* nature and according to how this fits their observed working. It might be possible thus to separate out the embarrassing intruders into the Baroque category whose profusion also seems "too much" but who assuredly are not baroque.

It is no wonder that through so open a door the wrong people have come in; while one theorist wears a distressed smile at the entrance of Lyly, another greets Marlowe without unease, and yet another asks him to leave. On what precise basis do we distinguish Eden's profuse "accumulation of sensory impressions" as baroque plenitude, and Comus' spawning seas and strangling fertility as "Renaissance"? The latter more like, we must suppose, to the "busy illustration" in a (quite truly) "busy," and poor, Spenser sonnet, or to the "decorative naturalism" of the *Prothalamion*.[5] We can of course avoid asking the question by somehow fishing out the *personage*, Comus, as a "baroque element" in a Renaissance piece (though to be sure his naturalistic argument is classical, medieval, Renaissance, and seventeenth-century). But then we have lost the merit which this criterion stressing sumptuousness, redundance, powerful simplified rhythm despite apparent crowding, and the like, had in the original formulation concerned with nonverbal arts: that the quality was experienced in demonstrable relation to unity of effect, though meanwhile no one could deny that the redundant elements were present. Differences of opinion as to how dangerously Comus topples over Milton's unified argument in praise of Temperance, and as to whether Comus' description of Nature's instructive fertility contains lush

---

groups under the label. Some will agree, some will not, but agreement in either case involves the double subjectivity: a standard located in a critic's mind, with which we agree when we too find figures over-used, and an inferred attitude in an author's mind, which we find ourselves able to label "self-indulgence" or "discipline," respectively.

[5] Examples are from Sypher (pp. 192, 92, 88). He relates the *Prothalamion* passage to Spenser's Renaissance "fractional seeing"—which in turn is useless for Comus' descriptions, that are as tightly argued as the Elder Brother's equally crowded ones, with each of the lavish images following veins in the old argument-systems. But the critic neglects all the *reasons* for the kind of "vision" in *Prothalamion*, just as his next comments on the disunity of the "anecdotal" *Faerie Queene* and its ornate "processional movement" show entire lack of interest in the complex kind of unity of *F.Q.*, with its hundreds of intertwined, never quite severed, threads. It would be easy to describe accurately the unity of *F.Q.* using solely the phrases popular in discussions of baroque form (which would place it in a very false category).

redundancies or just observation of natural fact, correlate suspiciously with a given reader's receptivity to *libertin* arguments. If anyone could argue that compounded orders and double domes and numerous *putti* were sometimes these and sometimes something else, things would be harder.

But there is a more usual way out of these confusions between one writer's profusion and another's, between enough and too much, between Renaissance fussy surface vitality, Mannerist virtuosity and contrivance, and Baroque plenitude and energy. The way out is, generally: to inquire whether, or not, the superabundance (of rhetorical devices, of image and conceit, of any observable stylistic element) is there because the writer wishes to surprise and startle. Curtius is only too forthright and simple: the Mannerist "wants to surprise, to astonish, to dazzle. While there is only one way of saying things naturally, there are a thousand forms of unnaturalness" (p. 282). Of course his bias is obvious, and we are not far from the grand Sophomore division of all literary styles into Flowery and Sincere. Nevertheless, the emphasis on the author's *wanting* to dazzle has never been lost; it was ancient before Curtius as a principle of disapproval but not as a ground for a literary category, and it appears in all kinds of phrasings, pejorative or not, according as the critic admires or dislikes baroque (or mannerist) artifice.

The overintellectualism, contrived ingenuity, and frigid learned niceties that can go with self-consciousness as with trying to astonish are generally attached now to Mannerism, for by many this term is uneasily kept as a kind of last box to house what could once be disliked in Baroque—though Curtius' charge of affectation is often simultaneously denied. We must with Sypher see these listed qualities as preeminent in "Lycidas," taking our pleasure as best we may in Milton's inexplicable private wilfullnesses, in the disconcerting shifts being expressive, and in the fact that the poem is complex (and, though false, inflated, frigid, callow, and erratic—"great"). Similar dissociations and shifts (not disconcerting as in "Lycidas") we must see as dictating a different categorization for *Paradise Lost* (which is Baroque, not Mannerist) by perceiving that here Milton is not awake to "the contradictions between his baroque sensuousness and his Puritanism," but has naïvely surrendered to his images, and hence does not suffer from the tensions inherent in them (as Donne each instant does, and the author of "Lycidas").

But what is disturbing is not the high price (a "self-seduced" Milton, ethically and theologically diddled) we here pay for a way out, when we must label a stylistically discoverable characteristic in one piece Baroque and in another Mannerist, and in one aesthetically satisfying, in another transcended with difficulty. What disturbs us most is not even the manifest difficulty of applying such a differentiating principle to a conceivably mannerist Carew or a debatably baroque Herbert. What is most disturbing to anyone who wishes to use a criterion to distinguish reliably is that this one is grounded in knowledge about the state of mind of an author which we can never have. We can suffer from what we see as contradictions, but we know less about whether an author did, or so saw them; we can tell whether we are surprised, or dazzled, but how high up this came in the author's motivations is a secret, except to those who like Curtius know exactly what the "one way of saying things naturally" would be. And with the latter, though at least we look at poem not poet, the subjective standard is in the critic's inner being, whereas in the statement "he chiefly wanted to astonish" we effortlessly enter the author's. (Even an occasional Marino who so declares his end would be hard to find in England.)

Criticism properly discusses such matters, but neither as a first step nor without safeguards touching evidence. Some intentions of an author can be reliably deduced from the nature of a work we have before us. But motivations in him inferred from the nature of our responses are something different, as also expressed meanings are a different thing to look for, from unconscious psychological needs or self-deceptions. De Mourgues' demonstrations of distortion and lack of balance as a distinguishing characteristic of Baroque show authors enthralled with the excitement of surprising primarily themselves, and stopping at nothing to indulge themselves in it; but in the use of a criterion based on knowledge of the motivation and overpowering psychological pressures behind profusion, over-plus, and extreme amplification of fancy, these demonstrations similarly classify according to what we can only think we know with sureness.[6] An unexpected

---

[6] The chief knowledge demanded in the application of O. de Mourgues' criteria is that we should know what is a balanced view of the universe. Since we try to know this whenever we read a book seriously, I do not mock it (even in Curtius' version—that Mannerists ought not to wish to say things abnormally but normally). Yet these necessarily self-flattering assumptions regarding eternal norms seem unfortunate as bases for knowing a baroque poem from another one. They seem peculiarly unhappy when we are awakened to a lively sense of history; there have been times when it was a mark of unbalance *not* to be impressed by the "disorder on a colossal scale" which would precede the Last Judgment. After all there are the Fifteen Signs, with all their history in OE, ME, and early Irish before they ever decorated the margins of xvi.c. *Horae,* and there are II Peter and Revelation. Can one be balanced and Metaphysical in one's time and

embarrassment turns up with keeping authors *out* of a category so based. Suppose Spenser's *Daphnaida* shows a man obsessed with death trying to indulge himself in it but failing to induce in us a similar obsession? Then we are at a loss where to put him; is he proto-Baroque—like Chaucer in the *Duchess?* We have, moreover, to measure the extent to which a man desired to startle or was impelled by psychological needs. Renaissance confession literature would be unmanageable; indeed, from the old difficulty of St. Augustine onward to Montaigne and Greene the problems germinate, multifarious, the data for solving them irrecoverable.

Certain older tests for knowing whether a thing we held in our hands was to be called Baroque, like Croll's "portraying in one's style exactly those athletic movements of the mind by which it arrives at a sense of reality," and once implicitly believed in, begin to seem more difficult to apply as the subdivisions multiply, and as modern literature has taught us more about what is produced when this "highly self-conscious simulation of the mind's actual operation" is indeed attempted. This was so attractive a thing to find in an author in the 1920's and '30's that it is only as the years pass that we realize we do not actually come upon statements by English "baroque" authors that they are trying to do precisely this (famous declarations by Montaigne and Burton do not regard total thought processes reproduced as by a recording instrument). It is significant that later writers on the Baroque have borrowed chiefly from Croll's remarks about this Senecan motive or desire, rather than from the analyses which accompanied them. It is also significant that one critic can adduce prose from Milton to exemplify this simulation of the movements of thoughts, while another quotes Milton's disapproval of, and analyzes his differences from, the style which the criterion aims to distinguish. I believe that one's gradually increasing sense of discomfort (experienced also as the years distance us from Daniells' suggestive descriptions of "baroque" exploratory prose) arises chiefly from the same element seen in other criteria, of inescapable conjecture and inference, increasingly distrusted as one attempts over the years to distinguish which authors are "trying" to do something, and which are not.[7] For these are not intentions concerning meanings,

---

get into the Baroque category later when one is seen to have been looking at an "unreal problem"? This would be the situation of many medieval lyrics on death and of most ME sermons on the Judgment.

[7] Croll did not come out for the classification "Baroque" until his latest appearing article of the famous five (from that on "Attic Prose," in *SP*, xviii [1921], I use some phrases above, as from Daniells' essay cited in n. 2). It is of some significance that

which can be sought, and found with considerable sureness, within a work.

As so often, difficulties come especially when one is keeping people out of some category; one has too often to avert the face from a criterion and simply "know better" than to let in what it would admit. In the very descriptions categorizing them as "Baroque," later authors who shared Bacon's or Lipsius' desideratum of a plain style, but whose zeal for honesty came out in the broken, loosely articulated style we confront in their works, are characterized stylistically through sets of phrases which suit point for point much earlier prose (Malory or some earlier Middle English writer). Though one would never confuse the two writers or periods, the offered descriptions do not separate them, as they have not in practice separated off Milton. For separation we must resort to the factor of the self-consciousness in later writers as they meticulously followed the trail of subtle thought; the earlier writer has to be assumed to be either naïve (medieval) or interested in his rhetoric rather than his thought (Elizabethan). These are all three suspect presuppositions; they belong to the end, not the beginning, of a critical examination.

Almost the same difficulty arises with the criterion of artistry "for its own sake." This used to seem simple applied to Lyly, but not if it covers as well, though with a difference in motive, mannerist writers and (to some theorists) baroque writers. Here again the differentiating factor depends on our knowing what *produced* an author's preoccupation with virtuosity—and the predilections of critics are ill-disguised as they assign orders of merit. One might have some success in examining whether technical cleverness functions toward a work's recognized end. But this turns out not to be a relevant point, for a differently based decision has instead to be made, in relation to antecedent decisions by which we suspect Renaissance virtuosity of being, unconfessed, its own end (Lyly), know Mannerist virtuosity to be the visible sign of unresolvable inner dissonance

---

George Williamson does not find the classification useful in the book which pursues, orders, and refines upon Croll's treatments with real care: *The Senecan Amble* (Chicago, 1951). Before one finds it easy to call Milton's prose baroque, or to separate seventeenth- and sixteenth-century styles, one must consult Williamson's careful working out of relations usually left to impressions and tastes, such as those between Euphuism and later styles; he also consistently demonstrates writers' ties with what they themselves would have thought to be the sources of their characteristics: numerous varieties of classical practice and theory, rather than baroque ways of seeing reality. Of course men see reality differently; it is our detection of this in their syntax that is too crude to use for categorizing them.

("Lycidas"), and enjoy Baroque virtuosity as *Lebensfülle* or honest report of complexity (Donne, Browne). Locatable qualities in pieces or how these function are no longer the point; our decisions turn upon why these have been attempted. It is difficult if one uses litmus paper not to go by whether it turns pink but by whether the subject tested intended to produce acid. One would like to call theatricality by that name even if baroque stylists produce it by mistake through zeal for "lifelike" delineation, would like to be enabled to differentiate qualities of prose, not be required to detect when and when not an intention to be direct unexpectedly produced effects that are spiral. In particular, "significant darkness" needs to be reliably differentiated, as to instrument and form, from the Renaissance *clarté* (luminousness, not the explicitness into which it is mistakenly translated—only *some* Renaissance poets made the mistake before us, the poorer ones). The styles differ, but not the aesthetic desideratum of "illumination"; hence the criterion which opposes a belief in significant enlightening "darkness," to content with unmeaningful noonday visibility, is a red herring.

It is that eminent baroque figure E. K. who claims, in the Preface to Spenser's *Shepheardes Calender*, that in the most exquisite pictures "they use to blaze and portraict not onely the daintie lineaments of beautye, but also rounde about it to shadow the rude thickets and craggy clifts," and maintains that, "I knowe not how" (this is the familiar *je ne sais quoi* in baroque strangeness-in-beauty), he takes "great pleasure in that disorderly order." All his maintaining cannot add one mannerist dissonance to his literary character, but the sleight of hand of looking sometimes at writers' desiderata and sometimes at their performance must be allowed to complicate matters all along the line, instead of merely where we are ready to consider a split between motive and resulting quality proper to the dissonance of the times.

These half-hidden difficulties in criteria touching stylistic matters seem all but trivial compared with those we meet in the second great division of criteria which enable us to classify works, and Milton's among them, as Mannerist or Baroque—those erected directly upon our conceptions of the author's state of mind. There is no treatment of the matter which does not use these as touchstones. The insecurity which one feels in observing their application can vary greatly. Exuberance, *Lebensfülle*, dynamism, energy, do seem observable in literary form, and in Milton's formal elements of style; and splendor, triumph, grandeur, do look like characteristics of themes, including

Milton's themes. On the other hand, all security disappears before the appalling problem of applying as a difference-finder between poems the Mannerist's sense of not being "at home in the world," which causes him to distort space, light, color, and contour and to take refuge in abstract art. The last being closed to the poet, and *formal* analogues to the first not possible,[8] critics have universally looked for characters not "at home" or speakers in moods of alienation, and difficulties naturally multiply. There is the fearful matter of men's changing views and moods; one cannot live without knowing that this particular stone "troubles the living stream" as it "changes minute by minute," and men's work has to be atomized to get the criterion to fit. A narrative's needs are a fatal complication. We must decide whether Chaucer agreed with Egeus, and if so how much of the *Knight's Tale* is mannerist. We have also on our hands some dozen centuries when *exules filii Hevae* and *hoc exilium* was doctrine seriously held; if we apply the differentiating factor as it has been applied to Milton, even saints would be hard to sort into, respectively, Baroque because they resolved the problem or Mannerist in case they suffered grievously under it. It is so basic a power of literature to portray attitudes progressively during imagined passing time, that from the spectacle of a man resolving such problems we cannot isolate the evidence which proves to us that a work of art's design does or does not do so.

"Disturbed balance" is the key to most phrasings of Mannerism, and many of Baroque, as a classification. In literature one does not only (or even chiefly) deduce, but is directly presented with, conceptually indicated balance and imbalance, and *in* persons' minds, whether characters or writers. It is uncomfortable to line authors up according to the "position" they take on such questions posed in their books; we have the alternative of turning reading into one long inquiry into the unrealized psychological state of poets. We are consulting the worst evidence in the world, an artist's deliberate reordering. It seems folly not to *expect* that a lyric which hopefully in-

---

[8] Analogues not purely formal, concerning distortion of actuality, are especially subject to confusion with the literary problem of probability-improbability. Moreover, happy and confident fairy tales distort most notably of all. Figurative speech makes distortions mean something totally unconnected with strain or alienation; the dragon's three-furlong tail which disturbs Sypher (p. 89) in *F.Q.* is a *probability* when a man is portraying the conquest of quintessential evil. But the whole Renaissance problem of finding a place among the learnings for the feigned truth of poetry becomes merely the "Renaissance" "tyranny of probability" in this critical discussion. Several examples in paragraphs following this one have been taken from the same critic (see above, end of n. 2).

vites a lady to put a kiss within the cup will "have a stability lacking in" one whose theme is the ineluctable shortness of the moments of enjoyment of a coy mistress. One (only one)is *about* instability.

It is a fatal shortcoming of all these criteria based on attitude and state of mind that in literature, a continual direct presentation of these through a conceptual medium, the criteria must immediately count on perfected decisions concerning the most problematic and the last thing we know about any work, the full nature and import of the entire poetic subject. Marvell's own invitation to love has a Jonsonian stability: "The grass I aim to feast thy sheep, The flowers I for thy temples keep." When Damon's next words show us that the subject is not what we expected, we move from the "stability" (it is not erased) to something else in a progressively discovered subject. No formal distortion marked the change; that was possible but not necessary—a naughty, confusing attribute in "evidence." The "troubled" *Lycidas* is Mannerist; it is hard to find a poem about the pain of early death and seeming unjust heavens, that is untroubled. Quite aside from the aesthetic doubtfulness of turning poets into mere sheaths of their subjects, we are stranded with the alternative of claiming either that only some eras have such attitudes (doubtful) or deal with such subjects (impossible), or else that any poet who does is mannerist out of his time. It must be noticed that we have only been saddled with the vast task of considering everything from *Job* to *In Memoriam*, or led toward any conceivable confusion between the pieces, because we sought the aid of this criterion, to classify—we should never confuse the things themselves. This is only the beginning, for we must ask of all these troubled pieces just *how* they are troubled (but here at this heart of the matter impressionistic phrases appear which aid us to no distinctions, because they commonly describe one item, usually one we are trying to classify, e.g., "Lycidas"). And if the essence of the criterion be that there is some special form of suffering under the way inescapable conditions impinge on men's wishes and their peace, we must find formal characteristics that reliably distinguish that form from all the others. We have further to discover, in all the other genres such as dramas and novels, whether it be the author who is tormented and torn, or his created characters—his own attitude being a thing to be otherwise discovered. All this comes close to making classification an end in itself merely by virtue of how long it takes. It can be rapid only if we deny authors the right to present trouble as troublingly as they can, or measure their sufferings and their resolutions against our incapacity to share them.

With every example we seek to classify, we are dogged by this intimate relation in literature between poetic subject and the decorum of
the piece, complicated by the fact that words have meanings, though
meanwhile *we* shape the forms we are asked to imagine. *Comus* is
serenely "Renaissance"; but if it is difficult to see how a tormented
treatment of Temperance could recommend it, it seems equally unfortunate to erect poetic categories on whether men are "for" or
"against" a virtue. Who shall not be a Tenebrist, or has not been, who
really set out to depict Hell? though with words the medium, capacities
to respond with imaged *tenebrae* both differ with persons and alter with
time. If we proceed to a Heaven without shadows we are uncertain
whether that should slip the poem into another classification. Milton's
description of Eden is quoted that we may observe its fleshly abundance. One would look long for a pre-Fall Paradise that had meager
instead of rich groves, unripe not burnished fruits, jungle-hot recesses,
and an Adam and Eve not eminently naked. Though we could tell a
Spenserian paradise from Milton's in an instant, this is because we
look elsewhere for differentiating characteristics than to the abundance which all Edens must possess.

That the innocence of prelapsarian fleshliness is part of Milton's
quite orthodox Christian point is apparent from his different post-
lapsarian fleshly lost-paradise; the Milton studies which make his
theological sophistication so clear could easily induce it in any critic
who finds the innocence of the flesh so out of square with Milton's
"Puritanism" that unconscious loss of his convictions must be called
in to explain it. Far from deserting his tenets for his images, it is
through the images that he makes sexual *temperance* his point; but it
is the same Christianized conception of temperance as in the "Renaissance" *Comus*, defined (as a long history had made possible) with
respect to its consonance with worshipping God rather than the flesh
which He had "created good" but not to take His place. To lock up a
thoughtful author, with a whole language and all the conceptual refinements language can get into images at his command, into the few
large oppositions which can be unambiguously the *conceptual* burden
of nonverbal works, is to give ourselves difficulties of interpretation at
every turn. Milton's Eden certainly reminds us of baroque rather than
Renaissance or medieval painting. Yet when the classification "Baroque," instead of giving us a name for certain indefinable likenesses,
imposes upon an author a pattern of thought derived from other examples in the classification, our poems have become tools to protect
our categories.

This can happen with any classifying. But perhaps it happens with special ease when the criteria are drawn over from arts in which form can only imply[9] a state of mind in a creator, into an art where such implications are obscured or short-circuited by the pre-eminent capacity of words: that they say meanings outright, counting upon an antecedent, very rough, resilient agreement on what these are. This capacity takes precedence over everything else, when we are watching the decorum with which style makes poetic subject manifest. If "Il Penseroso" is an example of "open form," and if open forms "imply . . . that there is no stable order in the world," so that the hermit at the close quite simply has nothing to "rightly spell," however old his experience—we have the choice of calling its form Milton's mistake, or questioning the applicability of our criterion. If we are willing to do the latter, we shall find that the peculiarly literary formal elements lead the poem toward the end he gives it with an almost perfect decorum. If Spenser's flower catalogue in *Prothalamion* has the "fractional seeing" of the Renaissance, and the "Lycidas" flower passage similarly taken alone and out of context has the same fastidious perception of single flowers despite the poem's mannerist "proximate seeing," it is possible that we should give up isolating and attributing a fixed significance to these images we have made and are "seeing," in favor of attending to literature's pre-eminent way of apprehending what it is we "see." That will lead us, in these two whole poems, including every flower and every other image, to "see" the difference of life from death. Dead flowers could not do it; they can say resurrection as easily as death, if asked to. If one wishes to classify with delicacy, it is better to use criteria which do not ignore, but take full cognizance of, the peculiar capacities of the medium of what one is classifying. Absolute clarity and relative clarity have a similar inadequacy; clarity in arts which use words is implacably connected with clearness as this is had by things to which shape, color, light are (except metaphorically) indifferent: ideas, impulses, notions. Criteria grounded in what our phenomena cannot possess can only be partial.

The bases of differentiating principles, that we have uncovered, do not make the outlook very cheerful for attempts to use "Baroque" or "Mannerist" as categories through which we will group poems more reliably and understand them more fully. In all this I have left out one great further difficulty. Nothing makes one more uneasy in reading

[9] In the merely apparent exception—when "images" or formal motifs have a history that makes their conceptual burden clear—it is natural and significant that we speak of "a language of images."

applications of these classifications to literature than to allow one's knowledge of literature of other periods to be at all awake. It is especially necessary to throttle all ghosts from the Middle Ages, and resolutely disallow that movement of mind which sees how neatly criteria as described suit writers who clearly do not belong with those being discussed. That the experience is painful is obvious from the exceptions others have taken. Alanus pops up at us out of one description; Adam of St. Victor agreeably inhabits another, Chaucer flies through all three time-divisions, his traits subsumable under the characterizations, though we know he belongs in none (we may be the last to know it); Augustine will not stay put unless we turn a deaf ear, deafened by his great history and by keeping away from numerous sermons, the *Enarrations* and the *Confessions;* the radical images of a *Somme le roi* or the subtle sustained metaphors of a *Queste del Saint Graal* insinuate themselves as the best possible examples of some described criterion identifying a category, inclusion in which we know would make the works misunderstood; lyrics on the Last Things or the Charter of Christ or the deceptions of *saeculum* beat through the brain; Chrétien's disputed *sen* and ambiguous comic ironies find yet another rubric and unsafe dwelling place; Jean de Meun, especially in his character as a master of extended ironic dialectic in large figurative sweeps covering thousands of lines, winks like a will-o'-the-wisp in and out of the descriptions of differentiating traits; both stylistically and as to psychological preoccupations, sermons (Latin and vernacular) are incorrigible uninvited guests; and Carolingian pastorals are a plain nuisance. I am not speaking of characteristics we can "find" in pieces, but of the traits we should have to describe in trying to come at their true quality.

It may be this kind of experience, finally, which makes one think: since one would not confuse the works themselves, nor the styles or themes of any of them with those of a mannerist or baroque Milton, however much the descriptions of wherein he is mannerist or baroque pull these unlike works into his company, would it not assist clarity and save time to avoid the machinery of categories so unable to isolate the true quiddity of a great poet's works? It is not only that this seems to elude the describing phrases, but that the categories which carve Milton up often differentiate what seems to matter least about literature: some dead man's problematic but possible, or temporary, state of mind which has little to do with what makes his poem memorable, some private motive or need that impelled him toward ornateness or spareness or profusion, but has little effect on our enjoyment of the ornaments or the brevity or the plenty, because his motive is not the subject he is writing about and has used these means to illumine. Meanwhile the categories, or the criteria advanced to help us put men into them, do not differentiate except by virtue of the antecedently sure taste of the most experienced critic, between things it is critically vital to distinguish; profound terror gets into the same drawer with melodrama, restraint into the same drawer with smothering of screams, poise with frigidity, truth of revelation with self-obsession. This is not true of the arts to which the criteria are directly applicable, for form is a supremely delicate carrier. But literature does not have forms in this sense; we make them out of meanings, suggestions, relations. The infinite complexity and stubborn uniqueness thus provided may be the reason why we have the uncomfortable sense—when we have ranged literary works under categories not merely arbitrary like chronology, but purporting to indicate a view of reality—that we have merely stuck names on them like tickets. And the names belie and circumscribe, rather than illumine, the nature of the thing we have labeled. To come out with names for things is one way of classifying; it does not order the phenomena.

This is not to say that our previous habit of using these categories to make suggestive relations with other arts was mistaken; I should be no more willing than another to forego the stimulation and insight into qualities of works which the series of such treatments has provided. If every critic past or future who has called attention (or will) to baroque elements in seventeenth-century poetry or Milton were to find that here attacked, a disservice to criticism would have been done. Dogmatic categorizing and the attaching of labels seems a different thing, and the more popular it threatens to become, the more different. It is moreover true that this may be one of the numerous ways in which English literature is less amenable to some kinds of arrangement than other literatures; the question at issue here is solely that of the usefulness of these criteria and categories for the literature to which Milton belongs, and for Milton's several works. It would not be the first time that John Milton, *Anglus*, resisted all efforts to get him whole into the order that justly suited others, and he would not be the first Englishman to show that recalcitrance.

LIMITS OF MILTONIC TOLERATION

Don M. Wolfe, Brooklyn College

I

No belief was more deeply rooted in Milton's thought than freedom for the individual to interpret religious truth for himself and publish it to the world.[1] It was in fact this belief that prepared the way for *Areopagitica:* the principle of toleration applied to secular ideas as well. But like almost every intellectual of his generation, Milton found himself fencing his tolerationist beliefs with decisive qualifications. Unlike Richard Overton and Roger Williams, he would have forbidden Roman Catholics the right of worship according to conscience. Unlike Cromwell, Williams, and Edward Nicholas, he did not speak out for the right of the Jews to return to England and set up synagogues free from molestation. Milton's rejection of Catholic freedom is emphatic and consistent. His attitude toward the Jews constitutes not so much rejection as ambivalence and withdrawal. In 1652 and 1656, years when readmission of the Jews to England was an issue much in agitation, Milton did not join Williams and Cromwell in extending tolerationist principles to enfold Hebraic consciences.

Though he wished toleration for all Protestant sects, whatever their aberrations, Milton would have prohibited Roman Catholics from exercise of their conscience even in mass conducted in private homes. In his most extreme plea for toleration, *Civil Power in Ecclesiastical Causes*, he restates his position a little uneasily: "Their religion the more considered, the less can be acknowledged a religion; but a Roman principality rather, endeavoring to keep up her old universal dominion under a new name. ... Nevertheless, if they ought not to be tolerated, it is for just reason of state, more than of religion."[2] This argument, as applied to Protestant sects, Milton himself had more than once refuted; it was indeed the dominant justification of "forcers of conscience," whatever the colors of their creeds. In *Civil Power*, for the first time in his career, Milton's rejection of Catholic freedom seems about to give way; but his most extreme passion, the

[1] See especially the statements in *Christian Doctrine*, Columbia edition of the *Works* (New York, 1930–39), XVI, 267, 395.
[2] Wolfe, *Milton in the Puritan Revolution* (New York, 1941), p. 111.

226

efficacy of a subjective approach to truth, aided by the traditional prejudices of his country, holds him in check. Milton's inconsistency is mirrored in Cromwell's statement to the Irish: "I meddle not with any man's conscience. But if by liberty of conscience you mean a liberty to exercise the mass, I judge it best to exercise plain dealing and to let you know where the Parliament of England have power, that will not be allowed of."[3] Around the campfires of the New Model, as Baxter found to his horror, strange notions fed on each other in wild and promiscuous array. Cromwell would allow no one of these, "God's children," to be persecuted. But freedom of Catholic conscience to Cromwell, as to Milton, was unthinkable.

In rejecting toleration of Catholic worship, Milton rejected as well the sensory beauty of the Anglican service he had known and loved as London boy and Cambridge student. He turned his back, in effect, on the poetic approach to religion, the magic of ritual, of color and smell and sound: the creation amid the bleakness of daily life of a world of mystic beauty and spiritual exaltation. As a poet Milton dealt with images that transported the reader in every scene to the world of the artist's imagination. But images in religious worship he despised as idols. Before the subjective searching of the Bible as the essence of religious experience, in Milton's mind the drama and color of song and ritual faded into dangerous unreality.[4]

Milton's reluctance to tolerate Catholicism yielded to no persuasion of his fellow-reformers. In *The Bloudy Tenent* (1644) Williams had spoken for the freedom of both Catholic and Jewish consciences, asserting that Catholics "for their *conscience* and *religion* . . . should not . . . be choaked and smothered, but suffered to breathe and walke upon the Deckes in the ayre of *civill liberty* and *conversation* in the Ship of the *commonwealth* upon good assurance given of *civill obedience* to the *Civill State*."[5] In 1644 *The Bloudy Tenent* had been burned by the common hangman. But by 1652, when the Commonwealth was three years old, Williams found that England still needed his message. In *The Hireling Ministry None of Christs* (April? 1652), referring to Ireland as "a field of blood," he asserts that the "consciences *of the Catholicks have been restrained by the* civil Sword *and* penalties."[6] In *The Bloody Tenent Yet More Bloody* (28 April 1652), Williams asked,

---

[3] *Ibid.*, p. 115.
[4] I am here following in part my *Milton in the Puritan Revolution*, p. 115.
[5] British Museum, E1(2), p. 107.
[6] British Museum, C.32.d.37, "Epistle Dedicatory," sig. A4.

"Why should their *Consciences* more than others be oppressed?"[7] Richard Overton, who was probably also a friend of Milton, had made a vigorous, whole-hearted plea for toleration of Catholics in his *The Araignment of Mr. Persecution* (1646).[8] Men as far apart socially as Henry Marten and Gerrard Winstanley favored toleration of Catholics, Marten in open Parliament, Winstanley in his utopian blueprint.[9] Of less learning and genius than Milton, these men (and others such as Henry Vane and George Fox) exhibited a maturity in their tolerationist views toward Catholics that Milton never attained. Even Cromwell, once secure in his power, was less of a Papist-hater than Milton. He was opposed to the repressive abjuration bill passed against Catholics in 1657 and as the executive consistently alleviated its oppressions.

II

An even sterner test for the tolerationists of Milton's time was their attitude toward the Jews. On this issue, as on freedom of Catholic consciences, Williams was blunt and outspoken. In *The Hireling Ministry None of Christs* Williams asserted that "a free and absolute *permission*" should be granted to the "*consciences* of all men," not excepting "the very *consciences* of the *Jews*, nor the *consciences* of the *Turkes* or *Papists*, or *Pagans*."[10] On 30 March 1652, when the Committee for Propagation of the Gospel was considering proposals for a modified state church, Roger Williams issued a blunt challenge in *The Fourth Paper:* "Whether it be not the duty of the Magistrate to permit the Jews, whose conversion we look for, to live freely and peaceably amongst us?"[11] Only ten days before, on March 20, Captain Robert Norwood had anticipated this question and given his answer: "Yes; because we would, if under their power, that they should tolerate us."[12] Williams' answer in *The Fourth Paper* to his own question is more

---

[7] British Museum, E661(6), p. 180.

[8] *The Araignment of Mr. Persecution*, pp. 11–12. This tract may be most easily examined in William Haller, *Tracts on Liberty in the Puritan Revolution* (New York, 1934), III, 205–56.

The extreme tolerationist positions of Overton and Williams, as applied to both Catholics and Jews, had been anticipated in Leonard Busher's *Religions Peace* (1614), which was reprinted in 1646, appearing on 25 April, E334(7). For a highly perceptive analysis of this crucial tract, see Wilbur K. Jordan, *The Development of Religious Toleration in England* (4 vols., London, 1932–40), II, 284–98.

[9] Winstanley, *Law of Freedom in a Platform* (1652), E655(8), p. 81.

[10] P. 24.

[11] *The Fourth Paper Presented by Major Butler*, 30 March 1652, E658(9), p. 3.

[12] *Proposals for Propagation of the Gospel*, E656(21), p. 17.

searching and detailed than his commentary in *Hireling Ministry* or *The Bloody Tenent Yet More Bloody*. The Jews, insists Williams, are a people more beloved of God than any other, blessed with "most gracious and express Promises." Were it not for the Jews, he continues, the Gentiles could not have possessed a savior. Moreover, insists Williams, the English have much to answer for in their treatment of Jews over the centuries. They have oppressed and mistreated the Jews in ways that "have cried to *Heaven* against this *Nation* and the *Kings* and *Princes* of it." Williams pleads with the Committee "to make way for their free and peaceable Habitation amongst us." Yes, he is aware of the ancient grounds of hostility toward the Jews: "of their known Industry of inriching themselves in all places where they come"; of the Jews' killing Jesus; of "their *cursing* themselves and their *posterity;* of the *wrath* of *God* upon them."[13] But such objections in Williams' mind would not prevent a great nation from the generous readmission of the Jews to the fellowship of unpersecuted English consciences.

III

The circumstances under which *The Fourth Letter* was written and discussed make it very unlikely that Milton could have been unaware of Williams' extreme position on toleration. Upon his arrival early in 1652, to seek new powers and protection for his Rhode Island settlement, Williams had renewed his friendship with Vane, Peters, Cromwell, Milton, and other leaders. Cromwell "sent for him and entertained many discourses with him at several times."[14] That Williams was often at Vane's house is suggested by Williams' letter of 20 April 1652, on which day he wrote Winthrop from Vane's lodgings at two in the morning.[15] In a letter written to Winthrop in 1654, Williams shows that he had been on familiar terms with Milton: "The Secretary of the Council, (Mr. Milton) for my Dutch I read him, read me many more languages."[16] The composition of *The Fourth Paper* shows Williams assuming leadership in presenting a strong appeal for toleration; the names of five others, including Charles Vane, brother of Henry, appear on the title page as subscribing to the ideas of the pamphlet, all of which except for Christopher Goad's letter to Major Butler, Wil-

[13] E658(9), pp. 18, 19.
[14] James Ernst, *Roger Williams* (New York, 1932), p. 317.
[15] *Letters of Roger Williams*, in *Publications of the Narragansett Club*, 1st ser. (Providence, 1874), VI, 234.
[16] James D. Knowles, *Memoir of Roger Williams* (Boston, 1834), p. 264.

liams acknowledges as his own. He had issued, or was about to issue, *The Hireling Ministry None of Christs;* a month hence he was to send forth *The Bloody Tenent Still More Bloody.* Williams therefore was in the thick of agitation for the cause he believed in most, this time with friends in power near at hand. The preface to *The Fourth Paper* shows that Williams was present at at least one meeting of the Committee when Cromwell spoke, saying, *"That he had rather* Mahumetanism *were permitted amongst us, then that one of Gods Children should be persecuted."*[17] At the end of *The Fourth Paper* Williams asks the ministers of John Owen's committee to retract their Fifteen Proposals and Fifteen Fundamentals. If they reject a retraction, Williams hopes that "the hearts of some of his Faithful Witnesses (against such *Graven Images)"* will be moved "to present some faithful and truly *Christian Observations."*[18] Whether or not Milton read this appeal for help, he could not have been unaware, as his two sonnets to Cromwell and Vane were shortly to show, of the agitation in which Williams had assumed such tenacious leadership. Milton was not present at the meetings of the Council of State in March and April; but he was closely following the march of events that mattered more to him than any other issues facing the new republic.

Milton's two sonnets to Cromwell and Vane in May and July 1652 do not delineate his tolerationist reservations; but they show his intense vigilance and preoccupation with the ebb and flow of argument as well as events. Cromwell was a member of the crucial committee and a close friend of John Owen, main author of the proposals. Even in the heading of his first sonnet Milton shows his resolution to make his appeal unmistakable in its immediate application: "To the Lord General Cromwell May 1652. On the proposalls of certaine ministers at ye Comm[i]tee for Propagation of the Gospell." After complimenting Cromwell on his military and civil achievements, Milton warns that "New foes arise, threatening to bind our souls with secular chaines." Then, writing as though Cromwell cannot fail to want the widest liberty of conscience, he concludes:

> Helpe us to save free Conscience from the paw
> Of hireling wolves whose Gospell is their maw.

In this sonnet Milton's emphasis is the state church as the main impediment to freedom of conscience, as shown in the words *hireling*

---

[17] Preface entitled "To the Truly Christian Reader," E658(9).
[18] E658(9), p. 23.

wolves and *Gospell is their maw.* Milton was afraid that Cromwell would yield, as Cromwell ultimately did, to the need for a state church. Cromwell was realistic enough to see that the abolition of the machinery of the state church, with its nine thousand parish ministers and its tithes irreversibly interwoven with the economy of the nation, would create a chaos impossible to cope with. Unlike Vane and Milton, Cromwell believed that a liberal state church would not necessarily mean persecution of conscience for those outside its fold. But Milton was saying to Cromwell that *any* hireling ministry would inevitably bring with it repression of Protestant consciences. Owen and the ministers had indeed proposed a careful selection of parish ministers, to be approved by a Parliamentary committee going from county to county. But who was an orthodox minister to this roving committee? He had to support certain beliefs, which the ministers had already set down as the Fifteen Fundamentals mentioned by Williams at the end of *The Fourth Paper.* So Milton was rightly fearful, both of the ministers' intention to create a new orthodoxy and of Cromwell's intention to support a hireling ministry.

When Vane received Milton's sonnet on July 8, the issue of the state church was still unresolved. If, as it seemed, Owen had Cromwell's support, Vane was resisting the proposals, as was evident from the open opposition of his brother Charles in endorsing *The Fourth Paper.* Milton reserves his highest tribute for Vane's understanding of the exact relationship that should exist between church and state:

> Both spiritual powre and civill, what each meanes
> What severs each thou 'hast learnt, wch few hav don.
> The bounds of either sword to thee wee ow.
> Therefore on the firme hand religion leanes
> In peace, & reck'ns thee her eldest son.

Milton was on firm ground in looking to Vane as the bulwark of tolerationist hopes. Even in his New England years, as the twenty-three-year-old governor of Massachusetts, Vane had championed Mrs. Hutchinson's right to expound her strange antinomian theories. In Parliament Vane had supported all extreme measures for liberty of conscience. Baillie regretfully reported that Vane "twyce at our table prolixlie, earnestlie, and passionatelie had reasoned for a full libertie of conscience for all religions."[19] In 1647 Vane had moved that the unitarian John Bidle be set free. In a commonwealth now at peace, Vane

---

[19] *Letters and Journals* (Edinburgh, 1841), II, 235.

was to Milton the "eldest son," the true statesman, trained as no other man in the Commonwealth in making distinctions between civil power and the rights of individual conscience.

On the issue of freedom for Catholic or Jewish consciences, Vane made no full statements such as those of Roger Williams. Indeed, on the question of the readmission of the Jews to England, a question much discussed in the early months of 1652, Vane was silent. Though he made no plea for Catholic conscience, Vane did attempt to protect Catholics from persecution. On 1 June 1652, when the Commons took up the question of Irish Catholics, "not to compel any the Recusants in this Nation to their Worship, or Divine Service, contrary to their Consciences," Vane voted against coercion.[20] On the same day, however, without division, the House voted not to tolerate "Exercise of the Popish Religion in *Ireland*"![21] Only a zealot prepared to lose all his influence over his contemporaries would have voted for toleration of the mass, particularly in royalist Ireland. But Williams' analysis of English persecution of Irish consciences in *The Hireling Ministry None of Christs*, published while Williams was intermittently a guest at Vane's house, and obviously written to crystallize opposition to Owen's scheme of a state church, would suggest that Williams' plea for Irish consciences was not unwelcome to Vane. Certainly Vane was more sympathetic to Papists than Milton or Cromwell. On the other

[20] *Commons' Journals*, VII, 138.

[21] *Ibid.*, VII, 138. Lingard states (*History of England* [London, 1825], XI, 179) that Vane voted in favor of a Catholic petition on 30 June 1652. The *Commons' Journals* for that day, however, show that Sir Henry Vane, Senior, voted against the reading of the petition. The motion to read the petition carried by vote of 33–28, but the petition itself was denied. I cannot find any record of the younger Vane's stand on this issue.

As Lingard points out, the petition, mild and moderate enough, asking for "such clemency and companion . . . as in the judgment of this honourable House may consist with the publike peace," may be found in John Austin's *Christian Moderator*, E1313(2), pp. 59–62. Austin's tracts contain some of the most searching pleas for toleration of Catholic conscience the Puritan Revolution produced. See the first part of *The Christian Moderator*, E640(1), August 1651, and the third part, E705(15), 14 July 1653; in the latter Austin deals with the oath of abjuration.

A case cited by Lingard from *Christian Moderator* shows the savagery of Parliament's treatment of the Papists. A Catholic orphan girl appealed to the commissioners for sequestration at Haberdashers Hall for relief from the sentence against her, payment of two-thirds of her estate to the state. Having served as a maid for seventeen years, she had saved twenty pounds (at an annual wage of seven nobles), and deposited her money with a friend. The commissioners discovered her estate and appropriated two-thirds of it, 13 pounds, 6 shillings, 4 pence. The sequestrators said "they had not the power to give her any relief, more than the bare thirds, unless she would take the oath of Abjuration." See *Christian Moderator*, E1313(2), p. 82. Austin's remarkable tracts deserve more attention than they have thus far received.

hand, so far as the evidence goes, Vane never spoke out for readmission of the Jews, as did Cromwell, or made any specific mention of their right to liberty of conscience, as did Williams.

IV

Despite the agitation for freedom of Jewish conscience in 1652 and 1656, Milton at no time spoke out decisively on this issue, the most searching tolerationist dilemma of his age. This fact is particularly striking when we reflect upon the agitation carried on by Williams in the early months of 1652 and the strenuous efforts made by Cromwell to secure readmission of the Jews to England. Milton's very aloofness from such a vital controversy is in itself a fact that deserves exploration and interpretation.

The nearest approach to a statement of Milton's attitude toward liberty for Jewish conscience is in *Observations on the Articles of Peace with the Irish Rebels*. By an official assignment of the Council of State, 28 March 1649, Milton had been called upon to justify the policies of the new republic, answering in part *A Necessary Representation* of the Belfast Presbytery, which the Council had ordered printed with the *Articles of Peace*. The Presbytery accused the new republic of embracing "even Paganisme, and Judaisme in the Armes of Toleration." Though Milton calls this charge "A most audacious calumny," he hastens to make a qualification: "And yet while we detest *Judaism*, we know ourselves commanded by St. *Paul, Rom*. II. to respect the *Jews*, and by all means to endeavor thir conversion."[22] When Milton writes, "we detest *Judaism*," he uses words repeated nowhere else in his writings. Nor do we find elsewhere in Milton Paul's admonition "to respect the Jews" or work for their conversion, though this injunction is found prominently in Williams (in *The Fourth Paper*, for example, as the leading justification). How, Williams had asked, can we hope to convert the Jews to Christianity if we forbid them to live in the land? But Milton did not expand the idea of conversion here or elsewhere. One can only conclude that he was only interpreting the official attitude of the new republic, respect for the Jewish people, without denying all complaints against the Jews or committing the government to the universal toleration mentioned by the horrified Belfast Presbyterians.

Denial of Jewish liberty of conscience had been based on accusations centuries deep in folk and intellectual custom. Milton resorts

[22] *Works*, Columbia edition, XVI, 238, 264.

only rarely to these traditional slurs. In *Doctrine and Discipline*, it is true, he wrote of the Jews: "Their hearts were set upon usury, and are to this day, no Nation more."[23] This accusation is particularly striking in view of the money-lending career of Milton's father and Milton's statement that his own livelihood had come "out of the sweat of other men."[24] Though he is very ambivalent on the subject, Milton elsewhere upholds usury, saying that it is not "against the word of God, nor the rule of charity."[25] In *Christian Doctrine* he asserts that usury is not to be ascribed to the "hardheartedness of the Jews." Moreover, God "would not have permitted the Israelites to lend upon usury to strangers" if it were wrong.[26] So that this attack upon the Jews, so common in Milton's time, indirectly referred to in Williams' statement "their known Industry in inriching themselves," Milton never took seriously enough in his own thinking to expand or justify.

The most persistent cause for persecution of the Jews had been the recurring simplification of the ages, "The Jews killed Christ," a charge repeated by Williams in *The Fourth Paper*. At no point does Milton expand or support this charge against the Jews as grounds for forbidding them home in England or denying them liberty of conscience. Milton refers most directly in *Second Defence* to the responsibility of the Hebrews for the death of Christ, when he says that by the clearest signs they might have identified him.[27] Milton refers obliquely to the recurring accusation to illustrate a distinction in his *Art of Logic:* "Long ago the proegumenic cause of the death of Christ was the ignorant zeal of the Jews; the procatarctic cause was the violation of the sabbath and the seditious assemblies with which he was charged."[28] Such a statement shows that Milton from time to time fell into the pattern of age-old rhetoric which had justified for centuries persecution of Jewish conscience. But his judgments of the Jews possess none of the blazing fury that dominate his passionate utterances against the Papists. He was not a champion of the Jews, like Edward Nicholas and William Tomlinson; but neither was he a fanatic opponent of their liberty of conscience, like William Prynne and James Howell.

[23] *Works*, Columbia edition, III, 436.
[24] *Complete Prose Works*, ed. Don M. Wolfe, I (New Haven, 1953), 804.
[25] *Works*, Columbia edition, III, 427.
[26] *Ibid.*, XVII, 39, 341.
[27] *Ibid.*, VIII, 95.
[28] *Ibid.*, XI, 37.

V

A number of Milton's contemporaries came to grips, as he did not, with the thorny question of admitting the Jews again to England, welcoming the expression of their consciences. On 21 February 1649, for example, Edward Nicholas sent forth his *Apologie for the Honorable Nation of the Jews*. Like a handful of other men, Nicholas welcomed the Jews without recalling the grievances of ages against them. Instead, he set before his readers the grievances of the Jews against the great nations, against "the rage of men in all countries." In Spain alone, "120000 Jews cast out and banisht, in the year 1493." Then Nicholas adds: "I hope better things of our Nation." Could one really assert that the nation of the Jews was guilty of the death of Christ? Not so, asserted Nicholas; only the "Elders, chief Priests, and Scribes," as the Gospel record shows.[29] A few sailors of England's far flung ships echoed the views of Nicholas. On 19 March 1652, a sailor from the ship *Phoenix*, resting at Leghorn, described a visit he had made with friends to a local synagogue. There they found a man who could speak a little English: "*We . . . asked him the meaning of such and such things.*" Then the writer asks: Is it possible that England will continue laws in force against the Jews when the Pope tolerates them, the Turks, the Duke of Florence?[30] In *A Bosome Opened to the Jewes*, William Tomlinson noted the irony of praying for outcasts one is not willing to embrace in his own land. He would not have England "a rejecter of them being strangers in the time of their calamity, they seeking to come in and live peaceably among us."[31] In *A Brief Answer* Thomas Collier asked "Must we take it into our hands, and become Executioners upon these poor dispersed people, let Turks and Indies do that, and not us who profess to know God in Christ." Almost alone among the commentators of his day, Collier considered Christ more Jew than Christian: "Our salvation came from them, our Jesus was one of them."[32] Such attitudes toward the Jews, if not foreign to Milton's outlook, found no expression in his letters, pamphlets, or poems.

Other thinkers who favored readmission of the Jews wrote with

[29] E544(16), pp. 11, 6. The books and articles of Professor Cecil Roth, of Oxford University, are an indispensable guide to Jewish life in England during the Cromwellian regime. His *History of the Jews in England* (Oxford, 1941) has been particularly helpful in this study.

[30] *Severall Proceedings*, 29 April–6 May 1652, E794(33), p. 2128.

[31] British Museum, 669f.20(22), 12 January 1656.

[32] 4 February 1656, E866(1).

varying degrees of caution and reserve. Milton's friend John Dury, for example, evidently in response to Hartlib's request, wrote *A Case of Conscience, Whether It Be Lawful to Admit Jews into a Christian Common-Wealth.* The tract is signed 8 January 1656. Dury's first impulse is a generous affirmative: "A People in misery and distresse . . . there is not doubt, but they may lawfully be received into any civil Societie."[33] Moreover, continues Dury, our indebtedness to them is far-reaching: "We have the Oracles of God by their meanes, preserved and conveyed to us, and the . . . accomplishment of all the promises, whereof we desire, that they may be made partakers again with us . . . to shew that mercie to them which he [Jesus] hathe shewed to us." It may even be a sin to refuse them admittance. But toward the end of his pamphlet Dury's doubts begin to mount. He warns Hartlib that the Jews "aspire to have . . . riches and power over others, where ever they can get it"; he fears "their covetous practices and biting usury." The state, he concludes, "*doth wisely to goe warily, and by degrees, in the busines of receiving them.*"[34] Dury is aware that the Commonwealth hopes to profit by the international experience of some Jewish business men; but in Dury's judgment the basis for admitting them should be rather "out of Christian love and compassion towards them." Thus, in contrast to Williams and Nicholas, Dury has many reservations. He is willing for the Jews to have liberty of conscience, provided they worship in their own tongue, do not blaspheme, proselite, or "profane the Christian Sabbath."

Unlike Milton, therefore, Dury at least put himself on record as desiring a limited toleration of Jewish conscience. Another friend of Milton, Moses Wall, translated Manasseh Ben Israel's book, *The Hope of Israel,* saying, "Do not think I aime by this Translation, to propagate or commend Judaisme . . . through Grace I have better learned the truth, as it is in Jesus."[35] But Wall writes to "remove our sinfull hatred from off that people, whose are the Promises, and who are beloved for their Fathers sakes."[36] Despite Manasseh's blunt warning against any such possibility, Wall and other writers hoped for the conversion of the Jews. Wall speaks of his great admiration for Manasseh; he "may wel be set for a pattern to us Christians."[37]

[33] 27 June 1656, E882(11), p. 3.
[34] *Ibid.*, pp. 8, 9.
[35] E650(1), "The Translator to the Reader," sig. B1.
[36] *Ibid.*
[37] *Ibid.*

The Parliamentarian Edward Spenser was willing also to admit the Jews to England, but conditionally: "My consent ye shall have, that you and your people shall live in *England*, and have meeting places to worship *Adonai*, but no place for sacrifices." Spenser doubts that England will permit circumcision, or marriage to Christians. Moreover, a third part of each Jew's estate will be forfeit to the state at his death; another third is to be used for the maintenance of converted Jews![38]

At the far right of England's commentators on the Jews were men with whom Milton and Dury had nothing in common; nevertheless such commentators carried on the resistless march of folk superstition; they were a political force that even the champions of free Jewish conscience could not ignore. In his preface to the translation of Josephus, *History of the Latter Times of the Jews*, 2 June 1652, James Howell repeated the ancient accusations: Jews over the centuries had poisoned wells, counterfeited coins, falsified seals, crucified Christian children. The Jews look strange, have "*uncouth looks and odd cast of eye . . . likewise that rankish kinde of sent . . . which is observed to be inherent. . . . I wish that England may not be troubled with that sent again.*"[39] William Prynne came forth in 1656 with two formidable volumes against the Jews, recapitulating the ancient grievances and conjuring up a new Jewish plot "*to seduce us unto Judaism,* to which many are now inclined."[40] Like Prynne, the anonymous writer of *Anglo-Judaeus* justifies the hostile treatment of Jews by English kings, attacks Manasseh for his appeal to Cromwell, accuses them of usury. "Lower we cannot prize any one of most abject condition," asserts the writer, "then by comparing him to a *Jew*." The author of this tract dedicated his volume to Cromwell, signing his epistle "W.H."[41] The strange royalist Arise Evans, who urged Cromwell repeatedly to set Charles II on his rightful throne, wrote that if kingship were not restored, the Jews would be to blame.[42] In his desire to resettle the Jews in England, granting them freedom of conscience, Cromwell found a steady resistance among some of his closest col-

[38] *An Epistle to the Learned Manasseh Ben Israel* (1650), British Museum, 701.a.40, pp. 11, 15–16.

[39] E1427, Epistle Dedicatory, "To Englands Imperial Chamber, the Renowned City of London," sigs. A6r–v.

[40] *A Short Demurrer to the Jews*, 7 January 1656, E483(1), and *The Second Part of a Short Demurrer to the Jews*, 30 March 1656, E483(2). The passage quoted is from E483(1), pp. 83–84.

[41] 8 January 1656, E863(3), p. 47.

[42] *An Echo from Heaven*, 24 March 1653, E1304(3), p. 135.

leagues in the Council of State. Only Hugh Peters was a militant worker for the return of the Jews. Lambert was silent. Harrison was silent. Milton was silent. Dury was sure of the case from trial by conscience but doubtful from the tests of expediency.

VI

The limits of Milton's toleration, then, are clearly defined in his undeviating hostility toward freedom of Catholic conscience; and his failure to speak for the Jews can only be interpreted, in the light of contemporary agitation, as a reluctance to permit them freedom of worship. Even the royalist Sir Thomas Browne was more outspoken for Jewish conscience than Milton, pointing out that "the persecution of fifteen hundred years hath but confirmed them [the Jews] in their errour." Was not persecution, asked Browne, the basis of the Anglican faith? "None can more justly boast of Persecutions, and glory in the number and valour of Martyrs." Milton's failure to speak for the Jews sprang from a tolerationist psyche unique among his contemporaries, informed by a vast learning, untouched by superstition, influenced by a reluctance yet to be unravelled. Though like his fellows Milton separated the Jew Jesus from the Christian Jesus, he never fell into the habit of separating as two species the Jews of the Bible from the Jews of his own time. He was an Old Testament Christian, more at home with the fire of the prophets than with the revolutionary love of the New Testament. He could not portray the meek and loving Christ in *Paradise Regained*, even as the Puritans could not glean their battle cries from the Gospels. But even a prolonged preoccupation with Old Testament Judaism did not induce Milton to take his stand with Richard Overton and Roger Williams for liberty of Jewish conscience.

BIBLIOGRAPHY OF THE WRITINGS OF
HARRIS FRANCIS FLETCHER

Isabelle F. Grant, University of Illinois

BOOKS

1926

Milton's Semitic Studies and Some Manifestations of Them in His Poetry . . . Chicago, University of Chicago Press [1926]. Pp. x+155. (Thesis, Ph.D., University of Michigan, 1926.) English edition, London, Cambridge University Press, 1929.

Books for College Men and Women. Selected by the Department of Rhetoric and Journalism, The University of Michigan. [Compiled by Harris Fletcher, Clarence De Witt Thorpe, and Charles E. Whittemore] Ann Arbor, Mich., George Wahr, Publisher [1926]. Pp. [23].

1929

The Use of the Bible in Milton's Prose . . . [Urbana] University of Illinois, 1929. Pp. 176. (University of Illinois Studies in Language and Literature, XIV, No. 3.)

1930

Milton's Rabbinical Readings . . . Urbana, University of Illinois Press, 1930. Pp. 344.

1931

Contributions to a Milton Bibliography, 1800–1930, Being a List of Addenda to Stevens's "Reference Guide to Milton" . . . [Urbana] University of Illinois, 1931. Pp. 166. (University of Illinois Studies in Language and Literature, XVI, No. 1.)

1941

Milton, John. *The Complete Poetical Works of John Milton.* A New Text Edited With Introduction and Notes by Harris Francis Fletcher . . . Boston [etc.] [1941] Pp. x+574. (New Cambridge Edition.)

1943–1948

Milton, John. *John Milton's Complete Poetical Works, Reproduced in Photographic Facsimile.* A Critical Text Edition Compiled and Edited by Harris Francis Fletcher . . . Urbana, University of Illinois Press, 1943–1948. 4 Vols.

1953

Illinois. University. Library. *Collection of First Editions of Milton's Works, University of Illinois Library; an Exhibition, October 1–31, 1953.* Introduction and Notes Prepared by Harris F. Fletcher. Urbana, University of Illinois, 1953. Pp. [6] 23, [1] port. (Adah Patton Memorial Fund. Publication No. 2.)

1954

Illinois. University. Library. *An Exhibition of Some Printed Geographical Works and Atlases, 1475–1675, University of Illinois Library, 15 October– 30 November, 1954.* Introductory Essay and Descriptions by Harris Fletcher. [Urbana, 1954] Pp. 24. port. (Adah Patton Memorial Fund. Publication No. 3.)

1955

Illinois. University. Library. *An Exhibition of Some Latin Grammars Used or Printed in England, 1471–1697. The First Printed Greek Grammar. The First Printed Hebrew Grammar. November 1 to December 15, 1955.* Introductions and Descriptions by Harris Fletcher. Urbana, 1955. Pp. 42 illus. (Adah Patton Memorial Fund. Publication No. 4.)

1956–1961

The Intellectual Development of John Milton. Urbana, University of Illinois Press, 1956–61. 2 Vols.

1957

Illinois. University. Library. *An Exhibition of Printed Latin-English and English-Latin Word Lists and Dictionaries, 1497?–1736, University of Illinois Library, January, 1957.* Introduction and Descriptions by Harris Fletcher . . . [Urbana, 1957] Pp. 48. (Adah Patton Memorial Fund. Publication No. 5.)

1961

"A Library for Younger Schollers." Compiled by an English Scholar-Priest *about 1655.* Edited, with Bibliographical Index, by Alma DeJordy and Harris Francis Fletcher. Urbana, University of Illinois Press, 1961. Pp. 152. (University of Illinois Studies in Language and Literature, XLVIII.)

ARTICLES

1924

"Milton and Yosippon." *SP*, XXI (July), 496–501.

1926

"Milton and Thomas Young." *TLS*, No. 1253 (January 21), p. 44.

1927

"Milton and Walton's *Biblia Sacra Polyglotta* (1657)." *MLN*, XLII (February), 84–87.

"Milton's Use of Biblical Quotations." *JEGP*, XXVI (April), 145–65.

1928

"Milton and Rashi." *JEGP*, XXVII (July), 300–17.

1929

"Grierson's Suggested Date for Milton's *Ad Patrem*." *The Fred Newton Scott*

Anniversary Papers . . . Chicago, University of Chicago Press, [1929] Pp. 199–205.

"Nathaniel Lee and Milton." *MLN*, XLIV (March), 173–75.

1930

"Milton and ben Gerson." *JEGP*, XXIX (January), 41–52.

1932

"Proficiency Examinations for Credit at the University of Illinois." *School and Society*, XXXVI (December 17), 792–93.

1935

"Index Making." *Practical Applications of the Punched Card Method in Colleges and Universities.* Edited by G. W. Baehne. New York, Columbia University Press, 1935. Part 9, Section 4, pp. 405–408.

"The Selection of Students at the College Level for the Study of Law." *School and Society*, XLI (May 18), 686–88.

"Tutorial Work in the College of Liberal Arts and Sciences of the University of Illinois." *School and Society*, XLII (November 30), 744–45.

1936

"The First Edition of Milton's *History of Britain.*" *JEGP*, XXXV (July), 405–14.

1937

"The Undergraduate College Student and the Library." *School and Society*, XLV (May 29), 735–40.

"The Inception of a Tutorial Plan." *Journal of Higher Education*, VIII (January), 33–38.

1938

"Small Film Photography and the Textual Scholar." *Journal of Microphotography* (Winter).

1939

"Milton's Homer." *JEGP*, XXXVIII (April), 229–32.

1941

"A Note on Two Words in Milton's *History of Moscovia.*" *Renaissance Studies in Honor of Hardin Craig.* Stanford University, Calif., Stanford Univ. Press, 1941. Pp. 309–19. Also in *PQ*, XX (July), 501–11.

1948

"Milton's Copy of Gesner's *Heraclides*, 1544." *JEGP*, XLVII (April), 182–87.

"Milton's 'Vicar of Hell.'" *JEGP*, XLVII (October), 387–89.

1949

"Milton's Private Library—An Additional Title." *PQ*, XXVIII (January), 72–76.

"A Second (?) Title-page of the Second Edition of *Paradise Lost.*" *PBSA*,
. XLIII (2nd quarter), 173–78. facsim.

1952

"Milton's 'E Nostro Suburbano.'" *JEGP*, LI (April), 154–59.

1954

"The Education of a Literary Genius." *Phi Delta Kappan*, XXXV (March),
243–46.

1955

"A Possible Origin of Milton's 'Counterpoint' or Double Rhythm." *Studies
by Members of the English Department, University of Illinois, in Memory
of John Jay Parry.* Urbana, University of Illinois Press, 1955. Pp. 61–65.
Also in *JEGP*, LIV (October), 521–25.

1956

"Milton's [Index Poeticus]—*The Theatrum Poetarum* by Edward Phillips."
JEGP, LV (January), 35–40.
"Milton's *Apologus* and Its Mantuan Model." *JEGP*, LV (April), 230–33.

1958

"The Earliest (?) Printing of Sir Thomas More's Two Epigrams to John
Holt." *Studies in Honor of T. W. Baldwin.* Edited by Don Cameron
Allen. Urbana, University of Illinois Press, 1958. Pp. 53–65.
"Milton's Demogorgon—*Prolusion I* and *Paradise Lost*, II, 960–65."
JEGP, LVII (October), 684–89.

1961

"Milton's 'Old Damoetas.'" *JEGP*, LX (April), 250–57.

REVIEWS
1927

Whipple, Thomas King. *Martial and the English Epigram, from Sir Thomas
Wyatt to Ben Jonson.* Berkeley, Calif., 1925. (University of California
Publications in Modern Philology, X, no. 4.)
JEGP, XXVI (1927), 598–99.

1929

Freund, Michael. *Die Idee der Toleranz im England der Grossen Revolution.*
Halle, Saale, 1927. (Deutsche Vierteljahrsschrift für Literaturwissen-
schaft und Geistergeschichte . . . *Buchreihe.* 12. Bd.)
JEGP, XXVIII (1929), 574–77.
Michigan. University. Department of English. *Studies in Shakespeare, Milton,
and Donne* . . . New York and London, 1925. (University of Michigan.
Publications. Language and Literature, Vol. I.)
JEGP, XXVIII (1929), 561–62.

1930

Hartwell, Kathleen Ellen. *Lactantius and Milton.* Cambridge, Mass., 1929.
JEGP, XXIX (1930), 465–66.

Milton, John. *Milton on Education, the Tractate "Of Education"* . . . Edited . . . by Oliver Morley Ainsworth . . . New Haven and London, 1928. (Cornell Studies in English, XII.)
JEGP, XXIX (1930), 464–65.

1931

Tillyard, Eustace Mandeville Wetenhall. *Milton*. London, 1930.
JEGP, XXX (1931), 592–94.
Stevens, David Harrison. *Reference Guide to Milton from 1800 to the Present Day*. Chicago [1930].
MLN, XLVI (1931), 539–41.

1932

Milton, John. *The Latin Poems of John Milton*. Edited . . . by Walter Mac-Kellar. New Haven, 1930. (Cornell Studies in English, XV.)
JEGP, XXXI (1932), 158–59.
Milton, John. *The Student's Milton* . . . Edited by Frank Allen Patterson. New York, 1930.
JEGP, XXXI (1932), 156–58.

1934–1941

Brunner, Hildegard. *Milton's persönliche und ideelle Welt in ihrer Beziehung zum Aristokratismus*. Bonn: Peter Hanstein Verlagsbuchhandlung, 1933. (Bonner Studien zur Englischen Philologie . . . Heft XIX.)
JEGP, XXXIII (1934), 338.
Milton, John. *The Cambridge Manuscript of John Milton* . . . with a Bibliographical Note by Frank A. Patterson. New York, 1933. (Facsimile Text Society. *Publications*. No. XVII.)
JEGP, XXXIII (1934), 338.
Milton, John. *The Works of John Milton* . . . New York, 1931–38. (The Columbia Milton.)
JEGP, XXXIII (1934), 132–44, 300–305; XXXVIII (1939), 147–52, 292–300; XL (1941), 146–48.

1935

Clyde, William McCallum. *The Struggle for the Freedom of the Press from Caxton to Cromwell*. Oxford, 1934. (St. Andrews University. *Publications*. No. XXXVII.)
JEGP, XXXIV (1935), 599–601.
Hardeland, Gertrud. *Miltons Anschauungen von Staat, Kirche, Toleranz*. Halle, 1934. (Studien zur englischen Philologie. LXXXI.)
JEGP, XXXIV (1935), 120–21.
Taylor, George Coffin. *Milton's Use of Du Bartas*. Cambridge, Mass., 1934.
JEGP, XXXIV (1935), 119–20.

1941

French, Joseph Milton. *Milton in Chancery* . . . New York, 1939. (Modern Language Association of America. *Monograph Series*. X.)
JEGP, XL (1941), 145–46.

1942

Cawley, Robert Ralston. *Milton's Literary Craftsmanship; A Study of "A Brief History of Moscovia"* . . . Princeton, New Jersey, 1941. (Princeton Studies in English, XXIV.)
JEGP, XLI (1942), 547-48.

1944

Ross, Malcolm Mackenzie. *Milton's Royalism, A Study of the Conflict of Symbol and Idea in the Poems* . . . Ithaca, New York, 1943. (Cornell Studies in English, XXXIV.)
JEGP, XLIII (1944), 253-54.

1946

Corcoran, Sister Mary Irma. *Milton's Paradise with Reference to the Hexameral Background* . . . Washington, D. C., 1945.
MLQ, VII (1946), 359-61.

1947

Bush, Douglas. *English Literature in the Earlier Seventeenth Century, 1600–1660.* Oxford, 1945. (Oxford History of English Literature, [5].)
JEGP, XLVI (1947), 315-17.

1948

Clark, Donald Lemen. *John Milton at St. Paul's School; A Study of Ancient Rhetoric in English Renaissance Education.* New York, 1948.
JEGP, XLVII (1948), 308-309.
Eisenring, Albert J. Th. *Milton's "De Doctrina Christiana": An Historical Introduction and Critical Analysis.* Fribourg, Switzerland, 1946.
JEGP, XLVII (1948), 309.
Gilbert, Allan H. *On the Composition of "Paradise Lost."* Chapel Hill, 1947.
JEGP, XLVII (1948), 202-203.
Pope, Elizabeth Marie. *"Paradise Regained": The Tradition and the Poem.* Baltimore, 1947.
JEGP, XLVII (1948), 203-204.
Waldock, Arthur John Alfred. *"Paradise Lost" and Its Critics.* Cambridge, [Eng.] 1947.
JEGP, XLVII (1948), 203.

1950-1959

Conklin, George. *Biblical Criticism and Heresy in Milton.* New York, 1949.
JEGP, XLIX (1950), 254-55.
French, Joseph Milton. *The Life Records of John Milton.* New Brunswick, New Jersey, 1949-58. 5 Vols. (Rutgers Studies in English. No. VII.)
JEGP, XLIX (1950), 416-21; LVIII (1959), 695-701.
Krouse, F. Michael. *Milton's Samson and the Christian Tradition.* Princeton, 1949.
JEGP, XLIX (1950), 115-17.
McGinn, Donald Joseph. *The Admonition Controversy.* New Brunswick, New

Jersey, 1949. (Rutgers Studies in English. No. V.)
JEGP, XLIX (1950), 255.

1952

Cawley, Robert Ralston. *Milton and the Literature of Travel.* Princeton, 1951.
(Princeton Studies in English, XXXII.)
JEGP, LI (1952), 294.
Talon, Henri Antoine. *John Bunyan, the Man and His Works . . .* [Translated
by Barbara Wall.] Cambridge, [Mass.] 1951.
JEGP, LI (1952), 294.

1956

Hart, John. *John Hart's Works*, Part I. Edited by Bror Danielson. Stockholm,
1955.
JEGP, LV (1956), 142–44.
Schultz, Howard. *Milton and Forbidden Knowledge.* New York, 1955.
JEGP, LV (1956), 322–23.
West, Robert Hunter. *Milton and the Angels.* Athens, [Ga., 1955].
JEGP, LV (1956), 323.

1957

Howell, Wilbur S. *Logic and Rhetoric in England, 1500–1700.* Princeton, 1956.
JEGP, LVI (1957), 266–68.

1959

Milton, John. *The Poetical Works . . .* Edited by Helen Darbishire . . . London and New York, 1958.
JEGP, LVIII (1959), 296–97.

1961

Huckabay, Calvin. *John Milton: A Bibliographical Supplement. 1929–1957.*
Pittsburgh, 1960. (Duquesne Studies in Philology. Series I.)
JEGP, LX (1961), 170–71.

DOCTORAL THESES OR THEIR EQUIVALENT
(I.E., SIXTH-YEAR MASTER'S IN LIBRARY SCIENCE)

WRITTEN UNDER PROFESSOR FLETCHER'S SUPERVISION

Theses (Ph.D.), University of Illinois

Baldwin, Ruth Marie. *Alexander Gill the Elder, High Master of St. Paul's
School; An Approach to Milton's Intellectual Development.* Urbana [1955]
v+202 ll. (Library School)
Condee, Ralph Waterbury. *Milton's Theories Concerning Epic Poetry: Their
Sources and Their Influence on "Paradise Lost."* Urbana [1949] 234 ll.
Deutsch, Alfred Henry. *Some Scholastic Elements in "Paradise Lost" . . .* Ur-
bana [1945] 206 ll.
Grabill, Paul Egidus. *Milton's Residences and Real Estate Holdings.* Urbana
[1953] vi+176 ll.
Harding, Davis Philoon. *Milton and Ovid, a Study of the Influence of Ovid and*

His Renaissance Editors and Commentators on Milton's Poetry. Urbana [1943] 196 ll. Under title: *Milton and the Renaissance Ovid* . . . (Illinois Studies in Language and Literature, xxx, No. 4.) Urbana, University of Illinois Press, 1946. Pp. 105.

Jochums, Milford Cyril. Milton, John. *John Milton's "An Apology," etc.—A Critical Edition* . . . Urbana [1948] 583 ll. mounted facsims. (Illinois Studies in Language and Literature xxxv, Nos. 1–2.) Urbana: University of Illinois Press, 1950. Pp. xii+255.

Kimmich, Paul Edward. *John Milton's Technical Handling of the Latin Elegy.* Urbana [1958] vi+521 ll.

Little, Marguerite. *Some Italian Elements in the Choral Practice of "Samson Agonistes"* . . . Urbana [1946] 86 ll.

Lowell, Virginia Maud. *English Metrical Paraphrases of the Bible* . . . Urbana [1947] 267 ll.

Miller, Sonia. *Milton, John. "Eikonoklastes."* An Annotated Edition by Sonia Miller. Urbana [1958] v+321 ll.

Moloney, Michael Francis. *John Donne, His Flight from Mediaevalism.* Urbana [1939] 257 ll. (Illinois Studies in Language and Literature, xxix, Nos. 2–3.) Urbana: University of Illinois Press, 1944. Pp. 223.

Nicholas, Constance. *Milton's Medieval British Readings.* Urbana [1951] 171 ll.

Stratman, Carl Joseph. *Dramatic Performances at Oxford and Cambridge, 1603–1642.* Urbana [1947]

Winger, Howard Woodrow. *Regulations Relating to the Book Trade in London from 1357 to 1586.* Urbana [1953] iii+257 ll. (Library School)

Theses (Master's), University of Illinois

This group of Master's theses is included for two reasons: (1) The theses represent a sixth year of college work. Before they started, Professor Fletcher told the writers that he would expect the equivalent of a doctoral dissertation. (2) They were written by students outside of Professor Fletcher's own department. All were written for the Master's degree in Library Science.

Baldwin, Ruth Marie. *Matthew, Mary, and Samuel Simmons, Printers and Booksellers, 1635(?)–1678(?).* Urbana [1945] 145 ll.

Coffin, Georgia. *John Macock, a Seventeenth Century Printer.* Urbana [1948] 166 ll.

Grant, Isabelle F. *The Publication of "Paradise Lost" from 1667 to 1800, with a Handlist of Editions.* Urbana [1937] 125 ll.

Halmos, Dorothy Emeline (Moyer). *Humphrey Moseley, a Seventeenth Century Publisher* . . . Urbana [1935] 147 ll.

Kusch, Edith (McRoberts). *The Publication of the Works of John Milton Before 1700, Excluding "Paradise Lost," "Paradise Regain'd" and "Samson Agonistes"* . . . Urbana [1936] 76 ll.

Lewis, Clarissa Olivia. *William Dugard, Printer and the Commonwealth, with Particular Reference to the Milton-Salmasian Controversy.* Urbana [1933] 126 ll.

Waltemade, Henry John. *Head and Tailpieces of English Printers, 1640–1649* . . . Urbana [1938] 162 ll. incl. 360 mounted facsim.